Altruism
in Later
Life

Volume 196 Sage Library of Social Research

RECENT VOLUMES IN . . .
SAGE LIBRARY OF SOCIAL RESEARCH

Altruism in Later Life

Elizabeth Midlarsky
Eva Kahana

Sage Library of Social Research 196

SAGE Publications
International Educational and Professional Publisher
Thousand Oaks   London   New Delhi

For information address:

SAGE Publications, Inc.
2455 Teller Road
Thousand Oaks, California 91320

SAGE Publications Ltd.
6 Bonhill Street
London EC2A 4PU
United Kingdom

SAGE Publications India Pvt. Ltd.
M-32 Market
Greater Kailash I
New Delhi 110 048 India

Printed in the United States of America

Library of Congress Cataloging-in-Publication Data

Midlarsky, Elizabeth.
  Altruism in later life/Elizabeth Midlarsky, Eva Kahana.
    p. cm.—(Sage library of social research: v. 196)
  Includes bibliographical references and index.
  ISBN 0-8039-2768-1.—ISBN 0-8039-2769-x (pbk.)
    1. Altruism in old age. 2. Helping behavior in old age.
  I. Kahana, Eva. II. Title. III. Series.
  BF724.85.A47M53   1994
  155.67—dc20   94-19448

94 95 96 97 98 10 9 8 7 6 5 4 3 2 1

Sage Production Editor: Diane S. Foster

Contents

List of Tables

List of Figures

Preface

This is a book about the elderly and about altruism. It is written about research resulting from the concatenation of methods and concepts from two fields of social science inquiry, psychology and sociology, in an era in which this may be increasingly necessary.

Nine years have elapsed since the initial research reported in this book was conceived. The passing time has given us the opportunity to enhance our understanding of altruism in late life. It is also our great fortune that, unlike some common enterprises in which altruism and self-centeredness collide, ours has continued to enjoy the pleasures of a fine and productive collaboration. In addition to the thanks from each of us to the other, there are many others who merit our gratitude.

The nature of the research enterprise in our times is such that scholars must turn to others for money, facilities, and help. We wish to acknowledge our debt to the National Institute on Aging for grant no. R01 AG03068 and to the American Association of Retired Persons for grants awarded to us by their Andrus Foundation. The directors and staff of these institutions, who provided support throughout the years, were Dr. Ronald Abeles, Dr. Kenneth Cook, Mary Louise Luna, Dr. Betsy Sprouse, and Dr. Frederick J. Ferris. Their interest and encouragement were as important to us as the financial support that they provided.

A great many individuals were instrumental, through their diligent and enthusiastic efforts, in ensuring that the data presented in this volume are of high quality. These include A. Lynn Burns, Howard Brubaker, Shirley Christian, Sarah Cilano, John Davis, Sarah Fein, Richard and Glenda Jacobs, Catherine Khaghani, Maria Rosa Macias, Vera McQuade, Jacqueline Oliphant, Sandra Pecora, and Elizabeth Ross. The skills of Mina Cuker and Barbara Sperl Monroe in sampling and supervising fieldwork activities are especially noteworthy.

In addition to those staff who worked primarily on data collection and preparation, thanks are due to Sheila Richard, librarian and information specialist par excellence, to Dr. Mary Elizabeth Hannah and Rosalea A. Schonbar, for providing contextual support and collegial consultation, to Evelyn O'Keefe, for her reliable and conscientious secretarial assistance, and to Janis Owen for her brilliant handling of the final manuscript. We also acknowledge the efforts of Robin Nemeroff, for her outstanding work as a graduate research assistant, and Drs. David Huizinga and Delbert Elliot, for their consultation regarding conceptual aspects of the data analyses. Special thanks are due to Dr. Robin Corley, who provided outstanding technical assistance throughout the analysis of project data and whose insights were informative at many critical junctures.

We also express our appreciation to the older adults residing in the Detroit metropolitan area who participated in the research and who responded thoughtfully to the lengthy and probing interviews. Their deeds, as well as their words, taught us much about prosocial functioning in late life.

Both authors, moreover, wish to offer their warmest thanks to their husbands, Manus Midlarsky and Boaz Kahana, for their unparalleled understanding and support and for giving of themselves both personally and professionally. Our children—Susan, Miriam, and Michael Midlarsky and Jeffrey and Michael Kahana— went through many developmental stages in the course of the research and writing. Throughout all of these stages they helped— first, by exhibiting patience and humor when their Moms seemed always to be busy, and later, by offering their own growing knowledge, insights, and skills as contributions to our efforts.

We thank "Grandpa" Abraham Steckel for reading drafts and for offering encouraging words. All of us also owe our heartfelt appreciation to Mrs. Sari Frost, "Mom" and "Grandma" to the Kahanas by blood and to all of us through love, who "cooked for the troops." Above all, we thank them for serving as constant reminders of altruism in late life.

Elizabeth Midlarsky
Eva Kahana

To the Midlarsky clan,
Manus, Susan, Miriam, and Michael
And the Kahana clan,
Boaz, Jeffrey, and Michael
with our love.

The righteous shall bloom like a date palm;
they thrive like a cedar in Lebanon; . . .
In old age they still produce fruit, they are
full of sap and freshness.
—Psalm 92: 12-14

ONE

Introduction

This is a book about productive contributions by older adults to the lives of others, through their altruism and helping. It examines the relative frequency, nature, correlates, and ramifications of helping by the elderly; it presents some ways in which both experimental and survey research methodologies can be, and have been, employed in the study of prosocial response in late life. By focusing on altruism by the elderly, we hope to provide an alternative to the lachrymose view of the elderly as "a handicapped population dangling at the end of the life span" (Ehrlich, 1979a, 1979b). A demonstration is provided, instead, of another proposition: Although the need exists to support those of our elders who are vulnerable and frail, the recipient character of the aged is far from all encompassing and ubiquitous. We summarize evidence, primarily from our own studies, which indicates that helping is an activity valued by the elderly and one in which they frequently engage.

Our aim in this book is to present the results of a series of investigations that we have performed on helping by the elderly, in the context of historical, philosophical, and theoretical trends in gerontology and altruism research. We begin with a brief examination of the treatment of aging in historical texts. The two subsequent chapters then present the seminal theories of altruism, followed by models that appear to underlie current investigations in social gerontology. Our own theoretical model, the contributory model of successful aging, is depicted next, and the preponderance of the volume is then devoted to the studies that were based on the model. In this introductory chapter, we start with attitudes, fears, and hopes expressed about late life, beginning in ancient times.

IMAGES OF AGING—AN HISTORICAL OVERVIEW

The Quest for Longevity

The human life span has historically been short. The 20th century has witnessed an augmentation in average life expectancy that is unprecedented in human history. In the year 1790, 2% of the population reached or exceeded age 65, a figure that had doubled by the year 1900, when 4% reached the later years of life. The subsequent increase—from 4% at the turn of the century to 11% in 1981, with an anticipated further increase to 20% by the year 2030—attests both to recent technological advances and to the strength and adaptability of individuals living in the modern era. On the other hand, neither the quest for longevity nor claims of exceptionally long life spans in individual cases are new. Chroniclers of antediluvian elders have claimed that Enos died at age 905, Adam at 930, and the nearly indestructible Methusaleh at 965. Of course, as Medawar (1955) has so aptly written, these reported ages may reflect errors in the placement of decimal points or divergent methods of calculating age.

Moving on in time, even during an era in which the average age at death was relatively low, Cagliosko—remembered, unfortunately, for his boastfulness more than for his veracity—attained a vast age. By his own account, Cagliosko's unusually long life was attributable to a potion concocted of dill, sandalwood, and senna. Luigi Cornaro (1913), a 14th-century Venetian nobleman, wrote of the power of fasting and sober but pleasurable activity as means for prolonging life. Thomas Parr, whose autopsy was performed by the famous William Harvey (1635), physician to King Charles I, died at the age of 156. Also recorded are the many claims of exceedingly advanced old age among residents of Central Asia, particularly in the Ochemchersky district of Abkhazia (Metchnikoff, 1912). Although these claims have not always been fully substantiated to the satisfaction of scholars, their existence indicates that although far from typical, very advanced old age has existed as a possibility, if not a probability, for many centuries.

The Fear of Old Age and Love of Youth

The desire and quest for a long life, however ardent, have rarely been accompanied by positive views of aging. The process of aging has traditionally been treated ambivalently at best, with the longing for longevity—and even immortality—paradoxically juxtaposed to the fear of losses associated with the aging process. When, as in the present book, the words *helping* and *aging* are paired, an image is almost invariably invoked of help that flows from young to old—the converse of our emphasis here.

The assumption that old age is always a period of catastrophic decline and dependency appears with considerable frequency in the texts of antiquity. The distaste for old age, provoked by the sight of an old man's wrinkled visage and unsteady gait, led Buddha to question the worth of sentient existence. Even among the Hebrews, who generally revered the elderly, vulnerability was apparent in the successful attempt by Rebecca and Jacob to deceive the failing Isaac. In contradistinction to the Hebrews, among whom 80 was deemed "old," the Greeks considered that age 60 signaled the onset of decline. In the work of the 6th-century poet Himnerus, one reads that

> when peaceful old age overtakes a man and makes him ugly outside and foul-minded within, then wretched cares eat away at his heart and no longer does he rejoice to gaze upon the sun, being hateful to children and despicable to women. Such a grievous affliction have the gods made old age. (Garland, 1987)

The Hellenic culture, unlike the Hebraic, glorified youth and the joys of an individualistically oriented, hedonistic existence. Even the Greek gods were lusty, beautiful, dexterous, and young—or at least ageless, as in the case of Zeus. In this climate, old age was deprecated and death was described as a blessed release from a late life filled with sorrow.

The militaristic Roman culture was similarly dominated by the young and powerful. The myriad losses of position, physical strength and agility, and loved ones, which sometimes encourage an apparently aimless garrulousness, led the Roman poet Horace to lament that "grey hairs have many evils." The authority vested in the older man over his family—as in *patria potestus* (the father's power), *manus* (the power, or hand, of husband over wife), and *pater familius* (family head)—was counterbalanced by the portrayal in Roman comedies of older men as tyrannical, vicious, mean, and miserly (Haynes, 1963). William Shakespeare, whose pessimistic views on the later years permeate his work, wrote, "Age, I do abhor thee; Youth, I do adore thee." After even the most brilliantly hued life, old age, for Shakespeare, stood as mockery of all that went before; an ironic epitaph—

> Last scene of all, that ends this strange eventful
> History, is second childishness and mere oblivion;
> sans eyes, sans taste, sans everything.
> (*As You Like It*, II, vii)

The solution to the many ills of old age has been concomitantly sought in techniques for averting the ravages of time. The best solution has been thought to lie in methods for halting the aging process while at the same time prolonging the joys of youth. Indeed, one of the most intense obsessions among the ancient alchemists was the quest for a youth elixir. It was this same quest—for a "fountain of youth"—which led Ponce de Leon to discover Florida.

Paracelsus said he discovered the secret of eternal youth, but he died at 58. According to legend, Medea, too, claimed to have discovered the secret of unending youth. The sorceress reputedly restored King Aeson's vigor by replacing all the blood in his veins with a potion of snake skins, roots, herbs, the flesh of an owl, and a black ram's blood. A favorite cure for the cooling of the blood in late life, used by historical figures such as L. Claudius Hermip, was the inhalation of the blood of young maidens, a method termed *the Geronomic.* Older Romans and Syrians, hopeful of regaining vigor, ingested the blood of youthful gladiators. As late as the 15th century, Pope Innocent VIII was given a transfusion of blood from a youth—and died immediately. Metchnikoff (1845-1916), the Russian physician, sought to avert aging by eating large quantities of yogurt, and in 1949, a Soviet woman, Lepeshinkaya, prescribed soda baths to achieve rejuvenation (Busse & Blazer, 1980). When old age could finally be prevented no longer, the pessimistic conclusion was—and frequently still is—that decrepitude and dependency become apparent. In extremis, the ultimate means for preserving the dignity of the aging sufferer has been through the act of suicide—from the ancient Romans and, episodically, to the present.

Positive Views in Antique Texts

An apparent exception to the generalization that age was viewed historically as a tragedy is found among the ancient Hebrews. For the people of Israel, the veneration of one's elders was mandated, as in the biblical injunctions, "Thou shalt rise up before a hoary head, and honor the face of the old man" (Leviticus, 19:32), and "Despise not thy mother when she is old" (Proverbs 23:22). Long life was granted, in part, for one's good deeds, as in the commandment, "Honor thy father and thy mother that thy own days be long." Death was described as a punishment, visited on the progeny of Adam and Eve because of the original sin in the Garden of Eden. The ancient Hebrew society was patriarchal in nature, a state of affairs traceable to the reliance of extended households on the desert patriarch and mirrored in the image of Jehovah as a powerful but benevolent old man. Even among the generally youth-oriented Greeks and Romans, changes associated with older age were seen as the source of certain gains. The ancient Greeks, for example, were occasionally seen to equate age with wisdom. Freed from the lusts of the flesh that characterize youth, elderly persons were viewed by some as capable of enjoying a good life through the exercise of moral and cognitive faculties. Thus we read that Plato was still making contributions through his writings in the year of his death at 81. From an article describing life in ancient Greece, we learn that "old people were expected to show superior judgment and ability . . . [and] to fill magisterial and political positions in the councils of elders" (Angel, 1947, p. 20).

Although in many respects the Romans, like the Greeks, apparently deprecated older people—despite official expressions of goodwill—there are instances in which respect for the special qualities associated with late life were acknowledged. Within Roman society, slaves were commonly important sources of revenue or were used for petty services by the rich and powerful; the role of the *paedagogus* emerges as an exception. This slave was assigned the job of safeguarding the welfare of a young man from a wealthy family. As his charge moved from home to school and back, the paedagogus accompanied him, serving as his moral guardian. This role was ordinarily reserved for a trustworthy individual who was the recipient of considerable respect. It is noteworthy that the paedagogus was typically an older man. The ancient Romans further acknowledged the potential for wisdom and social concern among older adults when they placed the responsibility for the affairs of state in the hands of their Senate, or Senatus. The word *Senatus* is, itself, derived from *senex*—a term meaning "old" and that referred to a gathering of *senes*, or elders.

LATE LIFE IN MODERN TIMES

We live in an era in which the aged are experiencing a monumental growth in visibility, as they increase in numbers and proportion of the population. As in ancient times, there is considerable ambivalence about the prolongation of life. The negative side of that ambivalence is found, for example, in the trajectory theory of aging that depicts an unmitigated downslope after the age of 65, when a series of losses in cognitive and sensory functioning, status, roles, and health lead inexorably to death. If, indeed, fully 20% of our population are to become entirely dependent by the year 2030, then we may find that we have outstripped our ability to deal with the weight of the added years.

In contrast to the typical image of the elderly as universally recipients of help, there has long been evidence that advanced age is not necessarily associated with dependency. Where the stereotyped view of old age has implied total inutility, as in primitive societies such as the Yakut, older adults have been treated so badly that further contributions have become impossible; "naked living skeletons" cast aside by society can do little for others (Whitehouse, 1989). On the other hand, in societies that value the importance of elders within the family structure—or their skills in dance, song, or storytelling— older adults continue to perform vital roles and to enjoy their place within the culture. Thus in Japan, where tradition is enshrined, ascribed status increases with age (Kimmel, 1988). Similarly, the elderly of Hawaii are vitally involved in the structure of the family (Jensen & Oakley, 1982-1983).

In recent years, there has been a growing body of literature suggesting that behavior characterized as altruistic or helpful may be manifested in a variety of situations and by individuals of diverse ages, including those in late life (e.g., Cohler, Borden, Groves, & Lazarus, 1989; Dovidio, 1984; Midlarsky & Hannah, 1989). In the popular press as well, instances abound wherein older adults engage in activities designed to help others. Some examples:

> Donnie Jones doesn't get around like she used to, but she does just fine for a woman who'll be 101 years old September 15. . . . Whenever she can, she visits senior citizens who are ill. . . . "I always go on the sick floor and pray and talk with them when I can."
>
> Benjamin Holme, 88, helps organize activities at the retirement center where he lives. "There's a great desire on the part of us to be helpful," he said. Leona Corrick, 90, of Roseville, makes alterations for her neighbors. . . . She and others donate craftwork to hospitals. "We first started making crafts for ourselves," Corrick said. "But then we just decided to start doing it for others. I figure if you can't help somebody, what's the use of living." (Spratling, 1982)

Gerry and Bob Davidson don't seem to cotton to the stereotype of a retired couple.... Two stints in the Peace Corps after Bob retired from years of teaching in a New York State public high school give a clue to the Davidsons' willingness to experience the unusual. But there's another motivation even stronger than adventure. It's the desire to serve. Sooner or later, they just have to do something for someone else. Most recently the Davidsons, who are both in their sixties, have signed on as Catholic Volunteers of Florida ... whose mission is to promote social justice by direct service to those in need ... supervising the young women to make sure they do their chores satisfactorily. "And," she adds, "I have the satisfaction of the babies. The goal is to save the babies." For his part, Bob works as night supervisor at the St. Francis Soup Kitchen and Emergency Shelter. The Davidsons think that the sixties are the best time of life to be volunteers.... Next, they are thinking about helping migrant workers in the Immokalee area. (Crum, 1988)

Among the winners of an award for "outstanding acts of bravery," awarded by the Carnegie Hero Fund Commission, we find 65-year-old Lucille Babcock:

Lucille Babcock rescued a woman from assault, Little Rock, Arkansas, July 29, 1987. A 22-year-old woman screamed as she was being assaulted (in a rape attempt) by a man outside her home. Miss Babcock, 65, writer, saw the assault from her nearby apartment. Although she was disabled, requiring back and leg braces, Miss Babcock approached the assailant and beat him with her cane. ("I whopped him upside the head," she told a reporter.) The assailant then turned on Miss Babcock, allowing the younger woman to escape. The assailant struck Miss Babcock, then fled. Men in the neighborhood captured the assailant and held him for police. The younger woman was treated for multiple injuries. (Carnegie Hero Fund Commission, 1987)

The competence and contributions by the elderly that are reflected in these and many other observations and anecdotes are frequently overlooked by gerontological researchers, service professionals, and many members of today's rapidly aging population. There is currently a marked emphasis on how to cope with the myriad stresses and concerns associated with aging in the minds of a youth-oriented population. Gerontology, the study of aging, has tended to focus on old age as a period of deterioration and loss as well. In studies combining sophisticated methodologies with concern for the plight of the elderly, research efforts deal primarily with the alleviation of problems of caretakers when autonomy is diminished.

The image of old age as an affliction for the individual and as a burden for society has the potential to cast an overwhelming shadow at this juncture in our history. We currently are witnessing unprecedented growth in longevity, with expansion of life into the 80s and 90s an increasingly common phenomenon. When today's young view their elders, they may see people who have had less formal education, fewer financial resources, and less access to excellent nutrition and health care than they had, people who in Troll's (1984) ungentle words are, comparatively speaking, "poor, dumb and ugly." In reality, however, as new cohorts—unravaged by world wars and economic deprivation—become older, there may be ever larger numbers of older persons who, as in the examples cited above, will be able to look beyond material and safety needs to the higher order human needs for meaning (Maslow, 1968).

In answer to the question "Why old age?" that is increasingly being raised (Mergler & Goldstein, 1983), the response by at least some writers is that old age may have an importance and significance of its own. Thus, in a recent work by Erikson, Erikson, and Kivnick (1986), old age is presented not as an afterthought but as a new critical period during which the resilient individual may review earlier themes in the quest to achieve integration while overcoming its opposite, despair. In this process, the new adaptive strength of wisdom may be achieved. According to David Gutmann (1987), the meaning of old age is that the elderly are repositories of culture and compassion, with time available for the transmission of love and accumulated knowledge in support of the young.

The current book is written about a productive alternative in the lives of the elderly, their altruistic and helpful behavior. In it we review literature on altruism and helping in late life. We also present the results from two types of investigation that we have conducted to explore helping in late life. Field experimental methodology was employed to investigate and compare helping behaviors by younger and older persons. Survey research also was conducted to determine the nature, determinants, and consequences of helping. In the following chapter, we begin by defining altruism and presenting current theoretical perspectives on altruism and its existence.

Theories and Concepts of Altruism and Helping

In this book two terms—*altruism* and *helping*—will be used in referring to positive social behavior by the elderly. Both terms are similar in implying that the actor intends a positive benefit for the recipient. The term *prosocial behavior,* although popular within the current psychology literature (e.g., Eisenberg, 1982; Olweus, Block, & Radke-Yarrow, 1986; Staub, Bar-Tal, Karylowski, & Reykowski, 1984), is not used because it includes forms of behavior not of interest in this presentation, such as cooperation.

DEFINITIONS OF ALTRUISM AND HELPING

Helping is used here as a general term referring to all instances in which one individual comes to the aid of another. On the other hand, *altruism*—a term sometimes used interchangeably with helping—may best be viewed as a subcategory of helping, in which the behavior is voluntary and motivated by concern for the welfare of the other, rather than by the anticipation of rewards. In this usage, helpful acts motivated by external rewards are not considered altruistic, in contrast to helpful acts that are internally rewarded (e.g., those that are vicariously reinforced and motivated by sympathy or the desire to engage in meaningful pursuits).

According to *Webster's Third International Dictionary*, altruism is "uncalculated consideration of, regard for or devotion to others' interests." In the *Encyclopedia of Social Sciences* (vol. 2, p. 14), altruism is defined as "the disposition of an individual to further the welfare or happiness of other individuals or groups." In the King James translation of the Bible, the word *charity* is synonymous with altruism and is defined as love which is given with no thought of return or reciprocation.

Budd (1956), in his review of the history of the construct, writes that the term *altruism* was coined in the 19th century by August Comte. Altruism is based on the Italian *altrui*, derived from the Latin root *alter*; the meaning of both is "other." The synonym for altruism is unselfishness. Its antonym is egoism, which is defined as behavior designed to achieve benefits for one's own sake, rather than for the sake of others.

Comte, who has been called the "founder" of social psychology (Allport, 1954), believed that altruism was an instinct that could be located anatomically in "the highest median portion of the frontal division" (Comte, 1875-1877, p. 569). The term altruism was used by Comte to denote a religion of humanity in which self-centeredness was to be eradicated through discipline, replaced by selfless love and devotion to society. It came into widespread use following its inclusion in the late-19th-century work of Herbert Spencer (1897), who wrote, "Self-sacrifice is no less primordial than self-preservation" (p. 249). Altruism gained popularity in the United States, largely because of the approval given by religious leaders, and incorporated into the plans of utopian theorists and social planners. Alcander Longley, a philanthropist, sponsored his plans for the good of humankind under the aegis of the Altruistic Society, and he promoted his utopian position in a newspaper first called *The Altruist* and later *The Altruistic Review*. Several communities founded on the basis of brotherly love and communal ownership of property were named Altruria.

Pitirim A. Sorokin (1950, 1954) believed the potential power of "altruistic love" to be so great that it should be cultivated as the basis for resolving world crises. In his influential work, comprising 30 published volumes, he rejected the need for formal definitions of the terms *altruism* and *love*, which he believed to be obvious to the individual experiencing them. His writings reflect his assumption that when we help our neighbors, we do so unselfishly, out of brotherly love. For Sorokin, the most perfect form of altruism greatly transcends the minimum level prescribed by the Romans, "Do good to others, harm no one, and render to each his own." It is the altruism of the Sermon on the Mount, appearing in the *New English Bible* as,

> Love your enemies, do good to those who hate you, pray for those who treat you spitefully. When a man hits you on the cheek, offer him the other cheek, too . . . give to everyone who asks you. . . . Treat others as you would like them to treat you.

Sorokin's optimism and humanistic bias toward the potential for altruism in all human beings is a refreshing contrast to the biases of other, purportedly objective and scientific approaches that argue against the possibility of compassion and humanity.

In recent years, concomitant with the burgeoning study of altruism among psychologists, numerous additional definitions have been proposed. Brabeck (1989) and Kurtines and Gewirtz (1984), cognitive-developmental theorists, define altruism as one's relationship to and responsibility for other human beings. Hoffman (1978) describes it as a part of basic human nature, an inherent disposition or motive to act that is under the control of a perceptual and cognitive process. In the work of Weiss, Boyer, Lombardo, and Stich (1973), altruism is viewed as a conditioned response that is, however, rooted deeply enough in human behavior to act as an intrinsic reinforcer.

Economic models, such as exchange theory, have been very influential in both sociology and psychology. Economic theories are founded on notions of self-interest, but their terminology permits one to make relatively clear definitional statements about altruism, in terms familiar within the culture. Hence altruism has also been defined as behavior that is voluntarily emitted on behalf of others and incurs some cost to the individual but brings either very little or nothing by way of extrinsic gain, relative to the magnitude of the investment. The two major manifestations of altruistic behavior are (a) generosity or sharing, in which the individual makes a personal sacrifice of some kind—whether of tangible goods, money, time, or effort—in order to benefit others; and (b) helping at risk to oneself, such as rescue, in which the helper accepts a certain degree of risk, discomfort, or pain in order to ease or prevent the suffering of another (Midlarsky, 1968; Midlarsky & Bryan, 1967). A wide range of behaviors may be encompassed by this definition, ranging from simple acts of kindness to so extreme an act of self-sacrifice as altruistic suicide (Durkheim, 1951).

For Eisenberg (1983), altruism is "behavior that benefits another, is voluntary and intentional, and is not consciously performed to promote one's own self-interest" (p. 195; see also Hoffman, 1982). Cialdini and his associates propose that "altruism becomes, through the socialization process, a learned response involving self-reward" (see Baumann, Cialdini, & Kenrick, 1983, p. 299). Bar-Tal and Raviv (1982) state that altruism represents the highest quality of helping and is defined as "voluntary and intentional behavior carried out for its own sake and to benefit a person, as a result of moral conviction in justice and without expectations for external rewards" (p. 149). H. S. Sullivan (1953) described altruism as the "common humanity of people," and for social psychologists such as Hornstein (1976), altruism is a universal human trait.

This chapter presents a review of the major conceptualizations among behavioral scientists and philosophers, followed by a discussion of criteria for attributions of altruism. Theories are divided into those antithetical to altruism (philosophical and theological views, as well as the economic, psychoanalytic, and behavioral models) and those congruent with altruism (philosophical views, evolutionary theory, and the newer psychoanalytic approaches). These views of human nature are listed in Table 2.1. The chapter ends with a discussion of criteria for the attribution of altruism.

THEORETICAL PERSPECTIVES
ANTITHETICAL TO ALTRUISM

Philosophical and Theological Views

Centuries before the word altruism was coined, the basic nature of human beings was the subject of inquiry and debate. Among

Table 2.1 Perspectives on Human Nature

	Exemplars	
Type of Viewpoint	*Antithetical to Altruism*	*Congruent With Altruism*
Philosophical/ Theological	Hebrew-Christian Religion Plato Sophists Bentham Kant Machiavelli Nietzche Stirner Ardrey Hobbes Lorenz	Confucius Mencius Wang-Ming Tagore Aristotle Hume Smith Rousseau

Economic	Arrow
	Downs
	Mauss
	Simon
	Social Exchange (e.g., Foa
	  & Foa; Homans; Dowd)
	Equity (Hatfield, Walster,
	  & Piliavin)	

Evolutionary/ Sociobiology	Darwin (some interpretations) Ardrey Hobbes Lorenz Trivers	Darwin (some interpretations) Campbell Wilson
Psychoanalytic	Sigmund Freud Anna Freud	Adler Erikson Fromm Jung White Kernberg

Behaviorist	Watson
	Radical Behaviorism
	  (Skinner)
	Social Learning Theory[a]
		Social Learning Theory
		  (e.g., Rosenhan)

NOTE: The roster of perspectives and examples of each is designed to be illustrative of the many who have written about the possibility of altruism and is by no means comprehensive.

a. The preponderance of experimental work in psychology investigating behavior that accords with operational definitions of altruism has been performed by the social learning theorists. The basic assumption by this group—that all behavior is developed and maintained by reinforcement—combined with the assumption by most other writers that all "reinforced" behavior is ultimately self-serving has led to the placement of social learning theory among the perspectives antithetical to altruism. Indeed, the basic reliance of this body of work on the law of effect, and its concomitant discomfort with the notion of *altruism* (i.e., concern for the welfare of the other), probably underlies the current preference for the term *prosocial*. On the other hand, the possibility of deriving intrinsic motivation from this theory leads to some degree of ambiguity. Hence it may be argued that certain social learning theoretic treatments may be congruent with altruism as well (Midlarsky & Suda, 1978).

the ancient Greeks, Plato (1954) posited a beast within containing our unpleasant desires, which

> bestir themselves in dreams, when the gentler part of the soul slumbers, and the control of Reason is withdrawn. Then the Wild Beast in us, full-fed with meat and drink, becomes rampant and shakes off sleep to go in quest of what will gratify his own instinct . . . it will cast off all shame and prudence at such moments and stick at nothing. It will go to any lengths of shamelessness and folly. (p. 271)

According to certain instinct theorists, the human species is characteristically aggressive in nature. For example, Ardrey (1962) stated that human beings have a Cain tendency, such that "man is a predator whose natural instinct is to kill with a weapon" (p. 316). Lorenz (1963) asserted that a characteristic of the human species is a drive to aggress that exhibits "irresistible outbreaks which occur with rhythmical regularity" (p. 17). Hobbes (1958) described human beings as possessed of a "killer" nature, whose "natural" tendency is to invade each others' territory for the purpose of destruction. As MacPherson (1962) has written, however, "Hobbes offers, as a confirmation of the 'natural' tendency of men . . . the observable behavior of men in present civil society." Thus, rather than exploring the fundamental nature of human beings who have not been socialized by a society dominated by egoism and individualism, "to get the state of nature, Hobbes has set aside the law, but not the socially acquired behavior and desires of men" (p. 22).

The view that human beings are basically evil, or entirely egoistic, was also held by the Sophists (Masters, 1978); it is evident in much of the Old and New Testaments (although not without a dialectic between good and evil) and in the works of such practical philosophers as Machiavelli and Hobbes. In at least some interpretations of the Hebrew-Christian religions, human beings are presented as the repositories of original sin. The love of the deity and of one another preached by the major religions is designed to overcome the basic human problems—sinfulness and self-centeredness. In Psalm 51:5 we read, "Behold, I was shapen in iniquity, and in sin did my mother conceive me." In the New Testament, St. Paul said,

"In his flesh dwelleth no good thing." Reflecting this tradition, some theologians

> are so anxious to prove that all that comes from human nature is sin, and that all good in man has a supernatural origin, that they mostly ignore the facts that cannot be produced as an example of higher inspiration or grace coming from above. (Kropotkin, 1902, p. 278)

Kant (1949) considers human beings innately selfish but capable of manifesting benevolence by silencing their basic instincts through the application of reason. When people do their duty—by helping others, if that is what duty dictates in a given situation—then by such acts self-worth is reaffirmed (Seidler, 1986, 1992).

John Aubrey (1898), in his biographical sketch of Thomas Hobbes, notes that Hobbes had a firm belief that egoism motivated all human behavior, including acts of charity. On one occasion, a clergyman, seeing Hobbes give alms, asked whether this act would have occurred if not commanded by Christ. Hobbes responded that his action was prompted only by the desire to relieve his own discomfort at the sight of so miserable a beggar. The fact that the beggar was helped was entirely incidental. Hobbes's thinking—in which existence is a struggle for personal survival and one's own good is placed above all others—is echoed in the writings of 19th-century philosophers Max Stirner (1907) and Friedrich Nietzsche (Levy, 1910). McDougall's (1908) classic social psychology textbook lists an "instinct of pugnacity."

Economic Models

Economic theory (e.g., rational choice theory, utility theory, cost-benefit analysis), at least from Bentham's time, has tended to emphasize that human choices are based on the degree to which the individual expects to maximize benefits and minimize costs (Hospers, 1961). For Bentham, a major proponent of psychological egoism (of which hedonism is a variant), people act to obtain maximum pleasure for themselves. So ubiquitous and rooted in human nature is egoism that it is futile to expect anything but personal gain to motivate behavior. If one wishes to encourage any behavior, then one must first ensure that people understand that the behavior will result in positive consequences for themselves— whether the consequences take the form of prestige, money, or just a warm glow of satisfaction. For Arrow (1979), too, preferences and behaviors are founded on what benefits the actor, and Herbert Simon's (1979) "substantial rationality" is reflected in behavior appropriate to the achievement of the individual's own goals.

The economic models emphasizing egoistic "rationality" were used originally to predict economic behavior almost exclusively. However, they have become influential in other social science domains as well. There are many social interactions and transactions that can be conceptualized as exchanges involving costs and benefits. In the field of political science, Downs (1957) has attempted to account for political phenomena by means of a cost-benefit analysis. In anthropology and sociology, gift giving has been analyzed from this perspective as well (Mauss, 1954).

These models have run into trouble, though, when the attempt is made to apply them to social welfare utility. Their primary prediction is that individuals should eschew any situation in which they are called upon to give up more than they can hope to obtain. How, then, can they explain financial contributions to causes, donations of blood or bone marrow, and other acts of charity in which givers may incur costs but can expect minimal gains, or no discernible gains at all? From a completely rational perspective, it would seem that the best strategy is to be a "free rider," who accepts the benefits of a society while making no contribution.

Some additional explanatory elements appear in theories by sociologists and psychologists who attempt to explain helpfulness through the application of economic principles. In *social exchange theory* (e.g., Foa & Foa, 1975; Homans, 1961), human interactions are seen as founded on social economics. As such they are governed by the individual's consideration of relative costs and rewards. Homans (1961), for example, views human behavior

as a function of its payoff . . . when what it fetches is behavior, similarly determined . . . the behavior becomes social. . . . .

Thus . . . social behavior . . . [is] an exchange of activity, tangible or intangible, and more or less rewarding or costly, between at least two persons. (p. 13)

With the addition of intangible costs and rewards to the calculus, we have the potential to exchange both material goods and such social goods as services and compassion in our social interactions. For the social exchange theorists, whether or not we consciously make note of economic factors, we use a minimax strategy—in which we strive always to maximize rewards while minimizing costs.

What does adoption of an exchange perspective do to our conceptions of altruism? In exchange theory, altruism is essentially a theoretical impossibility. The basic postulate of the exchange position is that egocentrism is at the root of all behavior, even behavior appearing on the surface to be allocentric. Selfless behavior on behalf of a friend, for example, is one of the goods exchanged to maintain the friendship, according to Homans (1961). With the possible exception of certain genuine saints, Homans (1961) wrote that people who seem benevolent are behaving benevolently in order to earn either social approval or gratitude from others or, in other instances, to accumulate social credits (Wright, 1971). Much of human behavior, according to these social theorists, is based on the "norm of reciprocity," whereby social exchange is maintained only when all of the individuals involved are making a profit and all payments made by individuals eventually balance out. Thus helping responses occur because one either has received a service, expects to receive one, or is attempting to be worthy of one. In any given situation, the individual currently "indebted" to others is the one most likely to be of service. Hence one may predict the likelihood that an individual will help from a calculus of positive social action based on costs, rewards, and prior indebtedness (Gergen & Gergen, 1981; Lynch & Cohen, 1978).

Equity theory, a model derived from economic theory by Hatfield, Walster, and Piliavin (1978), assumes that "individuals will try to maximize their outcomes [p. 116]. . . . When individuals find themselves participating in inequitable relationships, they become distressed ... [and] the greater the inequity that exists, the more distress they feel and the harder they try to restore equity" (p. 118). Equity, then, is defined as the condition in which the outcomes are equivalent to rewards minus costs. Despite the apparent objectivity of this statement, particularly because of the inclusion of intangibles, costs and benefits are not readily amenable to objective assessment and "ultimately, equity is in the eye of the beholder" (p. 117).

> For example, a wife—focusing on the fact that she is trapped in the house with toddlers all day, works long hours and is constantly engulfed by noise, mess and confusion—may feel that her relative outcomes are extremely low. Her husband—focusing on the fact that she can get out of bed whenever she pleases in the morning and can see whom she wants, when she wants—may disagree. (pp. 117-118)

Each individual tends to react to perceived injustice by employing a minimax, cost-benefit strategy to restore equity by distorting equality, or by some blend of the two. When these authors apply their model to helping interactions, they find that because of equity maintenance strategies, long-term relationships are likely to be characterized by reciprocity.

What role is there for altruism in the context of equity theory? Altruism, from this perspective, is good neither for the altruist nor for the recipient, and therefore genuine altruism has no place in the "real world" of social exchange.[1] What appears to be altruism, according to this essentially Hobbesian view, is most often disguised selfishness, and it is therefore readily transformed from the appearance of altruism to the reality of exploitation. Even when no immediate gain is obvious, apparently altruistic acts may be guided by an "enlightened self-interest," wherein future gains to the helper are expected to outweigh current costs.

How can social scientists give any credence to the possibility of altruism? In the words of these writers, "psychologists [occasionally] view altruism in a favorable light . . . [but] *scientists* [italics added] attribute apparent altruism to more selfish motives (Hatfield et al., 1978, p. 129). What is overlooked in this is that the addition to the calculus of positive action for future reciprocation, of intangible rewards and costs, and of the necessity of judging equity in subjective terms takes it several steps away from the original, more parsimonious, economic formulation. These additions also greatly diminish the predictive power of the model.

Hatfield et al. (1978) note that whatever motivates the helpfulness—altruism or selfishness—the consequences of altruistic relationships are likely to bring more evil than good to the recipients. Because altruistic relationships lack equity, they humiliate the recipient, rather than evoking positive reactions. Missing from this analysis is recognition of the fact that not all altruistically motivated charitableness is displayed in the types of personal relationships that have the potential to demean the recipient. Consider, for example, the individual donating blood marrow or blood to unknown strangers. Or the anecdote of the man standing in the street with his arms upraised. Asked what he was doing by a passerby, he responded, "I've heard the sky was about to fall, and I'm trying to stop it." "How can you, alone, do anything to help?" asked the stranger. "I must do as much as I can," the man replied. Although altruism of this disinterested kind may be a relatively rare occurrence, economic theories of the type reviewed here do little to explain it.

Psychoanalytic Theory

In contrast to the economic theorists, who view human beings as supremely rational, Sigmund Freud (1933) viewed the individual as driven largely by impulses that are irrational and unconscious. Personality, in this theory, is tripartite, consisting of three structures—the id, ego, and superego. The basis for all of personality resides in the one mental structure that is present at birth, the id (literally, the "it"). The id, Freud's "nasty beast," bears a strong resemblance to Plato's (1954) "Wild Beast," which will "stick at nothing . . . to gratify his own instincts" (p. 271). Like Plato's beast within, the id, residing at the core of every human personality, contains the instincts, is linked to the basic biological processes, and is the repository of all impulses and energy. The id is guided entirely by the pleasure principle, which urges immediate gratification of every primal wish and impulse, regardless of the consequences.

The ego is the part of the personality that is in contact with the world of external reality and, therefore, with other people—and their needs and desires. The ego is guided by the reality principle, but as it is energized by the organismic needs, transmitted through the id, its mission is to expedite need satisfaction in accordance with environmental conditions, thus ensuring the organism's survival. The superego represents the incorporation of standards and values of the society, transmitted to the individual by the same-sex parent between the ages of 4 and 6 years. The superego is guided by the search for perfection or the ideal. When the individual falls short of the ideal, he or she is punished by guilt. The ego, as executive of the personality, must mediate between the id and its need for immediate tension reduction, the superego and the punishment that it can mete out, and the constraints imposed by societal obstacles and hazards.

In psychoanalytic theory, Sigmund Freud paves the way for a comprehension of morality. However, traditional psychoanalysis, as originally proposed, is essentially antihumanistic because of its emphasis on the centrality of aggressiveness and self-centeredness. According to Freud (1930), "the inclination to aggression [present in the id] is an original, self-subsisting disposition in man," and the aggressive instinct "constitutes the greatest impediment to civilization" (p. 69). Human beings are naturally sadistic, and only the constraints of civilization prevent people from tearing one another apart. Aggression is a direct derivative of an intrinsic death instinct, which seeks to destroy the individual and return him to an inanimate state in which all tension would be eternally eliminated. Inhibitions against aggression are socially induced during the developmental process when the Oedipus complex is resolved and the superego is subsequently formed. Although the formation of the superego makes altruistic behavior possible, the tenor of Freud's argument is that altruistic or even nonaggressive responses are a harsh imposition upon a basically aggressive nature.

According to the traditional psychoanalysts—Anna Freud (1937), for example—seemingly altruistic behavior is produced by such

defense mechanisms as reaction formation and altruistic surrender. An exemplar of reaction formation is the middle-aged woman
whose brothers and sisters have all left home to establish independent married lives but who herself has remained at home to
care for their aging, ailing mother. This woman, described as
"saintly" by others, was most mistreated or neglected by the
mother during her childhood and has more reason to resent her
than any of her siblings. Her "altruistic stance" is thus interpret-
able as the operation of repression against her own underlying
hostility, which is then replaced by its opposite, altruism (i.e.,
through reaction formation).

Altruistic surrender is a form of defensive or aggressive identification in which, rather than satisfying one's own impulses by
seeking and then using material wealth, power, or sexual gratification, one instead satisfies one's needs through vicarious pleasure
in the achievements of others. In Anna Freud's (1937) interpretation, altruistic surrender occurs when the formation of a very strict
superego makes it impossible for individuals to experience direct
gratification of certain needs because of the threat of excessive
guilt. The "martyred," boastful wife, "matchmaking old maids,"
and other "altruists" may therefore be individuals who project
their own forbidden desires onto others. Only by helping those
others to secure fulfillment are they able to achieve some degree
of gratification for themselves.

Cases may be cited of the use of these mechanisms both in
pathological and in relatively nonpathological ways (Fenichel,
1945). The fact remains, however, that altruism is viewed by
traditional analysts with a high degree of ethical skepticism. The
interpretation of altruistic behavior—as, indeed, they interpret all
of human behavior—as being based on irrational motives results
in a loss of moral significance for those behaviors, at least by
implication.

Behaviorism

Altruism has been a problem for the id-oriented Freudian theorist, but it has caused problems for the social behaviorist as well.

In J. B. Watson's peripheralist theory, *behaviorism*, the concept of consciousness is rejected on somewhat metaphysical grounds (Heidbreder, 1933), thus rendering any consideration of ethics wholly meaningless.

B. F. Skinner's (1953) *radical behaviorism* also rejected inferred motives and dynamics, emphasizing instead the observation of overt behaviors exclusively. In order to avoid the circularity that comes from explaining behavior by naming needs or motives on which the behavior may be based, Skinner's goal has been to search instead for observable stimulus conditions that may control the observed behavior. The attribution of altruistic motivation, like the attribution of other motives, is meaningless in any event, according to Skinner's (1971) analysis of altruism. The only reason we could have to search for an "inner meaning" for a behavior is that we have not been successful in finding the true, external explanations (e.g., the need to relieve distress). In other words, we credit people with altruism only when we don't know what "really" caused the behavior, probably because its rewards are inconspicuous. Other social behaviorists go on to state that when we make attributions of altruism to others or to ourselves, these attributions may reflect biases of various types (Gelfand & Hartmann, 1982).

In the theoretical formulations promulgated by the behaviorists, the acquisition of all behavior is governed by the law of effect, so that no behavior may be emitted unless rewards are either present or anticipated, or the behavior serves to terminate or avoid aversive consequences. According to these investigators, altruistic responses should be acquired in the same manner as any other social behavior—primarily through reinforcement. People can, therefore, be trained to engage in behaviors that have positive consequences for others. These helpful acts, like any other behaviors, would follow the law of effect. Hence, by definition, they would be designed to benefit the actor at least as much as the recipient and therefore would not fit the definition of altruism. This perspective is strikingly similar to that articulated by Bentham, the economic theorist who argued that if society is to function optimally, each individual should help others. Although basic human nature is egoistic, it is possible to train people to obtain their maximum satisfaction by helping others (Hospers, 1961). With all of its apparent differences from classical psychoanalysis, the reliance of the behavioral approaches on the idea of reinforcement as a predominant motivating force comes very close to Freud's use of the pleasure principle.

Research evidence does exist in support of the position that individuals can acquire a habit of helping others through training in which the acts are positively reinforced. Parents and other socializing agents who wish their children to be generous should therefore reward them for sharing, thus setting in motion a habit of generosity. Experiments have demonstrated that it is indeed possible to encourage positive social behavior by the provision of material rewards. In an early study, Fischer (1963) showed that the degree to which children shared marbles with a peer with whom they were unacquainted was augmented when they were reinforced with bubble gum. Vogler, Masters, and Morrill (1970) increased children's cooperation by rewarding them with sweets. Control by positive consequences has also been demonstrated when praise was used as the reinforcer, both in laboratory investigations (e.g., Gelfand, Hartmann, Cromer, Smith, & Page, 1975; Midlarsky & Bryan, 1967; Midlarsky, Bryan, & Brickman, 1973) and in naturalistic settings (e.g., Slaby & Crowley, 1977). Results of other investigations have indicated that punishing helping responses can significantly decrease their probability of occurrence on subsequent occasions, both in children (Rushton & Teachman, 1978) and in adults (Moss & Page, 1972).

These and other studies have, then, provided empirical support for the position that the principles of learning based on the law of effect can explain generosity and helpfulness. The studies cited above have also done so without resorting to motivational constructs, such as altruism—a term that refers to positive behavior motivated by the concern for the welfare of others.

In response to the notion, however, that only overt behavior should be studied and that mentalist constructs such as motivation are useless baggage, we may note again that the possibility of altruism is linked to questions of consciousness and intent (Nagel, 1970), and it is difficult to justify the dismissal of these constructs out of hand. In Midgley's (1978) words:

There is nothing fishy about trying to study motives, and a great deal that is fishy about trying to avoid doing so. Motivation is a central human concern, a thing that gives constant trouble when it is not understood. And the "scientific" way to understand it is, as with everything else, to take it on its own terms and find concepts suitable for bringing out its typical patterns. We all need and use terms like fear and anger, interest and desire, hope and repression; we all look for motives that are not apparent and for patterns of motivation. What we need, therefore, is to do these things in a clearer, more organized way, not to outlaw them, or try to reduce them to reports of outer action. . . . There is, in fact, no need for . . . desperate measures of flight from the obvious subject matter of psychology. All they have done is to castrate that subject. It has been reduced, for fifty years or so, to the state in which the study of teapots would be if one half of the people engaged in it were sworn as a matter of professional pride never to mention the inside of a teapot, while the other half were just as unwilling ever to mention the outside. (p. 113)

The pervasive influence of behaviorism and its reliance on the law of effect is associated with what has been called the altruistic paradox, one version of which is as follows: "If organisms seek to maximize reward and minimize pain, how shall we account for altruistic phenomena that take their very definition from the unwillingness to forgo obvious and often significant rewards, even to give them up entirely?" (Rosenhan, 1978, p. 102).

Unlike the radical behaviorists, social learning theorists such as Rosenhan (1978) and Rotter (1966) have recognized that certain internal processes—such as expectancies and other cognitive processes, affect, and attentional processes—may contribute to our understanding of human behavior, including altruism. Rosenhan (1978), in particular, employed concepts derived from social learning theory to resolve the altruistic paradox, by invoking the process of internalization, whereby individuals help others because of the expectation of current rewards and/or the anticipation of future rewards. The notion that altruistic intentionality may exist in situations in which no reward is expected remains a challenge to all behavioristic notions (see Note a., Table 2.1). It is because of the basic view of human beings as responsive only to the law of effect that Allport (1954) referred to behaviorism as the "new hedonism" (p. 88).

THEORETICAL PERSPECTIVES CONGRUENT WITH ALTRUISM

Philosophical Views

Just as one can find support for the image of humankind as aggressive and egoistic, support exists for altruistic predisposi- tions. Balancing the view of "man as beast" or egoist who is satisfied only by preying on others are contrary views dating back to the early Chinese philosophers. Mencius asserted that "there is no greater delight than to be conscious of right within us. If one strives to treat others as he would be treated by them, he should not fail to come near the perfect life" (Brown, 1939, p. 67). Wang-Ming—a later Chinese philosopher, writing 2,000 years after Confucius— stated that each individual is endowed with a nature that is perfectly good and that can never be entirely changed (Matter, 1974).

Pure or intuitive goodness was emphasized in the ethical phi- losophies of India, as well. Tagore wrote of a spirit of unity that occurred at the moment in time in which human beings became truly self-conscious. Because of this spirit of unity, transcendence of self has the highest meaning (Sharma, 1965). Among the ancient Greeks, Aristotle (1962) expressed the view that goodness is not only a possibility, but that it is tied to the felicity and well-being of individuals and of the polity. The more one gives, the more one has: "To 'do well' is impossible unless you 'do right,' and there can be no doing right for a state any more than there can be for an individual, in the absence of goodness and wisdom" (p. 281).

During the 18th-century Enlightenment, the image of mankind as innately bad was challenged by the opposing view of an in- nately good and reasonable nature that becomes bad only when the influence of evil institutions is exerted. On the basis of original goodness, combined with the capacity to reason, the human spe- cies is seen as having the ability to design a great world. The 18th-century philosopher David Hume (1973) declared that human beings possess a primary drive or instinct of benevolence, and he wrote of such a "principle in our nature as concern for others" (p. 45), a view also expressed by Adam Smith (Coase, 1976).

Jean-Jacques Rousseau (1950) believed in a "force of natural compassion, which contributes to the species as a whole by moderating the violence of self-love in each person" and which "the greatest depravity of morals has as yet hardly been able to destroy" (pp. 225-226). His morality of *romanticism* was a positive morality that dictates purposes and actions based on love of others. This view was a form of goodness tied to pride, to achievement of positive consequences and mitigation of suffering, and it was also associated with generosity, creativity, and warmheartedness. Rousseau himself, influenced by the morality of romanticism, resolved "to do boldly everything which seemed good to him, and to pay no heed to the judgment of other men" (Carr, 1961, p. 63).

Evolutionary Theory

Evolutionary theory posits that social behaviors are caused by instincts that are present at birth. Behaviors such as altruism and aggression, whose precise manifestations may be attributable to culturally conditioned variations, nevertheless reflect phylogenetic adaptations.

The decision about *where* to include a discussion of evolutionary approaches in the current chapter—and, indeed, whether to include it—was a difficult one. In regard to *whether* the biological approaches are congruent with altruism or not, ethologists and others writing about genetic predispositions have debated on both sides of the issue. One group of writers has claimed primacy for an instinct toward aggression, or "original sin"—the "Cain tendency" (Ardrey, 1962; Lorenz, 1963).

In an attack on the views of such instinct theorists as Konrad Lorenz, Midgley (1978) points out that our descent from violent subhuman species has been depicted as the basis for our aggressive and self-centered nature. The origin of the beast within, according to this view, is the beasts from whom we have evolved.

However, in all the world there is no beast as lawless and unsavory as those depicted by Ardrey, Lorenz, and others. In the past, rather than basing their conclusions on systematic observations of animal behavior, many writers relied on animal folklore in which the wolf, for example, was seen as characterized by "lawless cruelty."

> We have thought of the wolf always as he appears to the shepherd at the moment when he finally decides to turn a sheep into lamb chops. Recently, ethologists have taken the trouble to watch wolves systematically, between mealtimes, and have found them to be . . . paragons of steadiness and good conduct. . . . These surveys have often been undertaken by authorities who were initially rather hostile to the wolf and inclined to hope that it could be blamed for various troubles. (Midgley, 1978, pp. 25-26)

In contrast to proponents of the "killer" instinct, others have suggested that altruism may reflect a hereditary predisposition (e.g., Eibl-Eibesfeldt, 1971) and that human beings are intrinsically good. Campbell's (1983) latest formulation is that perhaps human beings inherit a "weak" altruism, in which "the altruistic trait benefits the carrier but benefits the nonaltruists even more. The trait contributes positively to absolute fitness but negatively to relative fitness" (p. 15). In addition, if we strictly adhere to a definition of altruism that includes such concepts as intentionality—even for the phylogenetically lower species—then it becomes difficult to justify the inclusion of a paradigm that labels as altruistic any behaviors that appear helpful or involve self-sacrifice. Indeed, it appears absurd to attribute a higher-order cognitive process such as intentionality to social insects, which are cited as prime examples of altruism among animals (Campbell, 1983). Despite these misgivings, a discussion of this rapidly changing and far from monolithic domain of inquiry is included, both because it has captured the popular imagination and because it poses an important challenge to conceptualizations of altruism.

To begin with, the most powerful influence on theories regarding the biological substrate of human social behavior has historically been Darwin's theory. From the viewpoint of some influential interpreters of Darwin (who later were vigorously disputed by Holmes [1945], and Montague [1950], the principles of "natural selection" and "survival of the fittest" lead to the Hobbesian implication that only egoism and the ability to compete (presumably through aggressive means) with others are rooted in the biological heritage of human beings. This view of Darwinian theory is probably incorrect, however. Darwinian theory suggests only that the tendencies most likely to survive are those that are adaptive. It is possible to demonstrate that there are situations and species for which altruism is adaptive and that there are instances in which aggression is not adaptive—if only because aggressiveness is not always the best way to compete for survival. That is,

> individuals may "compete" in the "struggle for survival" without engaging anyone else in conflict. The ability to beat a quick retreat, to hide, to climb, to "play possum" . . . may well entail more adaptive modes of competition than fighting. . . . [Also], aggression generally requires a heavy investment of energy. An exhausted victor may be vulnerable to defeat from a second antagonist. . . . And . . . every individual who engages in a hostile encounter with another individual risks injury or death. (Krebs & Miller, 1985, pp. 7-8)

Whether or not human aggression is mandated by the biological substrate, how do investigators concerned with evolutionary and biological theories—comparative psychologists, sociobiologists, and ethologists—attempt to account for altruism? Ethologists, who study total patterns of animal behavior (e.g., Eibl-Eibesfeldt, 1971), have noted that there are many instances of what appears to be altruism among animals below human beings on the phylogenetic scale. Territory, food, and domiciles have reportedly been shared equitably and without a struggle; some restrain reproduction (in eusociality, for example); certain species nurture or defend unrelated young; and mammals, social insects, and birds signal the approach of predators to their group, despite the fact that danger to the self is thereby augmented.

The sociobiologists, who postulate a gene for altruism, have devoted considerable attention to the genetic transmission of altruism.

The research question, as stated in Edward O. Wilson's (1975) groundbreaking *Sociobiology: The New Synthesis*, is, "How can altruism, which by definition reduces personal fitness, possibly evolve by natural selection?" (p. 3). In other words, when we employ a "pure" definition of altruism as intentional self-sacrifice, so that the individual experiences a net loss in his or her own fitness to augment the fitness of another, then is that individual not less likely to reproduce and pass his or her genes on to new generations? If so, then the likelihood of altruism should decrease in that individual's species, as it is no longer a mechanism enabling survival. In a narrow interpretation of Darwin, "If self-sacrifice results in fewer descendants, the genes that allow heroes to be created can be expected to disappear gradually from the population" (Wilson, 1978, p. 153).

Setting aside questions of whether evidence from the lower animals is useful, because of the probable lack of conscious intentionality, how can biologically oriented theorists account for altruism? In recent years, three types of explanation have been attempted.

The first approach makes reference to a mechanism termed *reciprocal altruism* (Trivers, 1983). The organism helps, from this perspective, because of the expectation that the help will be returned. The value of such mutual dependency both at the individual and at the group level is quite clear. If one feeds the hungry, helps others during disasters, and protects others from danger in full knowledge that help will be readily available during one's own time of travail, an enabling mechanism for personal survival is thus directly provided. It is not at all difficult to understand how there can be natural selection for this sort of social exchange. Furthermore, reciprocal helping is important to society and probably is a frequent form of social interaction. However, helping of this kind is not what we usually refer to as altruism. Altruism is a form of behavior intended to help others, despite the probability that one will give more than one expects to receive; it is a form of self-sacrifice rather than an insurance policy. The altruist may potentially be the recipient of favors from others, as he or she may be a likable individual, so that others may wish to return generosity for favors freely given. However, a generous motive and not the expectation of reciprocation guides the initial behavior.

A second explanation of altruism is found in the concept of *group selection*. According to this model, as set forth by Campbell in 1965, a given group may include individuals with altruistic genes who are therefore willing to sacrifice themselves for the sake of others. The altruism of a man "who throws himself into an abyss to do honor to his god," "the many soldiers who every year increase the numbers of voluntary deaths" (Durkheim, 1951, pp. 239-240), and the ardent defense by individuals of home, community, and nation-state can be comprehended within this framework. The explanatory mechanism is that groups containing such individuals are more likely to compete well with other groups; thus the group would encourage altruism in its members.

Campbell (1975) later retreated from this notion, however. He pointed out that although the group with the higher number of altruists may be more likely to survive, the viability of the individual altruist is diminished because he or she will not be able to compete well within the group. Thus the gene may be lost, and altruism will not evolve. Although Campbell discarded group selection as a route to the evolution of altruism, other biologists have pointed out that group selection can lead to the evolution of a form of altruism that is at least closer to "true" altruism than can the concept of reciprocal altruism (Wilson, 1980).

The explanation for altruism that has been promulgated most vigorously in the past decade is *kin selection*. Sociobiologists note that genes are reproduced and transmitted either directly by the individual or by the individual's relatives. The closer the genetic relationship, the greater the likelihood that replications of the individual's genes are carried. Thus this theory quite readily accounts for self-sacrificial behavior for the sake of relatives, as in the case of sacrifices made by parents on behalf of their children. The theory must be stretched pretty far, though, to explain altruism toward nonrelatives (e.g., Krebs & Miller, 1985).

The fact that this is a serious deficiency in the kin selection theory becomes apparent when one examines the types of altruism prevalent in today's society, most of which appear to involve benefits to unrelated persons. People adopt, nurture, and protect children, and even kittens; they help members of scorned groups—as in the rescue of Jews by non-Jews during the Holocaust. The fact that members of nonhuman species also are known to adopt and defend members of nonkin species implies that the altruist gene that has evolved is considerably less selective than is suggested by the kin selection hypothesis (Dawkins, 1976). It is, in fact, difficult to imagine a gene that could trigger different impulses toward relatives than toward strangers: "Cousins, after all, can be strangers, so indeed, can uncles and brothers" (Midgley, 1978, p. 141). Scholars who wrestle with the reality that we often aid unrelated strangers have noted that when altruism transcends kinship, some form of group selection mechanism may need to be invoked (Tullock, 1978). Others write that instead of a gene for so complex a set of behaviors as those composing altruism, what may be transmitted is a "taste" for altruism (Silver, 1980) or an "innate predisposition toward the acquisition of altruistic behavior . . . as . . . for example in reactions to distress in others" (Aronfreed, 1968, p. 140).

One also wonders whether the sociobiological argument confuses cause and effect. If, for example, it is demonstrated that the closer the blood relations the more helping occurs, then the effect of helping is survival of the genes shared by the kinship group to which the helper belongs. What is missing is evidence that it is knowledge of kinship and the motivation to preserve one's genes that somehow lead to the helpfulness. However egoistic (or "kin egoistic") the ultimate outcome, the proximate cause may have been empathy or some other nonegoistic motive. Notable here is that sociobiology seemed highly supportive of the existence of altruism at first, because it provided a basis for the proposition that altruism—as well as aggression—has a genetic basis (Midlarsky & Suda, 1978). What is increasingly apparent, however, is that the prevailing theories of sociobiology, and particularly those that stress kin selection, provide little evidence for "true" altruism. Even the most dramatic self-sacrificial behavior may ultimately help those to whom we are most closely related. The dilemma of modern sociobiology, then, is that it takes the bloom off the rose that is altruism—because altruism can thus be viewed only as selfish from the biological perspective, as currently articulated (Baldwin & Baldwin, 1981).

Newer Psychoanalytic Approaches

The traditional psychoanalytic approach emphasized domination of the personality by the self-centered, pleasure-seeking impulses associated with the id and the organismic needs that energized it. Altruism in this context was viewed as founded on inner conflict and defenses against hostility and guilt, which in the most positive construction consisted of nonpathological transformations of self-interest (Fenichel, 1945; A. Freud, 1937). Almost from the outset, however, critics of psychoanalysis argued that Sigmund Freud greatly overemphasized the negative, irrational side of human nature. Modifications of the original theory, in psychoanalytic approaches variously referred to as neo-Freudianism, ego psychology, or object relations theory, have wrought important changes in the portrait of humanity as id-driven, narcissistic, and hostile.

Among the changes is an emphasis on the role of the cultural milieu in molding the individual and on the ego as autonomous, at least to some extent, from the id and from biological determinism. The more humanistic ego psychologists conceive of the ego as at least partly free of the conflict between society and the id (Hartmann, Kris, & Loewenstein, 1947). To the extent that it is conflict-free, the ego is released to employ functions of its own. These ego functions, in turn, are based not on biological imperatives but on abilities that are needed to aid the individual's adaptation to the environment—such as intelligence, perception, and memory (Allport, 1961). Motives for human action are therefore expanded to include not just narcissistic pleasure seeking but the exercise of competence (White, 1959) and, in the mature personality, of love and compassion (e.g., Fromm, 1973). Unconscious motivation still plays a role in these psychodynamic theories, but cognitive factors such as conscious plans and goals are elevated in significance as bases for human action. A woman once viewed as gleefully digging in the soil to plant a garden because of her fixation at the anal stage may now be viewed as gardening for its own sake, as a way of expressing her own interests and goals and actualizing her creative tendencies (Allport, 1961).

Carl Gustav Jung, who left Freud's inner circle to found his own school of analytic psychology, wrote that although the past is important in determining behavior, the individual's goal striving and purposes also play important roles. In contradistinction to Freud's postulate that cultural phenomena are produced by suppressions of libidinal urges, Erich Fromm (1973) felt that dominant character traits of individual members of society help to shape the cultural milieu. These character traits, which may include positive attributes such as sensitivity to others and the capacity for love, are, in turn, dynamic adaptations to the cultural milieu by personality elements that are inherent, either biologically or on the basis of cultural evolution. Harry Stack Sullivan (1953) gave so central a role to interpersonal processes in the development of personality that his model of psychiatry was viewed as a facet of social psychology (a "social psychiatry"). Similarly, Alfred Adler (1964) described humanity as a state of social being and assigned a central role to "social interest," a form of prosocial functioning.

Erik Erikson (1963) proposed a stage theory that differs from Freud's in certain important respects. This theory was, to begin with, termed a theory of psychosocial versus psychosexual stages. In this choice of terminology is reflected Erikson's neo-Freudian focus on the role of cultural factors in molding personality, instead of biological instincts alone. A second important contribution by Erikson is the expansion of the period in which development is expected to occur. Unlike Freud's developmental theory, in which the human personality is formed in infancy, Erikson's model describes a process in which the core of personality, the "ego identity," unfolds throughout life. In Erikson's words,

> The integration . . . is more than the sum of the childhood identifications. It is the accrued experience of the ego's ability to integrate all identifications with the vicissitudes of the libido, with the aptitudes developed out of endowment, and with the opportunities offered in social roles. (p. 261)

The view of altruism has changed within the context of alterations in traditional Freudianism as well. Current psychoanalytic theories emphasize the importance of the mother-child bond, which by aiding in the acquisition of hope and trust (Erikson, 1963), sets the stage for empathy and altruism later in life (Ekstein,

1972). In opposition to Freud's definition of altruism as pathological, Erich Fromm (1973) argues the reverse—that an interruption in normal development because of isolation during childhood results in a personality characterized by intense egoism and self-absorption—the "necrophilious" personality. The "biophilious" or altruistic personality is a manifestation of normal development produced by the close relationship between child and mother and the successful resolution of any conflicts that occur between them.

Among the modern psychoanalytic approaches, object relations theory seems particularly applicable to the comprehension of altruism. Self-other relations hold a central place in altruistic functioning, and object relations theory has, as its primary concern, the relations between the individual and the love object or significant other. Many proponents of this approach adopt a position that is diametrically opposed to Freud's approach in a critical respect. That is, in Freud's theory, an avaricious and narcissistic sexuality is the primary drive, to which other drives and needs are subordinated, so that positive social relations are a defensive distortion of this basic need. In object relations theory, on the other hand, a highly humanistic position is advanced in which the establishment of love relations is seen as the principal motive, from which sexual needs and drives are then derived (Kernberg, 1979).

From the perspective of object relations theory, altruism is a product not of guilt and maladjustment but of normal development. Individual differences in altruism are derived from natural variations in physiological endowment (constitution and inborn factors) and from the mother's adequacy as a caregiver. Both of these are among the determinants of the child's developmental success (Horner, 1980). The object relations—first with mother and later with others—are based both on the actual external reality of the object and on the internalized objects. These inner objects, which serve as the screen through which external objects pass, are determined by prior experience with significant others. As each new stage of development is reached, the success of relationships with new objects is then partly based on the inner objects derived from earlier stages. The greater the adjustment at earlier stages, the more positive the child's inner objects. According to Sharabany

(1984), when good inner objects are more salient, benign cycles are more likely to be set in motion, including higher levels of prosocial functioning. Thus in this conceptualization, "healthy and optimal lines of development produce altruistic potential" (Sharabany, 1984, p. 218).

In sum, modern renditions of psychoanalytic theory represent a major departure from the original Freudian theory, in ways that are highly salient to the study of altruism. Earlier approaches, emphasizing a determining role for self-centered libidinal urges and for the unconscious, portrayed altruism as a desire to manipulate others or a reflection of neurosis. The more recent approaches, focusing on the conscious mind, view altruism as "a function of personality . . . [which] in some cases reflects the genuine intentions of cognitively and emotionally mature individuals" (Losco, 1981, p. 29).

CRITERIA FOR ATTRIBUTIONS OF ALTRUISM

It is especially tempting for social scientists like ourselves, who have relatively few opportunities to deal with basic questions concerning human nature, to pursue the role and meaning of altruism for the species. Indeed, in recent years, discussions of the altruism construct have been the subject of numerous separate volumes (e.g., Eisenberg, 1982; Rushton & Sorrentino, 1981; Staub et al., 1984; Wispé, 1978). Yet even from a brief treatment like the one presented above, one becomes mindful of the complexity of the construct. Altruism is multifaceted both in its expression and in its implications. In altruism, one values others. That means that one is aware of others, is oriented to others, cares about others, is motivated to help others, and behaves in accordance with those values and motives. Hence altruism is a form of human functioning that refers to cognition and affect, to the individual's thoughts, values, feelings, motives, behaviors, and in some conceptions, to the consequences of the behavior.

What criteria should we apply, however? In order to study altruism, we must have some initial idea of the range of acts to which we are willing to apply the term. Some criteria that we may consider are the following.

Motives of the Benefactor. If the helper is motivated by the expectation of intrinsic rewards, in the form of financial remuneration,
praise, or an increase in social status, then however much the
recipient benefits, the act is not considered to be altruistic. Thus,
for example, the Swedish fisherman who ferried Jews fleeing Den-
mark or Germany to safer territories—for a hefty fee—and turned
back those who could not pay would not be described as an
altruist, even if those whom he saved numbered in the thousands.
Altruistic acts are motivated by concern for others, altruistic moral
judgment, the predisposition to respond in a socially responsible
manner, and altruistic values. The behavior is considered altruistic
even if it incidentally results in pleasure, satisfaction, or other
positive benefits for the benefactor—but not if the act is performed
for that purpose. Not all acts performed for the sake of others are
wisely or competently emitted. Therefore, they may not all succeed.
The lack of competence may actually diminish current success and
the probability of subsequent helping attempts, whereas competent
performance may encourage the helper to help again (Midlarsky,
1984). In any event, whether wisely or foolishly chosen and performed,
well-intended acts performed with no quid pro quos or other
ulterior motives are considered to be altruistic by this criterion.

The Degree to Which the Act Is Costly. An altruistic act, by definition,
involves some degree of self-sacrifice. What this means is that the
altruistic individual stands to lose more than she or he gains. If
people manifest compassion because it is easy to do so, costs little,
and because they fully expect to gain more than they lose by acting
in this way, then an attribution of altruism may be inappropriate.
If people drive to a blood donation center at least once every 2
months—even when they are away from the donation center in
their home city—for the express purpose of meeting the need to
increase the nation's blood supply (and they receive no pressure
at home or at the workplace and no money or other extrinsic
rewards), then an attribution of altruism does seem appropriate.

The Degree to Which an Act Is Voluntary. Many acts of help giving
or service occur not because of unselfish motives but in response
to a demand. One source of demand comes from the individual's

role. The teacher who praises a child's classroom performance in the context of a school district-wide decision to give positive reinforcement whenever feasible is not behaving altruistically, even if the praise is very beneficial to the child. That same teacher's visit to the home of a sick child, in a district in which home visits are not prescribed, is likely to be acting altruistically. A child who voluntarily donates part of her allowance to a charity (particularly if done anonymously) may be exhibiting altruism. If required to do so by his or her parents or minister, then the act is not altruistic. If an act is required, then it is not considered altruistic, even if the cost to the actor is relatively high.

The Degree to Which Alternative Acts Are Available. Even if an act is not prescribed, there are situations in which there is no choice but to be helpful. The older resident of a congregate housing facility may be introduced to a new resident and asked to show that person around. The only other choice may be to flatly refuse—a choice that many would deem equivalent to no choice at all. To be considered altruistic, the individual should have the genuine option to perform an act that does not serve to aid others or should have recourse to do nothing. Any alternative act must involve no greater cost to the actor than that entailed by a helpful act.

The above criteria specify a rather stringent definition of altruism. If one were to restrict the investigation of altruism to only those behaviors that demonstrably meet all of these criteria, then the study of altruism would probably come to a halt.

A common solution to the problem within the field of psychology has been to avoid problems of definition, either by using terms like *prosocial behavior* or by relying on the use of operational definitions of altruism—a solution that evokes difficulties by varying so much from study to study that generalizations regarding altruism become hard to achieve. A more satisfactory solution is one in which helpfulness is viewed as ranging on a continuum, from nonaltruistic helping (or very low degrees of altruism) to "pure" altruism (or high degrees of altruism). Rosenhan (1969), for example, noted that helpful acts can range from everyday kindness, which he termed *normative,* to acts that meet more stringent definitions of altruism, termed *autonomous* altruistic acts.

Most of the work reported in this volume is nomothetic rather than idiographic in its methodology. As such, it deals with personality variables, motives, and behaviors by groups of individuals. The goal is to make general statements about altruism, rather than to engage in case-oriented idiographic analyses. Particularly because a nomothetic strategy has been adopted, we feel justified in describing as altruistic those manifestations that have a high probability of exemplifying that form of behavior. For example, where a group of individuals reportedly engages in a high degree of cross-situational helping behavior, we have sometimes been willing to attribute altruism to them, in comparison with groups manifesting lower levels of helping. When the "high helpers" also evidence personality characteristics, values, and motives found in other studies to be associated with altruism, then we describe the motives for helping as altruistic. This approach is, of course, not without problems. However, when it is used thoughtfully and with appropriate caveats, we believe that it may lead to an enhanced understanding of the antecedents, nature, and outcomes of positive functioning in the older adults whom we have studied.

NOTE

1. Even love is reduced to behavior motivated by entirely selfish motives. Unless one is making "attribution errors" about one's passion, one will recognize that "the amount of romantic love a person feels is . . . a direct function of the benefits he or she derives from the relationship" (McClelland, 1986, p. 335).

Beyond Current Views of Aging: The Role of Altruism in Late Life

Those who fail to realize the intrinsic meaning of their old age will only feel the sufferings of age. There is a world of difference between a man [*sic*] who endures, wishes, experiences, and a man [*sic*] who takes what is given to him [*sic*], realizes it, shapes it. —Karl Jaspers

The foregoing chapter presents criteria for attributions of altruism and a glance at the complex labyrinth of perspectives regarding the possibility of altruism for the species as a whole. Within the species, however, diverse patterns of adaptation can potentially occur in subgroups, in response to internal and external factors. The elderly, conventionally defined as individuals whose chronological age is 65 years or older, compose one such subgroup. In order to continue the task of illuminating the background of our own empirical research, we turn now to an exploration of the place of altruism and helping in late life adaptation.

As a review of the gerontology literature readily indicates, interpersonal interactions of the elderly have been the subject of extensive investigation (Kahana, 1982; Lowenthal & Robinson, 1976; Rosow, 1967). An analysis of existing studies indicates that three theoretical frameworks or orientations underlie the preponderance of existing

---

AUTHORS' NOTE: This chapter is partly based on an article written in collaboration with Dr. Boaz Kahana (Kahana, Midlarsky, & Kahana, 1987) for the journal *Social Justice Research*.

research. Each of these three orientations—the dependency model, the autonomy model, and the exchange model—makes the implicit assumption that the social life of the older adult is marked by an egocentric orientation. This chapter presents a fourth model or conceptual orientation—the altruistic, other-oriented, or contributory model. Altruism, the subject of considerable scholarly interest as outlined in the preceding chapter, has seldom been systematically investigated as an explanation of interpersonal interactions among older adults.

Table 3.1 presents a diagrammatic outline of the formulations regarding the nature of giving and receiving during late life that are implicit in the four conceptualizations. Each of the frameworks depicted also reflects a different value orientation within the behavioral and social sciences. The frameworks are presented in their simplest form in order to illustrate their approach to specific issues regarding giving and receiving by older adults. We fully recognize that research based on these conceptualizations reflects far more complex and multidimensional orientations with respect to other aspects of interpersonal behavior. Furthermore, it is important to note that the conceptualizations presented are not always mutually exclusive and frequently refer to typologies of aging, need states, or modes of behavior. Finally, individual and situational characteristics of a given interaction may determine what conceptualization is most appropriate for explaining it.

This chapter, then, constitutes an effort to elucidate the possible role of altruism among the elderly. In it we outline the four theoretical frameworks and review empirical evidence regarding helping by the elderly. Finally, we turn to formulations that may provide support for the proposition that altruistic behavior has the potential to emerge, sometimes for the first time, during late life.

ALTERNATIVE FRAMEWORKS FOR CONSIDERING INTERPERSONAL INTERACTION IN LATE LIFE

The Dependency Model

Dependency and helplessness are stereotypically viewed as hallmarks of older adulthood (Carver & del la Garza, 1984), which

Table 3.1 Models of Interpersonal Behavior in Late Life

Theoretical Model	Primary Value Orientation	Model Levels of Giving	Model Levels of Receiving	Motives for Helping	Level and Type of Involvement With Others
Dependency	Medical/social service	Low	High	No—unable	High/passive
Autonomy	Anthropological	Low	Low	No—unwilling	Low
Exchange	Economic	High	High	Yes—Exchange	High or low active or passive
Altruistic	Humanistic	High	Low	Yes—Altruism	High/active

can be predicted with a high degree of accuracy from one's position on the chronological age scale (Walker, 1982). In American society, with its emphasis on individualism (Smith, 1978), dependency is generally viewed as extremely negative and, at the same time, a natural result of the passage of time.[1] If in older adulthood "change is change toward slowness, less behavior, less acquisition, less performance" (Baltes & Willis, 1977, p. 138), so that "aging is a process of becoming more dependent" (Thomasma, 1984, p. 86), then the process of aging is likely to be experienced as bleak.

Gerontology, the study of aging, is a multidisciplinary field. It is not surprising, therefore, that dependency in late life is described as multidimensional in nature. Declines and decrements have been reported in the physical, economic, cognitive, and social domains (e.g., Hendricks & Hendricks, 1986; Kalish, 1969). In much of the literature it seems almost axiomatic that older adults are harassed by illness, denuded of financial resources, cognitively deprived or impaired, and bereft of social roles, status, and loved ones.

In regard to physical health, for example, older adults tend to have a higher number of functional losses in sight, locomotion, and hearing as well as more acute and chronic disease and more hospitalizations than younger adults have (Yordy, 1986). Even more troubling, perhaps, is the perception that old age itself constitutes a medical problem (Zola, 1983). Indeed, "for Americans old age is seen as a kind of disease, a terminal illness that

uniformly begins in the sixties" (Sankar, 1984, p. 251). The stereotype that older persons are ill and dependent on others for their
care may be based, in part, on the statistic that approximately 80%
of older adults have at least one significant health problem. The
reality, however, is that there is great heterogeneity in activities of
daily living even among the oldest old, and the preponderance of
older people live in the community, where they are able to manage
their own care (Abeles & Ory, 1991). Indeed, the associate dean of
a large university, upon her retirement at age 65, recently con-
veyed her enthusiasm at having the time to engage in her favorite
avocation—flying small aircraft!

Stereotypes and anxieties aside, health-related dependencies do
not appear to be invariably associated with age. Although there is
certainly an increased probability of health problems with the
accrual of years, there are numerous instances of people who are
continually ill by the time they reach their 50s and of 70-year-olds
in excellent health. Nevertheless, when illness does strike an older
person, it is not uncommon for people to assume that the illness
is due to inevitable declines associated with aging. Of course, not
every older person can be expected to accept such attributions. As
a case in point, one respondent in our own study (Midlarsky &
Kahana, 1985a, 1985b) told us that she had considerable trouble
reading because of pain in her right eye. When she consulted her
physician about her problem, his unsympathetic reply was, "What
do you expect? Your eye, like the rest of you, is 82 years old." She
replied: "My left eye is 82 also, so how come it doesn't hurt when
I try to read?"

Currently, writers vary in the degree to which they attribute
changes in health to biological processes or environmental factors
(Barton, Baltes, & Orzech, 1980; Brody, 1977). Still others attribute
health-related (and other) dependencies to the interaction of per-
sonal/physiological factors with such environmental/contextual
factors as inability to gain access (perhaps for economic reasons)
to the fruits of continually evolving health-care technology (Yordy,
1986) or residence in debilitating environments (E. Kahana, 1982;
Lawton, 1975b; Lawton, Windley, & Byerts, 1982; Wack & Rodin,
1978). In a recent study, for example, 72 men and women whose
mean age was 78 were asked to perform a simple psychomotor

task after being exposed to one of three experimental training conditions to which they had been randomly assigned. Group 1 was given considerable instrumental assistance, Group 2 was encouraged but was given little help, and Group 3 was a control group, which received no training. Results indicated that the Group 2 subjects were superior to the other two in both completeness and speed of performance, were higher in self-confidence, and judged the task to be less difficult than did the other two groups. The task performance of Group 1 subjects deteriorated to a level lower than that of the control group. The authors concluded that excessive infantilization of older adults—based on the assumption that they are dependent and in need of extensive instrumental assistance—can lead to decreases in actual and perceived competence, while leading to concomitant increases in functional disability and perceived helplessness (Avorn & Langer, 1982).

Old age is also equated with economic dependency by some analysts. A widespread reflection of the propensity to view older adults as economically burdensome is the aged dependency ratio. In one description, we read:

> The most common version of this ratio is the number of persons 65 and over per 100 persons 15 to 64. The rationale for it and for its title is that it provides a crude index of the relative dependency load attributable to the older people in a population. It assumes that older people are not in the workforce, are consumers but not producers, and are dependent upon the active producers through transfer payments of some kind. It also assumes that the 15-69 group represents the productive population. (Cowgill, 1986, p. 16)

In a ratio of this kind, the assumption is made that there are two classes of citizens: workers and "dependents," the latter defined as those who are currently neither in the labor force nor seeking employment. As Adamchak and Friedmann (1983) note, "Workers represent assets in this model, and persons not in the labor force are liabilities" (p. 123). Left out of this purely economic ratio, of course, is any calculation of contributions that may be made by the "dependents"—particularly the community-dwelling "young old" outside of the paid labor force.

Late life is also frequently depicted as a period of inevitable declines in cognitive functioning and ability (Cerella, Poon, & Williams, 1980) in such domains as the processing of information (Salthouse & Somberg, 1982) and memory (Craik, 1977; Kausler, 1982; Light, 1991; Poon, 1985). Intellectual losses, often thought to be inevitable and irreversible in old age, provide another basis for the assumption that dependency is a salient characteristic of older adulthood. According to Reisberg (1981):

> Brain failure, like old age, is a condition which mankind has always recognized and always accepted. . . . So closely have people associated the loss of intellectual functioning with normal aging that they have not always found it necessary to have different words for the two conditions. Indeed, one word is currently used to refer to the two statuses of aging and loss of intellect: "senility." (p. 1)

The 1975 unabridged 2nd edition of *Webster's New Twentieth Century Dictionary* defines senility as

> old age,
> weakness,
> the characteristics of old age, and
> infirmity of mind and body.

Is old age synonymous with cognitive decline in actuality? The early cross-sectional studies of the relationship between age and intelligence indicated that intelligence declines with age, a decline that was erroneously attributed to biological aging rather than to cultural differences across cohorts, to which these findings were eventually attributed. Longitudinal studies, on the other hand, revealed no general declines until very late in life (Baltes & Labouvie, 1973; Schaie, 1974). Even at that point the declines are neither devastating for most older adults nor universal. Expectations of increments in dependency concomitant with chronological age are contradicted by findings that people in their 7th, 8th, and even their 9th decade of life may experience little or no diminution in cognitive ability. Indeed, results of neuropsychological investigations indicate that approximately 33% of 80- to 85-year-olds manifest no measurable decline. Conversely, benign senescent losses can occur as early as the 5th decade of life (Benton, Eslinger, & Damasio, 1981). Furthermore, adaptive development in late life may result in increased cognitive flexibility and complexity and in different modes of thinking—including a richer understanding of emotional processes and interpersonal behavior (Labouvie-Vief, 1982). Nevertheless, assumptions that the accrual of years is inevitably associated with cognitive deficits severe enough to constitute disability appear to be made not only by younger individuals but by the elderly themselves. Older adults are significantly more likely than younger adults to believe that they need help with intellectual tasks and less likely to take responsibility for maintaining or improving their intellectual functioning (Lachman, 1986; Lachman & McArthur, 1986).

Finally, the elderly are portrayed as dependent in the social/ interpersonal realm as well. Writers seem to assume that social dependency is the consequence of the stress experienced by older adults as they are increasingly exposed to inflexible and conflicting demands for far-reaching change at the same time that biological, financial, and cognitive declines are most apparent (Clark & Anderson, 1967). The assumption of increases in social stress as people age (Holmes & Rahe, 1967) appears to come, in turn, from the observation that older adults not only experience decreased physical capacity but also sustain losses in diverse social roles and occupations, so that their life space generally appears to shrink. As a result of mandatory retirement and changes in family composition, lifelong occupations both inside and outside of the home may cease, and few new opportunities for meaningful engagement may become available (Riley & Foner, 1968; Rosow, 1967). As perceived incompetence increases, concomitant with growing passivity, the need for external support increases as well—from both formal and informal sources. The dependence of older adults on their children and other network members is assumed, at least by some, to be a hallmark of late life (Brody, 1985; High, 1991). What is missing from this analysis is recognition that in regard to the limited physical capacities, what is most likely to be lost is some of the excess in physiological reserve with which human beings are equipped. There is generally enough physical capacity left to permit psychosocial interaction (Fries & Crapo, 1981). Also missing is the recognition that physiological losses and even role losses may be offset, at least to some degree, by gains in ego development, wisdom, experience, and skills.

The assumption or expectation of dependency has the potential to become a self-fulfilling prophecy. The assumption of dependency and infirmity may lead people to limit their activities because of feared incompetence and to experience decreases in their own effectiveness because of lowered performance expectations. Even effective behavior may go unrewarded. Consider instances in which an older person behaves in a way that would be considered competent or effective if exhibited by a younger person. As Figure 3.1 illustrates, when competent behavior is met by a negative response—perhaps because the behavior is not appropriately treated as competent, and/or because only dependent behaviors are recognized and reinforced—then perceptions of the self as incompetent may result. Perceived incompetence may, in turn, increase the probability of what may be variously designated as behavioral deficits, needs for external support, or excessive disability. Through this process, objectively competent behavior may decrease still further in the future (cf. Avorn & Langer, 1982; Langer, 1983; Midlarsky, 1984).

Research reflecting a dependency orientation has primarily focused on identifying determinants or on facilitating the amelioration of various deficiencies among the elderly (Butler & Lewis, 1982). The many studies on determinants and impacts of caregiving to older adults also reflect the influence of this framework (e.g., Cicirelli, 1983; Coward, 1987; Parmelee, 1983; Sivley & Fiegener, 1984; Stoller, 1984, 1989; Sussman & Romeis, 1982). Support for the dependency model was derived, for example, from early studies of personality change that indicated a more passive orientation among older persons than among younger persons (Riley & Foner, 1968). Typologies such as the "passive-dependent" personalities of the Kansas City studies of adult life (Neugarten, 1964) and the "rocking chair men" in the study by Reichard et al. (1962) also represented prototypes of dependent adaptations to aging. More recent exemplars of the dependency orientation in the interpersonal domain include the myriad studies on family caregiving (e.g., Reece, Walz, & Hagebaek, 1983; Stoller, 1983), social support

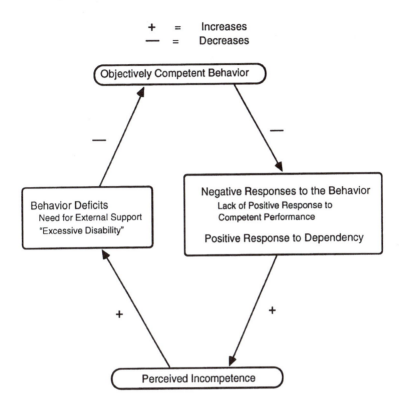

Figure 3.1 Model of Attribution-Based Dependency in Late Life

for the elderly (e.g., Antonucci & Akiyama, 1987; Biegel, 1984; Sauer & Coward, 1985; Wan, 1982), and service needs utilization and service provision (Cantor & Myer, 1978; Exton-Smith & Evans, 1977; Wack & Rodin, 1978; Ward, 1977). Where altruism is considered part of late-life interaction, it is often presumed that older persons are the recipients of help, as in the following: "Societies that sponsor an egocentric, self-seeking spirit in the population will be lethal to old and young alike. But societies that sponsor altruism and the formation of internalized objects provide security to these vulnerable cohorts" (Gutmann, 1987, p. 315).

As depicted in Table 3.1, research based on the dependency framework of aging typically grows out of the medical or social service orientation and often describes the elderly as showing great needs for succorance coupled with nurturance needs (Havighurst, 1975). As such, the dependency orientation presumes high levels of egocentricity. It predicts low levels of helping based on an inability to give, because of limited resources, and constitutes a perspective that is compatible with Sigmund Freud's (1959) notion that we are all born with a quantum of physical and, ultimately, of psychic energy that becomes depleted with age, with energy resources allocated to the ego-depleted first. The elderly are expected to show a desire for social interaction. However, such interactions are characterized by a passive orientation and reflect a search for social support by others (Goldfarb, 1969).

The Autonomy Model

There is an irony inherent in viewing old age as a period characterized by dependency—the interpersonal/social orientation that is associated with childhood. As noted in Chapter 1, the logical corollary of the view of old age as a host of declines, decrements, and dependencies is that when the cherished goal of longevity is achieved, this goal attainment is accompanied by a precipitous and probably unwelcome regression to a childlike, recipient role. In recent years, some investigators have concluded that the excessive focus on dependency has led to an acceptance, and even a reinforcement by gerontologists, of ageist stereotypes that may in many cases be founded on a lack of comprehension of the meaning of late life for the older adult (Gutmann, 1987; Kaufmann, 1986). Dowd (1980) speculates that "without knowledge of an old person's strength, many presume it to be weak . . . knowing nothing about an old person's intelligence, many also presume that to be in a weakened state . . . so that many aged persons are doubly disadvantaged" (p. 59).

According to Gadow (1983), an older adulthood that may appear to the observer to be nothing more than a seemingly endless series of days filled with misery and dependency may be experienced as a period rich with meaning as the individual engages in an existential exploration of the precarious nature of human life. Others have noted that the emphasis on dependency may have come, in part, from the fact that many of the older adults studied by the first generations of gerontologists are disadvantaged in relation to the more recent and future cohorts of elders (Troll, 1984).

In contradistinction to theory and research concerned with decrements and dependency is the focus on adaptive capacities and strategies of older adults who appear to cope maturely and successfully with changing resources and demands. Foremost among the features of successful adaptation, or mental health, is autonomy. One of the first people to describe positive mental health, Jahoda (1958) included autonomy among her six criteria. Others have proposed that autonomy and personal control are crucial for individual functioning and that their curtailment may seriously impede personal adjustment in late life (Fries & Crapo, 1981; Seligman, 1975; Thomae, 1980). According to Jung (1933), whereas socialization is the focal task of the younger years, adaptive development in later life requires individuation. Autonomy, along with separation and differentiation, is a trait that has traditionally been seen by developmental theorists as a hallmark of adult development (Giele, 1980).

For example, Gould's (1972) characterization of the unique features of late life refers to the freedom to act as a truly autonomous individual during late life. According to Gould (1980), the development of autonomy, which is necessary for maturity, comes only after a series of transformations that occur throughout adult life. It is not until the age of 50 that the individual recognizes that he or she is independent and self-governing. The ability to reach the apex of maturity represented by autonomy is based on the resolution of childhood separation anxiety, which resulted from the individual's first attempts at psychological independence. In Erikson's (1968) theory, although autonomy is the successful outcome of the second stage of development, corresponding to Freud's anal stage, it reappears as an issue in young adulthood, middle adulthood, and particularly in old age, when threats to autonomy may be diverse and frequent. Erikson also posits a movement from a focus on social relationships to greater reflectivity and interiority in old age. For Jane Loevinger (1976), as for Gould, autonomy represents a high level of maturity —that is, it is the 9th in a series of 10 developmental stages—and as such it is relatively rare. Autonomy and self-sufficiency have also been cited as elements of self-actualization, the realization of one's full potential during adulthood (Maslow, 1954). Kohlberg's (1969) stage theory of moral development posits autonomy as the highest developmental stage.

In a survey conducted by Shanas (1962), autonomy and self-reliance were among the highest values espoused by the older respondents. Furthermore, these older respondents were reluctant to give up their independent residences to join the households of their children and felt that they, and not their children, were responsible for their care and maintenance.

Longitudinal data also indicate that the autonomy motive generally increases throughout adulthood. The AT&T Studies of Male Managers (Bray & Howard, 1983) found that the need for autonomy rises from the age of 20 through at least the 50s, whereas a study by Veroff, Reuman, and Feld (1984) indicated that the autonomy motive generally increases after age 30.[2] The exercise of autonomy—defined, in this instance, as the avoidance of dependency on others—has been frequently linked in recent research to successful aging (Rodin, 1986; Rowe & Kahn, 1987). For women, in particular, autonomy shows a significant rise in later life, (Feldman, Biringen, & Nash, 1981). The joy reportedly experienced by at least some older women as they become free of earlier social roles is reflected in Helen Lawrence Brown's (1974) paean to autonomy in late life. In old age, wrote Brown,

> You no longer have to mind your image
> Or be a model . . .
> You don't have to prove anything . . .
> Little is required of you socially
> Except that you be neat, and pleasant, and don't whine. (p. 157)

The impact of the autonomy model, with its emphasis on the need for independence and self-determination in order to ensure well-being in late life, is reflected in advice given to the children of older parents, as in the following:

> The process of aging . . . [may lead to] the theft of autonomy, or control over one's own life. In the long run, that may even be the most painful loss of all. Most aging adults, with reason, hang onto their autonomy as long as possible . . . all people, including the old and the sick, are entitled to control over their own lives. They have a right to choose how to live and how to die. Even loving children have no right to impose on frail parents solutions the parents are unwilling to accept—even if the children have no doubt that these solutions are in the parents' best interests. (Otten & Shelley, 1977, p. 7)

The importance of this advice is underscored by recent findings that many older adults consider their independence—defined as control over one's life course within the context, wherever possible, of a normal community setting (National Advisory Council on Aging, 1990)—to be a critical determinant of their quality of life. Conversely, there are numerous instances in which dependency results in psychological distress for the older recipient (e.g., Markides & Krause, 1986). The swing of the pendulum to the extreme, in some instances, of attacking the role and prerogative of family members as surrogate decision makers even in cases of extreme cognitive impairment may, for many who prefer to rely on their families during times of adversity, be unrepresentative of their wishes.

According to the autonomy model, particularly as espoused by Cohler (1983), older adults generally aim to extricate themselves from social demands and obligations; social interactions are minimized, thus increasing inner-directedness. Several current theorists have characterized the emphasis on self-contained autonomy as "the North American cultural ideal, reflected in and legitimized by American psychology" (Meacham, 1989, p. 9). Both Sandler (1982) and Sampson (1988) have pointed out, however, that within Western culture, individual achievement and satisfaction ultimately rely, at least in part, on efforts by others—that is, upon interdependence—a phenomenon that Sampson describes as "ensembled individualism." In Cohler's view, it is a myth that the

Western cultural ideal is rugged individualism, in the sense of solitary and unaided pursuit of goals. Examination of Western texts indicates, instead, that it is interdependence and not complete independence or autonomy that is deemed necessary for success. Thus "even ragged Dick, the hero of the Horatio Alger series, had the good fortune to know a distant relative who could make the necessary connections . . . to assist his phenomenal rise to power and influence" (Cohler, 1983, p. 36).

The assumption that interdependence is the royal road to satisfaction is, however, unwarranted in the case of the elderly, according to Cohler. Unlike younger persons, the aged may experience withdrawal from life to reminisce, to ponder the meaning of life, and hence to attain inner calm as the most desirable mode of response—a fact that is more fully recognized in non-Western cultures than in Western cultures (Kakar, 1978). Cohler and Galatzer-Levy (1990) write:

> As a consequence of the increased awareness of the finitude of life, both men and women intensify concerns with self and display less patience for demands upon time and energy which are acutely experienced as in "short supply" . . . some of the easy empathy between elders and preschool children may reflect similarities in the experience of time. The sense that what is to be done must be done now can lead the creative individual to new and startling degrees of freedom and fearlessness. (pp. 219-220)

In contrast to respect for the older adult—and for manifestations of personal control that may, for example, lead to a contemplative mode—even well-meaning professionals may urge older adults to engage in activities chosen by others "for their own good." One model home for the aged "had an almost carnival atmosphere as old people were rushed from activity to activity . . . [indicating] profound disrespect for the psychological processes of their elderly charges . . . [which] bears witness to the intense anxiety stimulated in the staff" (Cohler & Galatzer-Levy, 1990, p. 228).

In Cohler's version of the autonomy model, therefore, the notion that autonomy is the natural mode of interpersonal interaction in late life shares some elements in common with disengagement theory (Cumming & Henry, 1961) and with the Jungian view of increasing constriction of personality in late life (Jung, 1933). Supporting an autonomy-based notion of social interaction is research indicating greater self-preoccupation in late life and greater "interiority" (Neugarten, 1979), in which the primary focus is on evaluating the meaning of one's life. Similarly, greater introversion has been observed in several developmental studies of personality (Leon, Gillum, Gillum, & Gouze, 1979; Neugarten, 1977; Schaie & Parham, 1976).

The autonomy model—at least as espoused in the disengagement position of Cumming and Henry (1961) and in Cohler's (1983) work—implies that older persons should find their greatest satisfaction in isolated, independent life patterns. There is evidence that some older people are quite content with solitary living arrangements, even within the current Western culture. Some degree of empirical support for the autonomy model may be derived from a study by Maas and Kuypers (1974), who found a subset of fathers of subjects in the Oakland and Berkeley longitudinal studies who appeared quite satisfied with life centered on a solitary hobby, such as bird-watching or wood-working. They called these men the "hobbyists." Similarly, Savage, Gaber, Britton, Bolton, and Cooper (1977) found that certain isolated older men in England appeared to be largely satisfied with their lives. In two other studies, elderly residents of Florida retirement communities were found to portray such autonomous value orientations (Kahana & Kahana, 1983; Streib, Folts, & Greca, 1983). Observations indicated that they found late-life gratifications in self-improvement and limited their involvement or interaction to family and significant others. In general, though, satisfaction appears to be associated with social involvement (Palmore, 1981), and in some cases, isolation may be attributable not to a positive motive such as desire for autonomy but to a negative, such as fear of crime if one ventures forth (e.g., Riger & Gordon, 1981).

This apparent contradiction between a strong autonomy motive and enjoyment of social relations may be resolved when we consider that for older adults, the key element in autonomy that may lead to satisfaction is not isolation from others but the ability to choose when and with whom to interact. Cohler makes the point that older people may wish to withdraw from obligatory, interdependent family relationships. On the other hand, in Loevinger's (1976) view, it is clear that autonomy does not imply that one must be indifferent to others. Instead, for some people, increased individualism may result in more nurturance, and for others it may result in less. What at least some older people may need is to become autonomous—or disengaged—from social role definitions (rather than from social relationships) as well as from other personal constraints. Only then, perhaps, will older adults be free to pursue broader metaphysical issues such as the meaning of their own lives (Labouvie-Vief, 1982; Labouvie-Vief et al., 1987).

In any event, as depicted in Table 3.1, the autonomy orientation to aging may be seen as arising primarily from an anthropological view of late-life adaptation (Cohler, 1983; Gutmann, 1977). It predicts low levels of helping, largely motivated by a desire to limit obligations to others. In this framework, the aged are seen as generally withdrawing from social interactions with others, portraying little need for giving or receiving in social domains. There may be a desire for self-fulfillment in relatively hedonistic ways centered around personal goals.

The Exchange Model

In contrast to the dependency and autonomy models, the exchange model acknowledges that older people engage in relationships that may be characterized by interdependence or mutuality. Like the dependency and autonomy models, however, this third model depicts interpersonal behavior as egoistically motivated.

Among theoretical orientations explaining social behavior and interactions among the elderly, exchange theory has been one of the most prominent and well-articulated conceptualizations (Dowd, 1980). The exchange model of aging is anchored in an economic perspective of human interactions (as is the exchange-based view of all other phenomena; cf. Chapter 2); indeed, exchange is employed to define influence patterns in most theories of economic behavior. The basic premise of this essentially Hobbesian position is that all human interactions can be viewed as social exchanges, in which resources and satisfactions are essentially the currency of the exchanges. The basic assumption in exchange relations is that in order to obtain what one wants, one must be able to provide what someone else wants in return. Furthermore, one must provide the desired service as a "favor" rather than as part of one's normal obligations. The service must be voluntarily tendered, and it must be received under the terms of an implicit agreement that the favor is to be returned. Social exchanges are treated as the building blocks of all encounters, and a wide range of phenomena—including, for example, cooperation, competence, helping, love, bargaining and negotiation, and intergroup conflict—are considered to be explainable as exchange transactions (Austin & Worchel, 1979; Gergen, Greenberg, & Willis, 1980; Piliavin et al., 1981; Walster, Walster, & Berscheid, 1978).

In exchange theory, generosity is based on norms that are based, in turn, on conceptions regarding the "good." Thus, for example, the basic concept for some cultures is the concept of limited good, which apparently prevails in certain peasant societies (Foster, 1965). In the context of limited good, because goodness is limited the giver experiences a loss of good, therefore being put at a relative disadvantage through acts of generosity. Thus the probability of giving is expected to decline where this concept is dominant. In cultures like our own, in which the concept of expanding good is used, each time "good" is given it is reciprocated, and so on, hence, it expands. Because reciprocation of good is anticipated by members of the society, helpers do not expect to lose anything as a result of their helping. The prediction from this is that where the concept of expanding good is operative, more helping behavior is likely to be observed (L'Armand & Pepitone, 1975).

A discussion of the treatment of altruism and helping in exchange theorists appears in Chapter 2. In sum, social exchange theorists describe all individuals in social interactions as attempting to maximize rewards and to minimize costs. The primary goal for all actors is to obtain outcomes that are most profitable for themselves (McDonald, 1981). Much of human behavior, in this view, is based on norms, prominent among which is the "norm of reciprocity," whereby social exchange is maintained only when all of the individuals involved are making a profit, and all payments made by individuals eventually balance out. Exchange theory predicts that help is given because one has received a service, expects to receive one, or is attempting to be worthy of one. In any given situation, the individual currently "indebted" to others is the one most likely to be of service. Hence giving would be closely related to the extrinsic rewards that one has either received or is expecting to receive.

In this conceptualization, the individual's self-presentation and self-concept are perpetually balanced on a fulcrum of mutual needs and comparative resources. Interpersonal relations are affected by the exchange values of the individual's power resources, and those with the greatest resources are able to dictate the terms of the exchange. Because the elderly in modern industrial U.S. society are seen as holding few power positions, their collective ability to benefit in social exchange relationships is viewed as limited (Blau, 1964; Clark & Anderson, 1967). Thus older men are more likely to retain power over their wives until late in life because the resources that are typically under their control (i.e., financial) are retained for a longer period of time than are the resources viewed as valuable in Western women (charm, beauty). As women increasingly work outside the home in the postparental years, women's resources—and consequently their power within their marriages—may decrease less rapidly or even increase (cf. Hess & Williamson, 1984).

In general, however, old age has been generally viewed in our society as carrying with it devalued status characteristics and even those resources that older persons possess are seen as providing little power. Accordingly, old people tend to internalize society's image of them as lacking in resources (Kahana, 1974) and hence, to feel that they are not entitled to power in social exchanges. Furthermore, to the extent that older persons are indeed more dependent on others than others are on them (because of perceived deficiencies in resources), they will experience power deficits. According to Hess and Williamson (1984), support for this theoretical perspective is found within families, in which one may observe a changing balance of power between children and their parents as the parents' resources decline and dependence increases with age. The deficiency in power comes, according to the principle of least interest, from the fact that those who feel more independent in a relationship, and more able to leave it, have greater power to dominate the relationship (Waller & Hill, 1951).

An example of the application of social exchange theory is found in work by Lozier (1975), who writes that the hallmark of successful aging is accommodation to the social order in a manner calculated to ensure some degree of personal security—Lozier's social equity-based thesis is that adequate security and influence in old age come from society's awareness of its obligation to, and commitment to, reimburse the individual on the basis of service credits that have been amassed. Support for Lozier's thesis is derived from examples of interpersonal interaction in the urban environment of New Orleans and in Laurel Creek, a rural Appalachian community.

In Lozier's analysis, reciprocity between people—including the young as a group and older adults as a group—is facilitated within communities that are small and cohesive enough for people to be fully aware of services by, and needs of, each individual. In Laurel Creek, for example, there is a clear expectation that all *good* [sic] men are expected to engage in gainful employment. A man unable to obtain paid employment, probably because of the paucity of available jobs, is expected to look for work, to work hard on his property, and perhaps to help others. Idleness, symbolized by sitting on the porch during working hours, is considered a sign of badness.

Men [sic] usually retire at 65, when they can no longer find work. With the onset of frailty, older persons can draw upon the credits earned in the many years of labor and service to others. When, at last, the man [sic] becomes a unilateral recipient, thus becoming a costly burden to his neighbors with no ability to reciprocate in the future, he is considered to be socially terminal and is expected to die shortly thereafter. In the highly mobile urban setting where no record is likely to be kept of service given when the individual was capable of performing service, little or no reciprocation of benefits can be expected. The assumption in all of this, of course, is that there is a positive relationship between increased chronological age and entrance into unilateral recipient status.

Table 3.1 depicts a paradigm of high levels of both giving and receiving in an exchange framework, reflecting expectations of reciprocity in giving (Payne & Bull, 1985; Wentowski, 1981). It is recognized, however, that exchange theorists, such as Dowd (1980), may consider the elderly to possess few power resources, and hence low levels of both giving and receiving are also compatible with this paradigm. Low or high levels of involvement with others may exist wherein elderly people alternatively assume passive or active roles, depending on the nature of specific exchanges.

THE CONTRIBUTORY MODEL
OF SUCCESSFUL AGING

The altruistic/contributory model differs from formulations based on the dependency, autonomy, and social exchange conceptualizations in regard to the motivational basis for the behavior. Social exchange theory provides a basis for understanding certain prosocial behavior—that is, behavior that is emitted in order to ensure that the actor will ultimately maximize his or her benefits— and minimize costs. For the older person, for example, an important concern would be that service credits accrued and kept on one's "record" for future recognition should be, at a minimum, proportional to the energy expended earlier in life. In that way, when one's own dependencies are at their peak, help from others would be available (e.g., Dowd, 1980, 1984; Lozier, 1975). In the social exchange model, as in other economic models (Arrow, 1979; Hatfield et al., 1978; Simon, 1979), egoistic motives are believed to be the primary motives for the helpful behavior.

Criteria for determining whether an act may be altruistic are summarized in Chapter 2. In the simplest terms, altruism is viewed as helpful behavior that, although it may be relatively costly for the benefactor, is voluntarily undertaken for the sake of the other. That is, the help is given in response to the recipient's needs, rather than in response to the helper's needs—because the helper anticipates either positive consequences for the other or alleviation of the other's suffering, danger, or pain. Instead of viewing the interpersonal transaction from a self-centered or egocentric perspective, the helper is genuinely other-oriented. The self-centered person views the world as one in which one's own needs are at the center and therefore are the basis for decision making and for action; others and their concerns are at the periphery. For the other-centered or allocentric person, interpersonal relationships are at the center, and a primary value and source of identity is derived from tangible and intangible care directed toward others. Decisions are made only after considering the ways in which the decisions would affect others.[3]

Altruistic contributions are made on the basis of motives that are more analogous to the "love" described by Sorokin (1954) than they are to exchange (Blau, 1964). This is not to say that helpers experience no positive consequences. On the contrary, in this volume we argue that people who take on contributory roles or even engage in episodic helping for allocentric reasons experience positive consequences. Gratifications experienced by the altruistic individual may include an enhanced sense of competence (Midlarsky, 1984) and self-esteem (Press & McKool, 1972; Trimakas & Nicolay, 1974), vicarious pleasure (Aronfreed, 1969; Midlarsky, 1968), social integration (Liang, Dvorkin, Kahana, & Mazian, 1980), and well-being (Midlarsky & Kahana, 1981, 1983a, 1983b). Nevertheless, in altruistic helping the helpfulness was not motivated by the anticipation of such positive outcomes. Rather, it was the expected benefit to the other that served as the impetus, despite anticipated costs to the giver. In the economic terminology used by exchange theorists, altruism refers to individuals behaving in a way designed to maximize rewards to another, even if it involves incurring costs to themselves that may outweigh any extrinsically based benefits (Bryan & London, 1970; Eisenberg, 1982; Midlarsky, 1984; Rushton, 1982). On the surface it may appear that the proposed altruistic or contributory orientation may be subsumed as a special case or extension of the exchange framework, which would allow for diverse definitions of costs and benefits, including intrinsic benefits. Interestingly, however, even Adam Smith (1759/ 1976), the prominent economic theorist, recognized that the self-interest (even enlightened self-interest) that dominates exchange relationships is inadequate to explain all human interactions. Moral, caring relationships, he acknowledged, may instead be based on empathy and compassion, so that

How selfish soever man may be supposed, there are evidently
principles in his nature, which interest him in the future of
others, and render their happiness necessary to him, though
he derives nothing from it . . . that we often derive sorrow
from the sorrow of others is a matter of fact too obvious to
require any instance to prove it. (p. 7)

When we base our view of all interpersonal behavior on an economic metaphor, we therefore ignore the many instances in which
one goes far beyond the call of duty—out of goodwill, love, and
compassion. Voluntary self-sacrifice that is based on recognition
of the other's need does not imply a bargain in which a concrete
material return is expected (cf. Selig, Tomlinson, & Hickey, 1991).

It is our position that differences between the social exchange
and contributory orientations are real and important, having great
heuristic value. To reiterate, in considering differences between
exchange and altruistic orientations it should be noted that the
difference in the two theoretical orientations lies not in the anticipated consequences for the actor but rather in the proposed motives. According to exchange theory, people help (or engage in
other behavior) because of anticipated rewards. Put another way,
people help because the anticipated benefits outweigh the anticipated costs. What we mean by altruism, however, is that although
the helpful actor may certainly experience positive consequences
as a result of assisting others, these positive consequences are
unintended outcomes. This position stands in marked contrast to
exchange theory, wherein all behavior is motivated by the expectation of financial rewards, social approval, or personal satisfaction.[4] Because social exchange theory is based primarily on an
egoistic and individualistic perspective (Campbell, 1975; Wallach
& Wallach, 1983) and assumes that individuals are motivated
entirely by their own self-interest, it may be quite limited in its
vision, particularly when dealing with the noninstrumental (e.g.,
moral, committed, and/or compassionate) facets of human functioning. Indeed, in Western societies, a significant part of the
economic system involves grant rather than exchange relationships. In grant relationships—which are apparent in charities,
public education, business subsidies, and scholarships—benevo-

lent values, rather than expectations of exchange or reciprocation, have been found to govern the relationship (Boulding, 1981). In the words of Singer (1979), a "practical ethicist,"

> The ethics we have now does go beyond a tacit understanding between beings capable of reciprocity, and the prospect of returning to such a basis is not appealing. Since no account of the origin of morality compels us to base our morality on reciprocity . . . we should reject this view of ethics. (p. 7)

In our view, contributory actions may be based on nonegoistic motives of several types. These may be viewed as personality and/or cognitive orientations and include altruistic values, moral judgment, social responsibility, and empathy. We have found that these may act together (in an additive fashion) to prompt helpful actions.

ALTRUISTIC MOTIVES

Altruism may be viewed as one of several types of intrinsic, allocentric motives. Altruism researchers have diverse definitions in this context. Some define altruistic behavior as that which is undertaken without any anticipation of external rewards, but allowing for the possibility that internal rewards may be anticipated (e.g., Macaulay & Berkowitz, 1970). Others restrict the definition of altruism to behavior motivated by the concern for others, excluding thereby any behavior motivated by either extrinsic or intrinsic rewards (Batson, Duncan, Ackerman, Buckley, & Birch, 1981). It is difficult to see how behavior fitting this latter definition is explicable by means of exchange theory.

If contributory behavior is not motivated by egoistic motives or favorable cost-benefit ratios as described by the exchange theorists, then what is the source of altruism? Some theorists argue, from a cognitive perspective, that altruism is part of a valuing process in which acting on behalf of others is assigned high value by the altruistic actor. Other altruistic motives or predispositions include moral judgment, empathy, and social responsibility.

Altruistic Values

One motive for giving help may come from the need or desire to express one's own values or ideals of conduct. People may choose to act benevolently for the reason that altruistic behavior is viewed as important. In a recent book chapter, Clary and Snyder (1991) referred to this reason for giving as a value-expressive function of altruism or prosocial behavior, a concept akin to what Paul Tillich (1952) described as "the affirmation of one's essential being." A study based on the analysis by Clary and Snyder (1991) found that older (55+) community volunteers, asked to specify their reasons for volunteering, rated the value-expressive motive as most important, in comparison to a set of egoistic motives referred to as the knowledge function, the social-adjustive function, the ego-defensive function, and the instrumental function (Okun & Eisenberg, 1991).

Moral Judgment

Moral judgment is conceptually related to altruistic values and to what Clary and Snyder (1991) call the "value-expressive function." Moral motives are quite distinct from the economic motives proposed by exchange theory. The person who is morally motivated is motivated by the intrinsic desire to adhere to moral principles, quite independently of any material rewards or self-satisfaction that may result.

Current thinking on moral judgment includes a debate between Kohlberg (1984) and Gilligan (1982). In Kohlberg's justice-based view, the highest form of morality is reflected in the fully individuated person who autonomously (i.e., free of dependency on relationships with others) and impartially applies ethical principles to moral dilemmas. Such an individual would help others because it is "right" or "just" to do so. Gilligan argues, however, that Kohlberg's view is based on studies conducted exclusively with male subjects. She asserts that highly moral women may rely, instead, on "caring." The woman's voice in moral reasoning, according to Gilligan, may rely more on connectedness with others than on disinterested principles and may reflect responsibility and compassion for others in social networks. Ultimately, the distinction may be that the highest level of morality is represented by a just society versus a caring community—both of which do ultimately imply an altruistic, allocentric orientation on the part of the helper.

In any event, investigators argue that in order to be considered altruistic, moral intentionality must be present. In other words, moral judgment (or intentionality) is viewed by some as the distinguishing characteristic of altruism, or at least of intrinsically motivated helping (e.g., Bar-Tal, 1976). Studies of helping among children tend to indicate that children with higher levels of moral reasoning are more likely to help others spontaneously and without the expectation of rewards (Eisenberg, 1982). In several studies, adults with higher levels of moral values were more likely to help others (e.g., Allen & Rushton, 1983; Zuckerman & Reis, 1978).

Social Responsibility

The social exchange position is one that tends to emphasize the norm of reciprocity wherein people help to reciprocate benefits already received or in anticipation of future benefits (Blau, 1964). In contrast, Berkowitz and Daniels (1967) offer the alternative of the norm of social responsibility, which requires people to help those who are dependent on them for help. In their view, the norm of social responsibility guides people to aid others without expectation of gain because it is the right thing to do. The operation of this norm is triggered by the dependency of others, notwithstanding considerations of self-gain. The norm of reciprocity (related to exchange theory), in contrast, leads to helping others performed in the expectation of self-gain, because benefits are expected to be reciprocated.

Empathy

Because the notion of empathy is defined by concern for the feelings of others, altruism theorists consider it a major organizing idea in the study of altruism (cf. Coke, Batson, & McDavis, 1978). Indeed, as in the case of moral judgment, some theorists (e.g., Aronfreed, 1969) even suggest that altruism should be restricted to actions controlled by empathic processes. Research indicates that human beings may be born with an innate capacity to respond with empathy to the distress of others, which may be related to attitudes and to the development of social bonds and social integration (Sagi & Hoffman, 1976). Others, such as Hornstein (1976), argue that empathy is most likely to be observed among members of groups characterized by a positive unit relationship. Where positive bonds exist, a "promotive tension" is created among the group members. Studies on community volunteers indicate that they tend to be higher in empathy than are nonvolunteers (e.g., Allen & Rushton, 1983).

In sum, the contributory model differs from exchange theory in that it views contributory behavior as that which is prompted by nonegoistic motives such as empathy, moral principles, and adherence to the norm of social responsibility. Although positive consequences are expected to accrue to the elderly contributor, in contrast to the exchange position, we propose that at least for some elderly contributors, the desire for positive consequences for themselves was not the initial reason for their prosocial action.

THEORETICAL PERSPECTIVES
ON ALTRUISM IN LATE LIFE

Evolutionary Theory

According to evolutionary theorists, senescence and ultimately death tend to occur subsequent to the reproductive period, with the time lapse between the end of reproduction and death varying with the species. Within the human species, it is possible to find postmiotic tissues that contain fixed populations of cells, that is, cells that no longer reproduce. The presence of these postmiotic tissues has been viewed as evidence for the position that although aging does not, at first glance, appear to be beneficial for the species, it has evolved. Indeed, in the human species, life expectancy is 30 or more years after the end of the reproductive period (Rockstein, Chesky, & Sussman, 1977).

What, exactly, are these benefits and how are they expressed? David Gutmann (1987) responds to this question from a perspective that he describes as a concatenation of elements from evolutionary, biological, and psychodynamic theories. In Gutmann's view, the later years of the life cycle are the locus for the development of capacities that can benefit the human species. Young adults in present-day society are employed outside the home in jobs that can best be performed, in many cases, by younger, more recently trained individuals. The most productive years for work coincide with the years in which reproduction is most viable, creating thereby an enormous tension between the pressures of the workplace and the need to create a stable and loving home, to develop supportive social relationships, and to transmit cultural values to one's offspring. This tension, which in some cases reaches crisis proportions, constitutes what Gutmann calls the "parental emergency." Other young adults, fearful of undertaking the stresses and demands of parenthood in combination with the stresses of the marketplace, may delay or entirely forgo parenthood.

In this context, the role of the older generation becomes critical. Rather than a useless, burdensome, and accidental addendum, the increased life span has evolved because the later years are necessary for optimal adaptation to our fast-paced society. Who but the older men among us, asks Gutmann, are better able to transmit our history and preserve our cultural continuity? Who but postparental older women can serve to bind the generations together to create the social structures that may serve as shelter to the nuclear family? Without these "parents emeritus," what assurance is there that the stressful critical period termed the *parental emergency* can be survived with grace? Who can better protect the nuclear family from stresses that cause fragmentation and abuse? In Gutmann's (1987) words, "We do not have elders because we have a human gift and modern capacity for keeping the weak alive; instead, we are human because we have elders" (p. 4).

Sociological Theory

A hallmark of gerontology in the 1960s was the debate between two groups of sociologists: the proponents of disengagement theory and the proponents of activity theory.

The term *disengagement* was originally proposed by Cumming and Henry (1961) to describe a process that they observed in a sample of 275 community-dwelling older adults, who were studied over a 5-year period. They described the process as one in which the number of roles, activities, and interpersonal interactions—and consequently the "life space"—shrinks with age. This is a process that the individual seems to anticipate, and in which he or she participates actively and voluntarily. It represents a mutual withdrawal of the individual from the society to which he or she belongs, and of society from the individual. It results in a state of freedom from the norms, rules, and obligations that are imposed by the society upon younger adults. The process of disengagement—which bears notable similarities both to the views of older adulthood that can be extrapolated from Freudian theory and to autonomy theory as espoused by Cohler (1983)—is described as natural, "healthy," biologically based, and therefore universal.

This highly heuristic theory sparked considerable research and a large number of proponents. There is evidence, some of which was reviewed under the autonomy orientation above, that for at least some older adults, the level of activity does decline (Labouvie-Vief, 1981; Maas & Kuypers, 1974; Savage et al., 1977). Thus Palmore (1981) found that older people see fewer friends and participate in fewer organized social and religious activities than younger people. There is no evidence, however, that disengagement is the only way in which people age. On the contrary, it represents one pattern of aging and may actually be representative of processes that began earlier in life for at least some older individuals. There also is little evidence, except in certain selected cases (Maas & Kuypers, 1974; Savage et al., 1977), that disengagement is related to higher satisfaction than is continued engagement with society. Furthermore, results of an anthropological case study by Hazan (1982) suggested that at least for one group of older London Jews faced with isolation and a social vacuum, a new reality was created in which the hallmark was prosocial interactions with one another. Within the group, fraternity and altruism (defined as nonreciprocal helping) as well as personal autonomy—and not disengagement and dependency—reportedly characterized the interpersonal relationships. For a significant portion of the community members, the observed behavior appeared to reflect behavior changes and was apparently not continuous with earlier patterns.

Activity theory, the opposing view, suggested that the route to satisfaction in late life is not through disengagement but through continued involvement in society in active, productive roles. The major proponent of this theory, George Maddox (1970), stated that older adults need to remain active and productive. Withdrawal from life is not the best way to adjust, even during late life, and those who remain active will be higher in life satisfaction. Critics of activity theory suggest that it constitutes an oversimplification of a highly complex issue. It is not activity per se that is needed but rather participation in activities that are meaningful for the individual.

The social reconstruction theory of Kuypers and Bengtson (1973) posits that self-esteem and well-being of the elderly are generally diminished because society deprives older people of meaningful role performance and then subjects the older person—now vulnerable because of the feedback vacuum accompanying role loss—to stereotyped negative labeling. The "expectable psychological consequences to [this] noxious social reorganization in late life" (p. 80) are, of course, negative, leading to what the authors refer to as the "social breakdown syndrome."

In contrast to activity theory, Kuypers and Bengtson note that activity, which fails to provide meaningful social roles, may fall short of enhancing life satisfaction. On the other hand, opportunities for greater social penetration and for an enhanced sense of control are seen as enhancing perceived competence and well-being among the aged. In her elaboration of the Kuypers and Bengtson (1973) theory, Payne (1977) suggests an intervention strategy to be initiated before the breakdown occurs. This strategy would include social role restructuring in which encouraging volunteer activity by older adults is an important element. On the basis of a longitudinal study of more than 200 older adult volunteers, Payne expects satisfaction and enhanced self-esteem to result from such a strategy. Thus, according to social reconstruction theory, helping roles may have the potential to provide older people with reconstructed social roles that help to combat the social breakdown syndrome.

Cognitive Theory

Cognitive theory has existed within American society at least since George Kelly's (1955) formulations in the mid-1950s, but it became an important force within American psychology only recently. The basic postulate of cognitive theory is that each individual actively engages in the process of constructing reality on the basis of the individual's idiosyncratic expectations and perceptions. It is the individual's construction of reality, rather than unconscious dynamics or purely environmental events such as reinforcement, that is the primary determinant of behavior.

An application of cognitive theory is found in the work of Robert White (1959), who suggested that an important human motive is the desire to control or master one's environment. Perceptions that one has been competent in demonstrating mastery are a source of considerable pleasure. In the face of role losses, crises associated with increased extrinsic and intrinsic dependencies, and threats to autonomy associated with increased age, the person's perception of his or her competence to handle environmental obstacles may well determine personal adjustment, according to the tenets of cognitive theory. One potential source of positive input into a person's sense of competence in old age, for example, may come from acts that have the observable consequence of helping others. The positive impact on the environment clearly evident in successful helping acts may therefore provide positive feedback, which may, in turn, enhance perceptions of mastery and result in personal satisfaction (Midlarsky, 1984, 1991).

Classical Psychoanalytic Theory

The theory of Sigmund Freud is generally incongruent with the concept of altruism. Based on his interpretation of Darwin's theory, Freud posited that human behavior is generally motivated by the need to achieve need satisfaction and thereby to ensure biological survival in a world of restricted resources. In a manner akin to what anthropologist George Foster (1965) terms the concept of limited good, in the traditional psychoanalytic view, behavior that appears to be altruistic "on the surface" is actually defensive. That is, helping behavior serves to disguise the "real" feelings of the helper. At best, altruism is a socially acceptable way in which to ensure that one's own needs are met. In other instances, altruistic-appearing behavior may be a reaction formation against aggressive or sexual impulses that are unacceptable to the ego (Freud, 1937). Thus, for example, in a case report of a 2-year analytic therapy with a 69-year-old woman, Sandler's (1982) interpretation of her patient's helping behavior was that it served as a means of manipulating others, so that her own needs would be met. That is, the patient lived through others and helped them to cope as a defense against recognizing the narcissistic injuries and object losses associated with her own aging, which in turn could help her find more appropriate [*sic*] ways of dealing with the developmental crisis she was experiencing.

The question of altruism in late life was not addressed by Freud, who dealt primarily with younger people, presumably because he felt that they were more likely to benefit from his treatment techniques. However, based on the tenets of Freud's theory, altruism—and even egoistically motivated helping—would be very improbable in late life, because of the biological changes that predictably occur.

As limited as resources may appear to be earlier in life, Freud's use of the quantum theory of energy dictates that bodily energy and, concomitantly, psychic energy are irretrievably lost in late life. If allocentric sharing is unlikely in healthy younger people, whose resources are at their peak, then how much less likely are older people to share their palpably more limited and diminishing resources?

The biological organs and systems from which, in Freud's view, all psychic energy is derived do not decline at equal rates in late life. Declines tend to occur first in the systems and skills that govern relations with the world of external reality and that combine to form the biological basis of the ego, that is, the sensory apparatus, memory, and mobility. The biological substratum of the id, that is, the involuntary (smooth) musculature and the endocrine systems, also experiences declines, but at a less rapid rate. As a result of the more precipitous reduction in ego strength, older adults may unconsciously fear a loss of control. This anxiety may prompt withdrawal from social contact as well as cautiousness and ego rigidity. Although adaptive in this context, ego rigidity and social isolation make socially extensive, allocentric activities even more improbable than they are earlier in life.

Newer Psychoanalytic Approaches: The Ego Analysts

Ego analysis differs from classical Freudian analysis primarily in its assignment of a more prominent role to the ego, or self. In contrast to Freud, some ego analysts espouse theories that allow for the development and creative expansion of the self through adulthood, into late life, and even until the moment of death.

Charlotte Buhler (1962), for example, believed that the basic human motives include conscious intentionality (rather than unconscious drives alone), goal-seeking behavior, and self-actualization. Different sets of motives are dominant at different ages. For older adults, the central motives include the development of an inner order and creative expansion of the self. Buhler's theory does not specifically address contributory roles in late life, but it allows for helping as a possible course of consciously chosen behavior.

Carl Gustav Jung, a disciple of Freud's, has been frequently cited as a proponent of increased interiority and autonomy in late life. In examining Jung's (1933, 1960) writings, we find his view that when people eschew social and biological concerns and activities during the second half of life, they turn instead to a world of spiritual concerns. It is at this juncture that people become more philosophical and religious, permitting the development of wisdom and patience. It is also in late life that people are able to move from total absorption with the material world and the material self to an identification with and, by extension, a concern for the larger community—and potentially with all living things. Although Jung's theory is congruent with autonomy theory (Cohler, 1983), it also appears to be congruent with the possibility of genuine altruism in late life.

Alfred Adler (1964) theorized that social interest, another term for the expression of concern for others, is a form of adaptive behavior. Extrapolating from Adler's theory, it is possible to predict that prosocial behavior would be particularly adaptive in late life, precisely because it is the period characterized by deterioration in capacities and by impending death. When one experiences organ (or social) inferiority, then the most positive approach is to compensate for the inferiority by establishing competence and creativity. In the face of impending death, one may feel it especially incumbent upon oneself to fight the sense of utter helplessness with uniquely creative efforts at self-perfection.

Erik Erikson, of all the neo-Freudians, paid the greatest heed to late-life development. Prior to Erikson's (1963) pioneering work on development through the life cycle, stage theories of human development were limited to the early years of life. Erikson's now classic formulation, on the other hand, delineates eight stages of psychosocial development, which begin in infancy but proceed through childhood, adulthood, and old age. Each age, from the cradle through the grave, is characterized by its own basic tensions that, when resolved, lend strength to the subsequent development of the individual. Most important for the field of gerontology is that old age is depicted, in Erikson's theory, not as an afterthought but as a new critical period.

Important for the study of contributory roles is Erik Erikson's identification of the development of generativity during middle adulthood (35-60 years). Maturity in middle age means for Erikson that the individual is able to make the transition from intimacy within a dyadic peer relationship to love and concern for the next generation. Without the capacity for care, the self-absorbed middle-aged or older individual stagnates, experiences boredom, and has a generally unsatisfying life. Such a self-absorbed person is also unlikely to be the recipient of care and concern by others.

In later adulthood (60 years and older) the need to achieve a sense of ego integrity through the process of reminiscence and introspection predominates. The task of achieving integration is particularly challenging, as the older adult is faced by the obvious finiteness of life and knowledge of past imperfections. The person who developed a generative, compassionate stance in middle age is likely to find care and support from others in his or her late life search for integration. But what about the need for late-life autonomy, in the sense of withdrawal from others in the search for integration? In apparent response, we read, "it is fascinating that we, as a people, should cling so tenaciously to our pipe dream of independence as we become increasingly dependent on our interconnectedness" (Erikson et al., 1986, p. 328).

Erikson and his collaborators (1986) place particular emphasis on the continued importance of vital involvement in the present, and especially the importance of caring, for the ultimate achievement of integration. Indeed, Erikson has stated that in light of the expansion of the years of life for a majority of the population, it may be necessary to expand his epigenetic theory to add a 9th stage. This new stage will be characterized by still further growth and development in later years, including the achievement of "the capacity for grand-generativity [which] incorporates care for the present with concern for the future—for today's younger generations in their futures, for generations not yet born, and for the survival of the world as a whole" (pp. 74-75).

This exegesis of grand-generativity may be epitomized in the passionate outpouring by George Bernard Shaw (1903):

This is the true joy in life, the being used for a purpose recognized by yourself as a mighty one; the being a force of nature instead of a feverish, selfish little clod of ailments and grievances complaining that the world will not devote itself to making you happy. . . . I am of the opinion that my life belongs to the whole community and as long as I live it is my privilege to do for it whatever I can.

I want to be thoroughly used up when I die, for the harder I work the more I live. I rejoice in life for its own sake. Life is no "brief candle" to me. It is a sort of splendid torch, which I have got hold of for the moment and I want to make it burn as brightly as possible before handing it on to future generations. (p. 11)

Erikson's (1963) theory of life span development has been important for the study of altruism in late life, first of all because it legitimizes the consideration of intrinsic motivations for helping during the second half of the life cycle. Second, by proposing the stage of "generativity" to precede the late-life stage of integrity, Erikson suggests that personal contributions arising from intrinsic motivations represent an important adult developmental task. The additional concept of grand-generativity, whose achievement may represent a necessary aspect of late life, further underscores the importance of the concern for others. In sum, then, the ability and propensity to give without expectation of a direct exchange is seen by Erikson (1963) as an important expression of maturity and successful resolution of midlife psychological development. In his recent work, Erikson (Erikson, 1977; Erikson et al., 1986) has placed even greater emphasis on caring as a primary task of both middle and later adulthood.

Another theoretical framework that has emphasized the necessity of role definition in order to achieve adjustment in late life is Peck's (1968) expanded treatment of Erikson's (1963) last stage. In Peck's treatment, the aged achieve healthy functioning by resolving three major crises. In the first, "ego-differentiation vs. work-role preoccupation," Peck stresses the need for an expanded ethic by noting that each person must face the question: Am I a worthwhile person only insofar as I can do a full-time job, or can I be worthwhile in other ways as a performer of several other roles, and also because of the kind of person I am? (Peck, 1968). In the second crisis, "body transcendence vs. bodily preoccupation," the elderly need to shift their focus from bodily strength, beauty, and well-being to social and mental faculties. The third crisis, "ego transcendence vs. ego-preoccupation," refers to the need by the elderly to deal with impending death through a shift in emphasis from the continuation of the self to the question of the enduring impact of one's contributions to others. According to Peck, ego transcendence may best be achieved through a focus on contributions to the welfare of others. Furthermore, the meaning of one's existence transcends concrete and immediate interactions with others. Symbolic definitions of one's contributions are likely to be more strongly valued in late life. An altruistic value orientation is thus consistent with existential mastery in late life.

Newer Psychoanalytic Approaches:
Object Relations

In the latest manifestation and expansion of the psychoanalytic perspective—object relations theory—we find that altruism is considered to be a product of normal development (see Chapter 2). In addition, the capacity for growth and development extends well into late life. According to Hildebrand (1990), because drive strength and ego strength are completely derived from physical organs and their energies in Freud's theory, people are expected to become too rigid to change by the age of 40. The revised approach has come, in part, from the fact that altruism, creativity, and wisdom are often observed in older adults—who present not an unmixed picture of degeneration but a mixed picture of strength and fragility.

Among object relations theorists in Great Britain, for example, acceptance of the viability of growth, creativity, and productivity in late life comes from the notion that the unconscious is not merely a pulsating membrane of libidinal drives but also the locus of meaning. This position contrasts with Freud's attribution of all meaning to the ego. The basic unconscious need for a meaningful existence may be met, at least in part, through meaningful contact with others. This need for meaning has the potential to be most powerful during late life, which presents the final opportunity to achieve meaning (Rycroft, 1985). Hence, in contrast to Freud's view that altruism is a defense in that it serves the function of other, "truer" motives, object relations theorists recognize that concern for others can be as "real" as other concerns and that the concern for others may be a feature of late life.

In object relations terminology, empathy—viewed by some theorists as a precondition of genuine altruism (e.g., Aronfreed, 1969)—is possible only in adulthood. Buie (1981) writes that what he calls full adult empathy includes the ability to focus on objects for their own sake. Such empathy "is object centered, not self-centered. Adult [object centered] empathy [as opposed to self-centered empathy] is concerned with much more than the other person's giving, no-giving, or threatening attitudes toward oneself" (p. 281). In a manner reminiscent of Erikson (Erickson, 1963; Erikson et al., 1986), Shane and Shane (1990) write:

> Altruism . . . is another aspect of adult development. The range of experiences in adult life where one serves the needs of another, where that other's emotional requirements are perceived to have priority over one's own comprises a state of being we call otherhood. It is a general term that defines the many adult relationships wherein mature empathy and healthy altruism are seen as prerequisite to performing functions on behalf of another person. To illustrate, we can cite being a parent or grandparent, a mentor, a teacher, a physician or attorney, or an analyst or therapist and yes, a friend and lover, for while these last two examples are between two people who share the same gradient, who presumably exist on the same emotional developmental level . . . there are important respects in which a friend and lover, to function adequately, must become an other dedicated to serving his or her partner's needs and desires. (p. 477)

Even Cohler, a major proponent of the autonomy model, recognizes the positive nature of help giving in late life, at least under conditions in which the help is given voluntarily and is based on a personal choice and a system of altruistic values, rather than in response to onerous obligation. There are instances in which family connections and loyalties allow members of a family

> to realize their ideals of providing care for one another at times of distress. Much of the discussion of caregiving for

psychologically or physically impaired family members over-
looks the enhanced sense of meaning and personal integration associated with "doing what is right" and expectable in
a family or community. (Cohler & Galatzer-Levy, 1990, p. 228)

Of course, one must recognize that the performance of roles,
even roles characterized by caregiving, is not in itself evidence of
altruism. Helpful behaviors are enacted for diverse reasons, including quite selfish ones,[5] so that in some cases, what appears to
be altruism can be a disguise for egoism. In contrast to the use of
altruism as a defense in which the "benefactor" actually aims to
restrict, harm, manipulate, or otherwise dominate the other (Sandler
& Freud, 1985), "authentic altruism . . . aims to expand the other's
self and to foster the other's sense of freedom" (Shane & Shane,
1990, p. 475).

Even when altruism is viewed as a "defense," it is possible for
it to be essentially nonneurotic. In Vaillant's (1977) work, four
levels of defense are listed: psychotic, immature, neurotic, and
mature. Altruism is included among the mature defenses, along
with humor, suppression, anticipation, and sublimation. Altruism
is instinctually based, according to Vaillant. It serves as a source
of vicarious satisfaction, based on the individual's knowledge that
genuine service or benefit has been received.[6]

According to the newer psychoanalytic approaches, then, the
classical position that altruism is a manifestation of the individual's neurotic problems unnecessarily excluded consideration of
a critical facet of normal—and even optimal—adult functioning.

Theories of Moral and Spiritual Development

If, indeed, altruism is a manifestation of optimal adult development that is based at least partly on systems of meaning and value,
then questions about the development of meaning through adulthood gain particular relevance.

Among theorists concerned with the development of spiritual
meaning, Lawrence Kohlberg (1973) has been highly influential.
Working from a combination of Piaget's (1952) theory of cognitive

development and Dewey's (1964) theory of "development, both intellectual and moral" (p. 213), Kohlberg examined moral development in a manner that parallels Erikson's (1963) stage theory of personality and Loevinger's (1976) theory of ego development. Moral judgment is of interest here because of the contention that a critical element in determining whether a helpful act is altruistic lies in the intentionality, or level of moral reasoning behind the act (Bar-Tal, Raviv, & Leiser, 1980).

The major issue in morality, in Kohlberg's theory, has been not what the individual does or believes should be done but why the action should be taken. The "whys" or reasons are of three types, which are described as six stages of moral reasoning,[7] two within each of the three levels that were originally defined by Dewey (1964). Within the preconventional level, Stage 1 reasoners view conduct as external to the self, and perceptions of "goodness" and "badness" are based on obedience to authority and the physical consequences of behavior. Stage 2 is represented by an instrumental, marketplace mentality in which reciprocity is based on concrete and pragmatic expectations about exchange, rather than on such abstract concepts as loyalty, justice, or gratitude. Within the conventional level, Stage 3 is governed by conformity to stereotypical images of goodness, and approval is sought for nice, or at least well-intended, behavior. Questions about moral intentionality become important at this stage. Stage 4 morality, on the other hand, is one in which considerations of "law and order" predominate. Stage 4 reasoners identify with law and with authority and attempt to do their duty.

At the level variously referred to as the principled, postconventional, or autonomous level—a level that becomes a consistent mode of reasoning for only a minority of adults—the individual goes beyond laws and contracts as handed down, in a search for the principles that inform those laws. In the event that the law is at variance with the principle, the individual anticipates being guided by the principle rather than by the law. In Stage 5 morality, the social-contract legalistic stage, the individual's concern is with human rights and standards agreed upon by societal consensus. Rational factors and social utility are the bases for action at this legalistic stage. Stage 6, reached only by a very few individuals, is one in which the emphasis is on "universal ethical principles of justice, of the reciprocity and equality of human rights, and of respect for the dignity of human beings as individual persons" (Kohlberg, 1973, p. 631).

In Kohlberg's theory, stages are viewed as organized systems of thought, or "structured wholes" that form an invariant sequence. People may vary in their stage of moral reasoning, but people do not skip stages, do not reverse the order in which the stages are traversed (e.g., first Stage 5 and only later, Stage 2), and rarely regress to earlier stages. In Kohlberg's words, "Under all conditions except extreme trauma, movement is always forward, never backward . . . movement is always up" (Kohlberg & Wasserman, 1980, p. 561). Akin to Piaget's (1952) notion of decentering, the movement through the three levels can be seen as a progression from the Level 1 concern with the rewards and punishments for the self, to the Level 2 concern with family and society, and ultimately, in some cases, to the Level 3 concern with universal principles underlying the social structure. In some respects, this decentering mirrors distinctions between degrees of egocentricism/allocentrism as well as issues of meaning beyond the narrow confines of the self.

Critics of Kohlberg's theory point to its equation of morality with prohibition-related issues, such as questions of formal obligations and rules, "oughts" and "ought nots." This exclusive emphasis on justice and "fairness" has been challenged for omitting certain facets of morality that may be more closely associated with helping behavior. These include responsibility and caring for others, which are more closely associated with the broader search for meaning (Eisenberg, 1979; Gilligan, 1982; Ward, 1979b). Despite the charge of narrowness, Kohlberg's theory has been extremely heuristic, so that both extensive theoretical and empirical efforts by numerous individuals have been devoted to extensions and elaborations of the theory. These, in turn, serve to enrich our comprehension of meaning and faith as well as of justice.

Foremost among the theorists who apparently used Kohlberg's work as their starting point is James Fowler (1981). In contrast to the theories of personality, developmental theorists such as Erikson and Loevinger, for whom the development of meaning was of peripheral concern, Fowler's theory of faith development focused on the individual's spiritual life and worldview as its central concerns. Despite the religious overtones of the word *faith*, Fowler did not equate faith with religious belief but with the struggle by all human beings to acquire a sense of meaning, identity, and community. Fowler's definition of faith, quoted in a volume by Smith (1979), is as follows:

> Faith is deeper, richer, more personal. It is engendered by a religious tradition, in some cases, and to some extent by its doctrines, but it is a quality of the person, not the system. It is an orientation of the personality, to oneself, to one's neighbors, to the universe; a total response; a way of seeing whatever one sees and of handling whatever one handles; a capacity to live at more than a mundane level; to see, to feel, to act in terms of a transcending dimension. (p. 12)

Essentially, then, *faith* is a term referring to the structured elements common to the world's religions, however diverse their forms. Faith, to Fowler, is a concept broader than moral judgment and broader than adherence to any specific religion. It refers to the individual's model of her or his connections, both with others and with the universe; it is the individual's stance toward life, which includes personal responses to questions about who is ultimately "in charge" and how to make life good, worthy, and meaningful.

Fowler, like Erikson, Kohlberg, and Loevinger, proposes that development can best be represented by a series of stages. First undifferentiated faith (like Erikson's mistrust/trust, in which the child is still largely undifferentiated from the major caretaker), and then:

1. intuitive-projective faith (ages 2-7),
2. mythic-literal faith (school age to adolescence or beyond),
3. synthetic-conventional faith (adolescence through adulthood, for some),
4. individuative-reflective faith (beginning in young adulthood, for some),
5. conjunctive faith (usually not before middle age), and
6. universalizing faith (rather rare, even in late life).

Development, in this model, is based on an interactional process in which the individual first progresses toward individuation, a process that may begin early in life and continue through early adulthood and only later move "backward" toward closer connection and unity, or oneness. Throughout the progression, "each stage represents a widening of vision and valuing, correlated with a parallel increase in the certainty and depth of selfhood, making for qualitative increases in intimacy with self-others-world" (Fowler, 1981, p. 274).

Fowler expects the sequence of stages to correspond only approximately to age. Some rare individuals may achieve "higher" levels at relatively young ages, and others may carry a stage achieved in early adulthood with them into late life. Nevertheless, whereas progress through the stages is not invariant, there is a progressive sequence with approximate ages of onset, and those moving through them in a timely fashion have optimal life experiences.

These interesting notions may all, of course, be phrased as empirical questions that require careful research examination. What is important in the current treatment, though, is that Fowler's theory emphasizes that it is at least possible to develop a kind of universalizing faith that would be very compatible with altruism and that the level of faith development encompassing such universal love is likely to be achieved in late life, if it is achieved at all. The development of a worldview focused on absolute love and justice, and in which one's own self-interest—and even one's own self-preservation—is deemed relatively inconsequential, is most expectable in the over-65 period, which is notable also for life review and involvement with what Kubler-Ross (1975) calls "death-work."

What all of the developmental theories have in common, then, is the notion that extreme extensivity of concern (unselfishness, or unself-centeredness) becomes increasingly probable as the individual grows older. The capacity for a genuine, allocentric caring may be a later accretion than is the focus on rules and expectations (Kohlberg, 1973; Loevinger, 1976) and on individuation (Fowler, 1981). Even Erikson (1977), who originally wrote of generativity as a midlife phenomenon, has more recently posited an even more extensive and universal allocentric orientation as a feature of very late life (Erikson et al., 1986).

The theories reviewed in this section are not necessarily mutually exclusive alternatives to the dependency and autonomy orientations. Some older people may indeed become so overwhelmed by their own growing dependencies that they may succumb to a "patient" or "recipient" role wherein they consider that a one-way allocation of resources to them constitutes repayment for their own efforts earlier in life (Dowd, 1980; Lozier, 1975). This may be far from a universal phenomenon, however. Other older persons may find the need to be a participating member of the community, and to contribute to the welfare of others, to be as strong as it was earlier in life or stronger (Midlarsky, 1991). The need to contribute may be part of a process of "meaning making," which may, in turn, reflect the process of spiritual development in late life (Clements, 1990), particularly as death appears imminent. Becker (1975) has written that what is feared by most human beings is not so much extinction but extinction with insignificance: "Man [sic] wants to know his [sic] life has somehow counted, if not for himself, then at least in the larger scheme of things, that is, has left a trace, a trace that has meaning" (p. 4).

Even people who may have led a penurious existence may wish to leave behind them a life emblematic in its generosity and nobility, rather than miserliness and cowardice. Of some relevance here may be the finding that 75% of Americans over age 65 consider religion "very important" in their lives, and 80% assert that religious faith—centered in a personal relationship with God—is the most important influence in their lives (Moberg, 1983).

None of this is necessarily inconsistent with views concerning autonomy. One can make critical contributions even—and in some cases, especially—subsequent to a process of reviewing one's lifelong patterns of responsibility, during which one disengages from the social role obligations prevalent earlier in life. Once free, at last, from earlier constraints, individuals who have achieved the highest levels or stages may choose contributory roles that transcend the narrow confines that dominated their earlier lives. Some of these individuals may, for the first time, move beyond exchange to a focus on genuinely allocentric, contributory roles.

According to the theoretical orientations reviewed thus far, it is plausible that older adults can choose to be helpful to others. For at least some older adults it is also theoretically possible that altruistic, rather than economic or other egocentric, motives may impel the behavior (at least part of the time). We turn now to an examination of the research evidence.

EMPIRICAL PERSPECTIVES
ON HELPING BY THE AGED

Evidence of Altruistic Orientations Among Older Adults

Evidence of altruistic orientations among the elderly has been obtained in a number of recent studies by the authors (Kahana & Midlarsky, 1982; Midlarsky & Kahana, 1981, 1983a, 1983b). In a study considering the relationship between internal-external locus of control, self-concept, and altruistic attitudes among residents of a retirement community, the great majority of elderly interviewed (84%) expressed altruistic attitudes. These respondents placed high positive values on personally costly and unreciprocated forms of helping. Furthermore, those respondents who exhibited altruistic attitudes had significantly better self-concepts and perceived health than those with less altruistic attitudes (Midlarsky & Kahana, 1981).

These findings are consistent with observations by Christenson (1977) and with results of several empirical investigations. Thus interviews conducted with 13 males and 38 females residing in a Midwestern retirement community indicated that personal qualities such as concern for others and social responsibility are valued over socioeconomic and other forms of status (Perkinson, 1980). In Crandall's (1981) cross-sectional investigation of age differences in social interest—an Adlerian construct defined as interest in and concern for others—results indicated that in a sample of 20- to 65-year-old adults there was a significant positive relationship between social interest and age. Similarly, in a longitudinal study of 19 personality and attitudinal variables in a sample of 2,500 people aged 21 to 84, only two characteristics were found to change over a 7-year period. Both of these characteristics, excitability and humanitarian concerns, showed increases (Schaie & Parham, 1976).

In a cross-sectional study of 370 people aged 5 to 95, Weiner and Graham (1989) found increases in sympathy and self-reported helping and decreases in expression of anger concomitant with age. Labouvie-Vief, Hakim-Larson, and Hobart (1987) have also reported that the tendencies to project one's own negative impulses onto others, to turn against others, and to avoid/distance oneself from others decrease from adolescence to later adulthood. Furthermore, in considering value orientations characteristic of diverse life transitions, Lowenthal, Thurnher, and Chiriboga (1975) noted that for their older age group, the most distinctive feature was an increase in humanitarian and moral purposes. These concerns manifested themselves through an expression of altruistic values in terms of personal contributions for women, stressing the need to be kind to people, to help, and to be useful to others. Men tended to stress the desire to make a tangible contribution to society.

Data from studies of older persons relocating and undertaking long-distance moves indicate that the assumption of contributory roles is seen as a central life task during late life by a significant proportion of adventurous elderly (Kahana & Kahana, 1983). Respondents often expressed a sense of relief and freedom in escaping the exchange-oriented culture of work life and in being able to channel their energies into doing for others for intrinsic reasons. A frequently heard motive for their desire to migrate, expressed by Israel-bound respondents, was: "All my life I have done for my children and my family—now I am free to do for others." Satisfaction with the move, in turn, proved to be significantly related to actual helping opportunities and fulfillment of the desire to engage in helpful behaviors.

Evidence of Helping Behavior Among Older Adults

The following discussion examines research evidence regarding the nature of helping by the aged. Underlying motives for helping are considered as they are relevant to the above outlined theoretical orientations regarding social interactions of the elderly.

A traditional focus of gerontological research has been on older adults as recipients of services (Brickman et al., 1982). On the other hand, until recently, little systematic attention has been paid to the extent and nature of helping provided to others by the elderly (Stewart & Smith, 1983). Findings of studies that have been conducted indicate that older persons not only engage in reciprocal helping and the active exchange of assistance but also provide help to others in the absence of direct reciprocity.

Research on older adults and their social networks has called attention to the importance of reciprocity in the social relations of this group. Accordingly, results of Hill's (1970) three-generational study of families indicated that family members do receive assistance if needed, but also that they continue to provide help to younger family members.

Bromberg (1983) found that in late life, relationships between mothers and their middle-aged daughters are characterized not by a role reversal, in which formerly nurturant mothers have necessarily become passive and dependent, but rather by interdependence. Similarly, Stueve (1982) has argued against the prevailing view of older adults as passive, dependent members of their social networks. She has provided evidence both that older people unilaterally help others and that they reciprocate for services rendered within their families, neighborhoods, and communities.

A study by Wentowski (1981) also provided data in support of the importance of reciprocity between older adults and those who provide help to them. Research based on a representative sample of 2,146 community elderly, age 60 and older, indicates that even older recipients of assistance continue to give help to others (Prohaska & McAuley, 1984). Direct reciprocation by the recipients was most likely for social and interpersonal activities. Findings clearly showed the older respondents to be providers as well as recipients of help. Indeed, in a study that set out to explore service needs of the urban aged (Kahana & Felton, 1977), community-dwelling older adults reported that they provide more help than they receive. Reports of a help-giving balance in favor of aged helpers has been provided by others as well (Akiyama & Antonucci, 1986; Fairchild, Pruchno, & Kahana, 1978).

Goodman (1984) studied 67 older widows with a mean age of 76, living in a retirement community, in order to identify patterns of help giving and receiving among them. Although her research was apparently conducted in accordance with assumptions derived from the social exchange model—as is much research of this type (e.g., Prohaska & McAuley, 1984; Wentowski, 1981)—so that reciprocal helping was assumed to be the most appropriate and beneficial form of helping, three types of older natural helpers were found. These were high helpers, who help without reciprocation, mutual (i.e., reciprocal) helpers, and neighborhood isolates, whose ties, if any, are to others outside of the retirement community.

Reciprocal patterns of helping were found to characterize elderly persons and their families in a survey of social support networks of 302 urban elderly (Fairchild et al., 1978). This study considered both reciprocal exchanges (elderly give as well as receive help) and complementary exchanges whereby the elderly are only providers or only recipients of assistance. Findings revealed that older people generally give more tangibles than they receive. Furthermore, in exchanges with relatives, "giving only" surpassed in frequency "receiving only." Findings also indicated that high morale was more frequently associated with giving-only than with receiving-only interactions.

Provision of assistance to others appears to be a normative activity for the elderly. In a representative sample of 400 community elderly, Chappell and Havens (1983) found that 55% of respondents said that they regularly provided assistance to others. Members of a comparison group of 400 frail elderly who used home care services were less likely than the well elders to be providers of aid. Yet even members of this frail group included numerous providers of assistance to others. Helping others and altruistic orientations have also been found to be normative in a study of elderly Holocaust survivors, which included samples of survivors in both the United States and Israel (Kahana, Kahana, Harel, & Segal, 1986). These data suggest that helping others continues to be normative, even among elderly people who had been victims, and also includes those who are currently receiving aid from others.

Older persons tend to emerge as critical providers of help within the family context. In answer to the question, "Who helps the frail elderly?" the answer is often "the elderly." At present, there are indications that the primary caretakers of older people with disabilities are their spouses (Chappell, 1990). Indeed, spousal caregiving is often the single most important factor in the aged person's ability to remain in the community (Johnson, 1980). In addition, as the over-85 population increases, greater amounts of help are apparently given to people over 85 by their children, who in many cases are themselves over 65 years of age (Selig et al., 1991).

In their relationships with the younger generations, older adults frequently emerge as helpers as well. Thus older persons generally serve as providers of financial assistance to their adult children (Morgan, 1983, Troll, Miller, & Atchley, 1979). According to Cantor (1973), 75% of minority elderly report that they provide help to their children. Elderly persons report helping their families regularly by providing repair work, housekeeping, nursing care, money, and gifts to family members (Harris & Associates, Inc., 1975). Community surveys of older persons have also provided evidence that in living arrangements involving three generations, the grandparent generation generally takes the role of caregiver to children and/or grandchildren who are experiencing life crises such as divorce or widowhood (Kahana & Kahana, 1980; Troll et al., 1979). During periods of crisis, even when they are not residing with their children, half of the elderly persons in a national sample reported giving their grandchildren some form of assistance (Shanas, 1967). In a study of three generations of ethnic women (Krause, 1978), grandmothers were found to be significantly more likely to be providers of support and assistance than were members of the mother or daughter generations. In a survey of Detroit area aged (Kahana & Felton, 1977), older people living in three-generation households were typically heads of families. Rather than the older parents being the dependents who moved in with the children, it was divorced or widowed children and grandchildren who moved back with the older parents.

Provision of help by the retired elderly is also prevalent in the nonfamilial residential context. Elderly neighbors tend to help each other in diverse ways, ranging from advice and social support to daily chores (Harel & Linderberg, 1981). The most important category of helping activities among neighbors has been found to be that of crisis or emergency intervention. Especially among neighbors who know each other well, there is reportedly a high likelihood (66%) of offering help in times of illness, which may take such forms as escorting neighbors to medical services. The role of neighbor is especially important for the elderly poor with no living relatives. For this group, help provided by elderly neighbors was found to be the primary way of coping with illness. In his classic study of 1,200 older adults, Rosow (1967) found that help from neighbors was apparently the primary way of coping with illness for the elderly poor with no living relatives or financial resources. Among the elderly at all levels, neighbors almost never approached one another for monetary help, but help in times of illness was frequently given, most notably among those who lived alone. Rosow (1967) found that:

> These neighbors take care of more solitary people in longer illness than do friends, as many as relatives, and almost as many as children. This attention is not confined to brief sickness, but is sustained longer if necessary. For all their stoicism and self-reliance, solitary residents do use neighbors' help for longer illness when they can get it, but dense apartments are the only ones that can provide this to any significant extent. (p. 308)

A review of anthropological research (Keith, 1982) on collectives for the elderly, ranging from mobile home parks and high-rise public housing to luxury condominiums, suggests that there is extensive aid given by peers. A helping network of peers allows many older residents to feel secure without giving up their independence. Furthermore, it is a special benefit of peer aid that it may be less likely to induce a feeling of dependency in recipients than is receipt of assistance from children or from formal organizations.

In addition to the literature on older persons' helping neighbors and family members, there is growing evidence that the elderly provide services to the wider community through their donations of time, money, and energy, most notably through volunteer and charity work (Babic, 1972; Chambré, 1984; Dye, Goodman, Roth, Bley, & Jensen, 1973; Harel & Lindberg, 1981). Payne's (1977) work yields estimates of regularly occurring volunteer work by 14-22%

of the elderly. The survey by Harris and Associates (1975) indicated that the elderly are most frequently involved in service activities in health and mental health, transportation, civic affairs, psychological and social support services, give-away programs, and family, youth, and child-oriented services. The Harris survey indicated that 22% of the elderly engaged in organized volunteer work, and an additional 10% expressed interest in being so involved. As of 1975, approximately 4.5 million elderly persons were actively involved in volunteer work, and an additional 2.1 million expressed a desire to volunteer their services.

On a more concrete note, Petersen (1981) reported that the mean age of volunteers working with the elderly through an urban social service program was 68.9 years, indicating that those caring for the elderly are older persons themselves. Financial contributions to charitable organizations are also made by the elderly, and sharing with others may be observed in bequests made to nonkin recipients—including community organizations—as well as to kin (Rosenfeld, 1979).

Which older adults provide help to the wider community, and what reasons do they cite for doing so? Research by Harris and Associates (1975) indicates that both men (20%) and women (23%) serve as volunteers, and people who perceive themselves as healthier are more likely to help in this way. Volunteers are also distinguished from nonvolunteers on the basis of prior participation, with those having a history of service through organizations more likely to volunteer during the older years (Dye et al., 1973).

In regard to stated motives for volunteering, results of the Harris Poll suggest that prosocial impulses may guide the actions of a sizable number of older persons. When asked what makes someone a useful member of society, 50% of older people cited helping and serving others, 43% cited involvement in community activities and organizations, and an additional 34% mentioned being a good neighbor. "Helping others" was also frequently cited as a basis for membership in voluntary organizations by group leaders and by people involved in charity or volunteer work, in a study conducted by Ward (1979b).

CONCLUSIONS

The research evidence reviewed above regarding altruistic orientations and helping behavior among the elderly raises important questions about both the dependency- and autonomy-based views of late life. It underscores the need by many older adults to engage in active social interactions wherein they provide diverse resources to family, friends, neighbors, and even strangers. Thus, even if one were to accept the notion that the elderly possess few power resources on the macro "societal" level, generalizing such powerlessness and lack of resources to the individual level of interpersonal interactions may well be misleading. There are compelling theoretical and empirical reasons to consider contributory roles of older adults and implications of these roles for previously discussed theoretical formulations.

Consideration of the interpersonal behavior of older people reveals that there may well be altruistic or contributory potential throughout the life span. It may be argued that help giving may continue to be important—or, in some cases, even increase in importance—even when functional capacities of the older helper are diminished in certain respects. It is possible that with increasing age and the waning of physical prowess, one may be less likely than during the earlier years to engage in dangerous rescue activities, under the extremely stressful conditions associated, for example, with natural disaster or war. On the other hand, even with advancing years, older persons may engage in numerous types of helping, ranging from obtaining medical assistance for neighbors to fund-raising for charitable organizations or participation in volunteer activities. In this sense, a focus on altruistic activities of the elderly may enhance the scope of behaviors legitimately considered by altruism researchers as well.

Furthermore, neither the theoretical orientations nor the initial exploratory research on motives for helping among the elderly provides support for the universality of exchange formulations in describing social interactions of the elderly. In essence, exchange theory, whose hallmark assumptions are egoistic in the extreme, leaves unanswered questions when invoked to explain apparently altruistic behavior patterns of older adults. Exchange theory's reliance on economic principles not only yields a pessimistic view of personal and social options for late life but also depicts older adults as passive, dependent respondents to situations they cannot control.

An alternative formulation focusing on a contributory model of aging is proposed, which recognizes the possible existence and operation of altruistic motives in social interactions in general, and among older persons in particular. It is argued that such a view is consistent with a humanistic and developmental view of the aging process. A prosaic model of interactions in late life is posited as an important complement to frameworks that have been previously articulated.

In sum, all of the above implies that older adults may be involved in helping others and that altruistic dispositions may exist in this age group. Ultimately, however, these conceptions must be put to further empirical testing. It is to this task that the remainder of this volume will be devoted.

NOTES

1. An alternate view is that dependency may occur at any age at which demands exceed the individual's capacity to cope with those demands—and not as part of either normal aging or irreversible decline (Baltes, 1988; Lawton & Nahemow, 1973).

2. Not all investigators have supported the finding of increased interiority in late life. In a series of studies that explored perceptions by adults of their own personality stability or change, Ryff found that whereas the peak for "integrity" was in old age, interiority showed no significant age differences. The methodology of these studies differed from others in that rather than asking people to describe their current selves, Ryff directly asked older adults to describe themselves at younger ages and asked young adults to describe the way that they were likely to be later in life (Ryff, 1984; Ryff & Heincke, 1983).

3. A distinction can be made between the allocentric person, who is characteristically or at least frequently other-centered, and the allocentric act. In the latter, a person who is not "an altruist" may engage in a behavior or series of behaviors that is genuinely altruistic. The rare individuals who not only do good but spontaneously exemplify goodness in all that they do are generally identified as "saints" or "self-transcendent" altruists.

4. The current pervasiveness of the egoistic bias may be illustrated with a personal experience. One of the authors of this volume recently wrote a chapter for an edited volume in which she argued that people who help others when they themselves are experiencing stress may benefit from the help that they render to

others (Midlarsky, 1991). In presenting the argument, several positive consequences for the helpful actor were listed. The discussant for the volume made an
assumption that may well be "natural" for many social scientists—that is, that
these consequences also serve as motives for the observed behavior.

5. Employing a similar logic, aggression can also be viewed as defensive. If we
consider that the need to engage in meaningful social action is intrinsic and lodged
in the unconscious (Rycroft, 1985), then especially as the time remaining for
altruistic/contributory roles shrinks with advanced age, the urge for meaningful
participation may increase. Concomitant with increases in overt dependencies and
the imposition of a "sick role" on the older person, opportunities for altruism may
be reduced even further. In this context, the anger expressed by some older adults
may represent a movement toward other people that, according to Jankofsky and
Stuecher (1984, p. 346), represents a manifestation of the older person's desperate
attempts to reengage in the social process as a frustrated giver.

6. Vaillant's (1977) formulation, like others appearing in recent psychoanalytic
theory on altruism and empathy, is strongly evocative of the rich program of
research carried out primarily under the general aegis of social learning theory. For
a review of research pertinent to these concerns see, for example, Midlarsky (1968),
Midlarsky and Suda (1978), and Eisenberg (1982).

7. These three levels represent a refinement of Dewey's (1964) three stages: the
premoral or preconventional level, the conventional level, and the autonomous
level, wherein "conduct is guided by the individual thinking and judging for
himself, whether a purpose is good" (p. 213).

Helping Across the Life Span: Naturalistic Experiments

In this chapter, we discuss a series of naturalistic experiments that consider helping behavior by people of varying ages as well as situational factors that may facilitate or inhibit helping. In the simplest terms, we were interested, first of all, in determining how helpful older people are in comparison with younger people.

To address this question, two separate sets of experiments were performed, investigating the antecedents of donations and rescue, respectively. Each of these types of helping requires at least some degree of self-sacrifice, but each varies in the type of resource shared. Thus donation behavior, also termed *generosity* or *sharing of the wealth*, is behavior in which the individual helps by incurring costs—primarily in terms of money or time—on behalf of another. Rescue, also termed *sharing of the pain*, consists of helping wherein the helper incurs risks in the form of discomfort or danger on behalf of another (Midlarsky, 1968). Inclusion of two distinct forms of prosocial functioning was thought to permit a broader comprehension of altruistic phenomena.

The ultimate purpose of the research program reported in this volume was to test a theoretical model of helping by older adults. In contrast to the prevailing tendency to focus on the dependency, autonomy, and exchange needs of older people, our studies sought to explore the altruism and helping behaviors among this large and growing segment of the population. We begin our discussion of the research and its findings with naturalistic-experimental perspectives on helping by the elderly.

DONATION BEHAVIOR[1]

Much of the research conducted on altruism in the Brobdingnagian literature on this subject has used experimental or observational methodologies to investigate the development of prosocial behavior in children and adolescents, under the apparent assumption that such development may lead to the adoption of contributory roles throughout one's adult life. Research on altruism among adults has typically comprised social psychological investigations of factors eliciting or maintaining altruism in specific situations.

Empirical investigations of altruism among younger persons have generally indicated that expressions of concern for others begin at a very early age (Yarrow & Waxler, 1976). Investigators of the form of altruism treated here, donating or generosity, have found a linear relation between age and altruism, upholding the prediction that altruistic behavior increases with age (Barnett, King, & Howard, 1979). However, these developmental studies have typically included respondents no older than late adolescence (Midlarsky & Hannah, 1985).

Turning to the literature of gerontology (reviewed in Chapter 3) one finds a shift in emphasis, wherein older persons are most frequently viewed as needy recipients rather than as helpers (Brickman et al., 1982). Several theoretical perspectives combine to predict that elderly adults are less likely to be altruistic than are younger individuals. For some writers, older adulthood is viewed as a period in which individuals aim to extricate themselves from social demands and obligations so that they can, at last, please themselves (Cohler, 1983). Other theorists argue that a central characteristic of older persons is dependency, just as it is conspicuous in the very early years of life (Baltes, Hann, Barton, Orzech, & Lago, 1983). Exchange theory, which predicts decreased helping by elderly individuals, at least in situations in which the rule of justice prevails, is another perspective. According to Dowd (1980), older adults as a group have "invested their lives in society. . . . Yet, their rewards, in terms of income, prestige or autonomy fall far below our usual definitions of proportionality" (p. 598). Hence there is reason for elderly persons to lack generous impulses. From all of these positions, one would predict a curvilinear relation between age and altruism, with the lowest degrees of concern for others manifested in the early and late years of life and the pinnacle of altruism occurring in midlife. In addition, in a recent historical analysis, Covey (1991) argues for the existence of a stereotype of older adults as greedy and miserly throughout Western literature and art.

Mitigating against the curvilinear hypothesis, however, is recent evidence that altruistic behavior and motives may exhibit a linear increase from middle to later adulthood. In a cross-sectional study of 572 pairs of twins from 19 to 60 years of age, paper-and-pencil measures of altruism, empathy, and nurturance increased with age (Rushton, Fuller, Neale, Nias, & Eysenck, 1986). Furthermore, if as Eron (1987) argued, aggression is a form of behavior directly opposed to altruism, then age-related decreases in aggression and psychopathy (Pfeiffer & Busse, 1973) suggest an increased potential for late-life altruism. In their recent cross-sectional survey of 370 people age 5 to 95, Weiner and Graham (1989) also found age-related decreases in self-reported expressions of anger on the one hand and helping on the other. Some theories also support the possibility of increased altruism through to the latest years of life (see Chapter 3). Buhler (1961), for example, viewed the later years as a period in which at least some individuals creatively strive to engage in meaningful action. Also, contrary to Dowd's (1980) position, wherein inequities experienced by elderly adults should lead to withdrawal from intergenerational relations, Erikson et al. (1986) posited that adaptation in the later years requires vital involvement in the social world, with caring as an important basis for one's primary bonds.

In addition to these two positions—that age is related to altruism in a curvilinear fashion, with the oldest adults helping less than the younger adults, and that age has a linear relation to altruism, with the oldest adults helping most—a third hypothesis may be advanced. This third possibility is that the relation between age and altruism may be affected by situational factors, two of which are considered here.

The goal of this first set of naturalistic-experimental investigations was, therefore, to determine (a) whether the relation of age to altruism is linear or curvilinear and (b) whether two situational factors— type of resource to be donated and a characteristic of the solicitor (pregnant, nonpregnant)—affect the form of the relation. First, in regard to resource type, a shortcoming of the altruism literature is that conclusions are usually derived from studies in which only one form of helping is observed, "for example, if the response of interest is donating money, this is the only means of helping that subjects are allowed to express" (Brickman et al., 1982, p. 368). This investigation included two studies in which the primary difference consisted of the operational definition of donation. In Study A1, money—a resource potentially less available to retired adults than to younger respondents—was the resource to be donated. In Study A2, generosity was exhibited by subjects pulling a lever on behalf of charity—a mode of expression equally feasible for persons of all ages.

A second situational variable in the investigation was the appearance of the solicitor. The potential importance of solicitor characteristics comes from the fact that the solicitor is the sole representative of the charitable organization at the time of the appeal and serves as the obvious conduit of donations to the beneficiaries. Prior studies have found significant positive relations between donations and both the race of the solicitor (Bryan & Test, 1967) and statements by the solicitor designed to appeal to charitable impulses (Dressel & Midlarsky, 1978). When the solicitor's appeal (a) seems particularly demanding, (b) introduces distracting complexities, or (c) induces negative moods, then donations tend to decrease (Isen & Noonberg, 1979). In the current investigation, we varied solicitor appearance in a way designed to precipitate socially responsible action through triggering what Leventhal (1976) has termed the *needs rule*. We anticipated that contact with a pregnant solicitor might arouse enough concern to evoke generosity, without producing the type of negative arousal that could backfire and thus lessen prosocial action (Brehm, 1966).

Another question concerned the degree to which the stimulus effect of the solicitor's appearance may vary across the age groups.

If, as Dowd (1980) has argued, perception of intergenerational inequities may inhibit generosity by elderly persons, then the presence of a young adult as solicitor for the charity may exacerbate this effect. Conversely, the presence of a pregnant solicitor with an appeal for infants with birth defects may remind the elderly person that whatever inequities he or she experiences in general are less severe than the potential difficulties faced by the obviously vulnerable person conducting the appeal. Thus, in addition to predicting a main effect for solicitor condition, the hypothesis of an interactive effect may be derived from Dowd's (1980) application of exchange theory to older adults. Hence, in the condition in which a nonpregnant woman is the charitable solicitor, the relation between age and generosity should be curvilinear. In the condition in which an apparently pregnant solicitor is used, however, the relation between age and generosity should be linear.

In sum, the solicitor's condition (pregnant, nonpregnant) was introduced as an independent variable to test the hypothesis that perceptions of intergenerational inequity, rather than altruistic motives, are critical determinants of generosity among elderly persons. A two-experiment design was used, each one requiring donation of a different commodity (money vs. time and effort) to test the hypothesis that observed differences in helping behavior are based on availability of resource to be donated, rather than variations in altruistic motives.

Study A1

Study A1 was designed to investigate the relation between age and donations to a fund for infants with birth defects, using a 2 × 8 factorial design. The independent variables were solicitor's condition (pregnant or nonpregnant) and age of the donor (5 to 14, 15 to 24, 25 to 34, 45 to 54, 55 to 64, 65 to 74, and 75+).

Method

The standard condition consisted of a woman in her 20s sitting in a booth that was open on three sides, near a table that held a donation canister. All around the outside of the booth and hanging at its rear were large, black and white posters inviting donations to a fund for infants with birth defects. The choice of a single, dramatic format for the posters accorded with findings regarding the most efficacious way to attract donors (Isen & Noonberg, 1979). For people approaching the table, the visual appeal was supplemented by a request from the solicitor to make monetary donations to a fund for infants with birth defects. The donation situation was carefully designed and pretested to ensure that it had maximal appeal and that only one potential donor could be in a position to donate at a time. The rationale for this latter procedure was based on the widely replicated finding that the presence of more than one potential helper may inhibit helping behavior (Latané, 1981). The donation canister had the name of the fund on the side facing the donor, but it was transparent on the solicitor's side to permit the unobtrusive counting of donation amounts.

The study was conducted on 2 successive weekends in several shopping centers, malls, and parks in a major metropolitan area in the western United States (population of about 2 million). The specific research sites were randomly chosen from among those known to be frequented, particularly on weekends, by individuals of highly diverse ages. Census data, supplemented by regional community health center neighborhood surveys, indicated that the six sites chosen varied widely in socioeconomic status.

The three charitable solicitors, women between the ages of 25 and 28 years, were randomly assigned to appeal sites and to the pregnant-nonpregnant condition. Solicitors simulated pregnancy with the help of a foam prosthesis of the type used in maternity shops when clothes are fitted; they wore maternity clothes over the prosthesis. Observers were upper-division undergraduate psychology students chosen from among 50 volunteers on the basis of their ability to rapidly determine age from videotapes of naturalistic settings similar to those used in the study. Triads of assistants were intensively trained to determine narrow age ranges in actual natural settings. Pilot tests were conducted in which the observers guessed ages of persons in naturalistic settings and then target persons were asked their actual ages. Results indicated that mean age estimates by triads of observers compared with actual ages had a very high degree of accuracy, $r = .96$, $p < .001$.

Results

Preliminary Analyses. In this study, three young women served as charitable solicitors. Our first question was whether the phenomena under investigation were sufficiently robust so that the specific identity of the solicitor would have minimal impact on the study results (cf. Scheier & Geller, 1979). Two analyses were, therefore, conducted. First, a one-way chi-square was calculated, in which the independent variable was charitable solicitor (collaborator) and the dependent variable was number of persons donating. Second, a one-way analysis of variance (ANOVA) was performed, in which the independent variable was again collaborator and the dependent variable was amount of money donated. Neither analysis produced significant results. Consequently, the collaborator to whom respondents were exposed was not included as a variable in subsequent analyses.

Primary Analyses. Table 4.1 presents the number of persons exposed to the appeal, the number and percentage of persons donating, and the mean donation in each condition. A 2×8 chi-square analysis of the numbers of persons donating, by age of donor, indicated that the overall differences among groups were significant, $\chi^2(1, N = 2,715) = 34.57, p < .001$. A phi coefficient ($\phi$) indicated that this relationship accounted for 11% of the variance. As predicted, significantly more people contributed in the presence of a pregnant solicitor (55%) than in the presence of a solicitor who was not pregnant (45%), $\chi^2(1, N = 2,715) = 26.06, p < .001, \phi = .10$. Furthermore, there was an increase in numbers of persons donating from the youngest age group (5 to 14 years: 32%) through the early adult years (25 to 34: 59%), followed by a plateau in the middle-adult years (35 to 64 years: 73%), a rise at age 65 (65 to 74 years: 93%), and then a decrease in the 75+ age group (85%).

In order to test the significance of observed differences among the eight age groups, Ryan's (1960) procedure for pairwise comparison in chi-square was used. This procedure yielded the findings that more people 15 to 24 years of age donated than did 5- to 14-year-olds, $\chi^2(1, N = 2,715) = 25.08, p < .001$, and more 24- to 34-year-olds donated than did those 15 to 24 years of age, $\chi^2(1, N =$

Table 4.1 Number and Percentage of Donors and Mean Donation by
             Age of Donor and Solicitor Condition in Study A1

| Age of Donor | Pregnant Solicitor | | | | Nonpregnant Solicitor | | | |
	Mean Donation	n	%	Total Solicited	Mean Donation	n	%	Total Solicited
5 to 14	30	107	34	315	24	96	30	323
15 to 24	50	150	52	289	41	120	40	301
25 to 34	75	203	66	308	59	154	52	297
35 to 44	101	236	85	278	83	177	62	287
45 to 54	102	251	86	293	85	179	61	295
55 to 64	104	253	84	302	84	184	62	298
65 to 74	87	198	100	198	68	161	85	190
75+	48	93	97	96	40	153	80	192

NOTE: Mean (M) donations are given in pennies.

2,715) = 21.01, $p < .001$. The three groups from 35 to 64 years of age donated significantly more frequently than did all of the younger groups, $p < .001$, but did not differ significantly from one another. In addition, more individuals 65 to 74 years of age donated than did those in any other age group studied here. Fewer of the oldest group, ages 75 and older, donated than did those in the 65- to 74-year-old group, $\chi^2(1, N = 2,715) = 8.89, p < .01$. However, more of the oldest group donated than did those in any of the under-65 age groups who were exposed to the charitable appeal, $p < .001$ for all comparisons.

An ANOVA was then performed to examine the impacts of donor age and solicitor condition on amount of money donated to the charity. This analysis yielded a significant main effect for condition of the solicitor, with the pregnant solicitors evoking a higher level of donations, $M = 75$ cents, than did the nonpregnant solicitors, $M = 61$ cents, $F(1,2700) = 217.3, p < .001$. The main effect of donor age was significant as well, $F(7,2700) = 194.13, p < .001$. The interaction between donor age and solicitor condition failed to reach significance. For the significant main effect of solicitor condition, eta-squared was 6%, and the eta-squared for the significant main effect of donor age was 41%.

Newman-Keuls tests performed on the mean amounts donated for the significant main effect of age indicated that the youngest respondents, 5- to 14-years-old, donated the smallest amounts, followed by the oldest group, 75 years of age and older. Following the oldest group in amounts donated were, respectively, the 15- to 24- and 25- to 34-year-olds; differences among all three groups were significant at $p < .001$. However, although the young old were the most frequent donors, on the average they donated significantly less money than did all three groups of adults in the 35- to 64-year-old group. None of the latter three groups differed significantly from one another, and observed mean differences among them were small in magnitude as well.

Study A2

Study A2 was designed to explore the question of whether the relation between age and donations was due to a decline in perceived financial resources and a concomitant increase in costs of donating among the elderly persons, rather than a disinclination to give.

Method

The standard condition (including the pregnant/nonpregnant solicitor) was identical to the one described in Study A1, with the exception of the apparatus for collecting donations. In this study, individuals approaching the donation table saw a two-lever device, rather than a donation canister. They were told that if they wanted to help the infants with birth defects, they should operate the lever labeled "For the Children" and a record would be made on a counter of the number of such pulls. They were also told that local merchants had agreed that for each pull of the lever "For the Children," 5 cents would be donated to the fund. The few people who asked about the second lever were told that it "came with the machine" but had no purpose in the current charity drive. For one half of the donation periods, the donation lever was to the left of the neutral lever, and for the other half, it was to the right.

The purpose of including the neutral lever was that a plausible rival hypothesis is that "gadgetorial seduction" inherent in a novel machine, and not an altruistic impulse, may predispose lever pulls. What makes a lever pull charitable is not just the motor response but the motive for the response. The neutral lever was introduced in order to reduce ambiguity about what motivated the observed behavior.

As in Study A1, this investigation was conducted on 3 successive weekends in shopping centers, malls, and parks in a major metropolitan area in the western United States. Locations for all of the donations were selected on a random basis from the list of such locations described earlier, but with the restriction that none of the locations had been used in the prior study. In Study A2, research assistants recorded the sex of the donor in addition to age and amounts donated.

Results

Preliminary Analyses. Results of an ANOVA indicated that collaborator identity did not significantly affect pulls of either the donation lever or the neutral lever. Chi-squares performed on numbers of persons donating revealed that neither collaborator identity nor sex of the donor had significant effects.

Primary Analyses. Table 4.2 presents the number and percentages of persons donating in each of the conditions formed by the factorial combination of age group and solicitor condition. Chi-squares performed on these results indicated that despite the difference in the nature of the donation requested, the relation of the two independent variables (age and solicitor condition) to numbers donating was replicated.

First, a 2 × 8 chi-square revealed that, overall, the observed differences were significant, $\chi^2(7, N = 2,735) = 34.17, p < .001, \phi = .11$. As before, significantly more individuals (55%) donated in the presence of a pregnant solicitor, when compared with donations to the nonpregnant solicitor (45%), $\chi^2(1, N = 2,735) = 25.87, p < .001, \phi = .10$. Again, using pairwise mean comparisons, evidence was found for a linear increase in numbers of persons donating with age. Results also indicated that the age trends and significance levels were virtually identical in the two studies, with one exception.

Table 4.2 Number and Percentage of Donors and Mean Donation by
             Age of Donor and Solicitor Condition in Study A2

| Age of Donor | Pregnant Solicitor | | | | Nonpregnant Solicitor | | | |
	Mean Donation	n	%	Total Solicited	Mean Donation	n	%	Total Solicited
5 to 14	8	95	31	307	5	93	29	319
15 to 24	13	157	54	291	13	128	42	304
25 to 34	18	202	67	302	18	156	52	300
35 to 44	27	243	85	286	23	182	61	299
45 to 54	27	247	84	294	23	179	60	298
55 to 64	29	255	86	297	23	190	62	307
65 to 74	33	182	99	184	28	173	86	201
75+	37	106	97	109	33	147	81	181

NOTE: Mean (M) donations are given in pulls of the donation lever.

Although a larger proportion of young-old individuals, 65 to 74 years of age (92%), donated in comparison with the old-old persons, ages 75 and older (87%), the difference between the two oldest age groups failed to reach significance.

Table 4.2 also depicts the number of pulls of the donations lever by age of donor, sex of donor, and solicitor condition. An ANOVA of donations, operationally defined as the number of pulls of the lever labeled "For the Children," yielded significant main effects for solicitor condition, $F(1,2681) = 196.87$, $p < .001$, donor age, $F(7,2681) = 611.08$, $p < .001$, and donor sex, $F(1,1681) = 15.83$, $p < .001$. More donations were given in the presence of pregnant solicitors, $M = 23.25$, than nonpregnant solicitors, $M = 20.88$, and more help was given by women, $M = 22.63$, than by men, $M = 21.5$. Etas-squared indicating percentages of variance explained were 3%, 58%, and 0.2% for the respective main effects. Newman-Keuls tests, performed on the mean amounts helped for the main effect of age, provided evidence of a steady increase in amount donated, with each age group donating more than the group below it in age. The youngest (5 to 14 years) respondents donated least, and the oldest respondents (75+ years) donated most. All of the age groups differed from one another, with the exception of those age 35 to 44, 45 to 54, and 55 to 64, which once again were not significantly different in amounts donated.

Three interactions affected the amount of helping as well. Significant effects were found for solicitor condition and age, $F(7,2681) = 13.98$, $p < .001$; donor age × donor sex, $F(7,2681) = 9.13$, $p < .001$; and condition × age × sex, $F(7,2681) = 9.18$, $p < .001$. Etas-squared performed for the significant interactions yielded results of 1%, 1%, and 1%, respectively, of the variance accounted for. Of particular interest from a theoretical perspective was the explanation of what accounted for the significant interaction between solicitor condition and age. Newman-Keuls analysis performed on that interaction revealed that men age 15 to 24 and 25 to 34 were more generous in the presence of nonpregnant solicitors than they were with the pregnant solicitors—a finding that is not in accord with predictions from equity theory. As all three of the interactions failed to reach significance in Study A1, and each accounted for quite a small amount of variance, results of additional post hoc analyses are not presented here.[2]

In Study A2, the neutral or unlabeled lever was included to provide an indication of the extent to which lever pulling in the donation booth was based on charitable impulses rather than on curiosity and other nonaltruistic motives. Hence an additional dependent variable in Study A2 was the number of times each respondent pulled the neutral lever.

Table 4.3 depicts the numbers of neutral lever pulls, by age of donor, gender of donor, and solicitor condition. Inspection of the means for neutral lever pulls in Table 4.3 indicates that in no group studied here was there a tendency to alternately pull the left and right levers, which suggests that pulls for charity were apparently a form of purposeful behavior. Pulls of the neutral lever were relatively rare phenomena, ranging from a mean of 1.16 for the highest responders, the youngest individuals (5 to 14), to a mean of 0 for both the 65 to 74 and 75+ age groups. Indeed, the oldest persons in this study were the only respondents who entirely ignored this lever.

An ANOVA calculated on the neutral pulls yielded only a significant effect for age, $F(7,2681) = 40.17$, $p < .001$, accounting for 8% of the variance. A Newman-Keuls indicated that individuals age 5 to 14 and 15 to 24 pulled the neutral lever significantly more than all other age groups, and that they were significantly different

Table 4.3 Numbers of "Neutral" (unlabeled) Pulls, by Age of Donor, Gender of Donor, and Solicitor Conditions: Study A2

Age of Donor	Pregnant Solicitor	Nonpregnant Solicitor
Males		
5 to 14	1.11	1.16
15 to 24	1.03	0.98
25 to 34	0.26	0.36
35 to 44	0.09	0.20
45 to 54	0.09	0.18
55 to 64	0.07	0.09
65 to 74	0.00	0.00
75 +	0.00	0.00
Females		
5 to 14	1.25	1.11
15 to 24	0.88	1.15
25 to 34	0.11	0.25
35 to 44	0.10	0.11
45 to 54	0.09	0.12
55 to 64	0.06	0.07
65 to 74	0.00	0.00
75 +	0.00	0.00

from one another, $p < .05$, with the youngest pulling the lever significantly more.

Discussion

An important goal of this investigation was to extend research concerning the relation between age and generosity earlier in life to cross-age comparisons ranging from early childhood to old age. The results of this investigation indicate that in naturalistic settings in which an opportunity to be generous was readily accessible to people of diverse ages, more elderly persons made donations than did younger persons. This finding was replicated across three types of naturalistic settings, two time periods, and three charitable solicitors, and it was obtained in samples that varied widely in socioeconomic status and that included individuals ranging from 5 to well over 90 years of age.

Three theoretical perspectives—dependency theory, autonomy theory, and exchange theory—lead to predictions of a curvilinear relation between age and altruism, with the apex of altruistic responding in the middle years, followed by decrements in old age (Kahana et al., 1987). In this investigation we found, first of all, a linear relation between age and numbers donating. After an increase from the youngest ages until a plateau was reached in the middle-adult years, older persons, 65 years and above, donated more frequently than did any group of persons under the age of 65.

In contrast to findings regarding the frequency of persons helping, when monetary contributions were treated as the dependent variable, the oldest donors (75+) gave relatively small amounts, exceeding only the amounts given by the very youngest donors (5 to 14 years old). The young old, 65 to 74 years of age, gave less than the three groups of middle-aged adults (35 to 44, 45 to 54, and 55 to 64), who were the most generous in regard to amounts of money given.

We considered the possibility, however, that despite the willingness to donate that was apparent in the numbers of persons making donations to charity, the costs of the financial donations for older adults, whose monetary resources may have shrunk following retirement, may have been disproportionately high in comparison with the costs to the younger adults. Costs of helping have, themselves, been found to be important determinants of helping in a wide variety of situations (Piliavin, Dovidio, Gaertner, & Clark, 1981). Hence, in Study A2, in addition to holding opportunities for helping relatively constant for the diverse ages, the costs of helping were also controlled to the extent possible. Where donations of time and effort were requested, in place of money, older adults were not only the most frequent donors but also gave more than any other age group. This finding supported the hypothesis of a linear relation between age and altruism.

A plausible rival hypothesis that may be invoked is that donations in the form of expenditures of time may be disproportionately less costly for the oldest respondents, many of whom are retired, have empty nests, and therefore have a great deal of leisure time. We did, however, attempt to control for that exigency by conducting the studies during weekends and in locations in which the preponderance of persons of all ages were involved in leisure pursuits.

In addition, the effort required to operate the rather stiff ratchet mechanism within the lever, associated with apparent physical strain only for the older persons, did not deter them from pulling the lever more often than any of the younger respondents did. Also relevant is the fact that no individual over the age of 65 showed any interest in the neutral lever at all, indicating that responses were based on altruistic dispositions rather than on simply the desire to spend some excess leisure time in a novel way.

A second goal of this investigation was to determine the effect of solicitor condition on donations to charity. As predicted, significantly larger donations, whether of money or of time and effort, were made when the solicitor was pregnant, and larger numbers of individuals donated as well. The main reason for including condition of the solicitor as an independent variable was to test a prediction derived from exchange theory (Dowd, 1980). As previously discussed, this theory would predict an interaction between solicitor condition and age, so that a curvilinear relation could be obtained in the presence of a nonpregnant solicitor and a linear relation in the presence of a pregnant solicitor. The lack of support in either of the two studies regarding the functional form of the relation under the two solicitor conditions, combined with the total lack of interest by elderly persons in the neutral lever, suggests that altruistic motivations were indeed the primary determinants of the observed behavior.

Of principal interest in this investigation is the finding that older persons helped more than young individuals did and that perceptions of intergenerational inequities did not inhibit generosity. In fact, when the needed resource was accessible to the elderly adults, they displayed a great deal of generosity. However, in an investigation of this kind, certain caveats may be introduced. For example, donations were made in public settings, and the degree of impact on donating in public versus private settings may vary with age. Also, the increase in donations with age found in this cross-sectional research study may reflect a cohort effect. Only studies using cross-sequential designs can definitively establish the degree to which there are linear developmental trends in generosity from the earliest to the latest years. On the other hand, the consistency and magnitude of the increase in donations with age indicate that further research in this domain is clearly warranted.

RESCUE BEHAVIOR

The second set of naturalistic experiments investigated the relationship between age and rescue. In speculating about this relationship, it seemed to us that even more than in the case of donations, one may argue that help in the form of rescue is inversely related to age.

Age is often considered to be associated with financial deficits and dependencies for many older persons (Adamchak & Friedmann, 1983; Cowgill, 1986). However, decrements in health are considered to be even more probable to the extent that old age itself is virtually equated with terminal disease which, in turn, necessitates dependencies on other, presumably younger individuals (Sankar, 1984; Zola, 1983). If aged persons are indeed a handicapped population, as the dependency model implies, then how can they be expected to contribute to the physical well-being of others? In addition to illness, two physical resources often needed in rescue—strength and speed—appear to be markedly diminished in late life (Kausler, 1982).

On the other hand, there is growing evidence that although the preponderance of older people do have health problems, the degree to which daily functioning is limited by ill health may have been overestimated. Indeed, late life is characterized by considerable heterogeneity in regard to health, and many older persons continue to function quite well until very late in life (Abeles & Ory, 1991).

There is also evidence from self-report data that assertiveness is related to age, at least from ages 19 to 60 (Rushton et al., 1986). Whereas assertiveness was only inconsistently related to a measure of altruism in which people reported the frequency with which they engaged in 20 specific helping behaviors (Rushton, Chrisjohn, & Fekken, 1981), we speculated that in regard to rescue, assertiveness might be an important attribute of the potential rescuer (more so than for donations or advice giving, for example). If this is indeed the case, then rescue is a form of helping that may show increases with age.

An additional factor that may be related to rescue is that older people are continually exposed to health problems (e.g., hypertension, heart disease, arthritis) both in themselves and in their peers (e.g., spouse, siblings, friends, and neighbors). Even among community-dwelling older persons who function well most of the time, and among their age-mates, there may be an increased probability of dramatic episodic illnesses that require emergency intervention. Such exposure may, in turn, evoke concern for the physical well-being of others and even provide some degree of rehearsal for emergency intervention—to a greater degree than among younger people. Although some older adults may become physically self-protective because of their own physical limitations, exposure to illness among one's peers may provide increased opportunities to be altruistic. These opportunities may prompt helpful responses by those older adults who are predisposed to be altruistic by higher levels of empathy, moral judgment, social responsibility, altruistic values, internal locus of control, or through some combination of those (or related) motives. It is, therefore, possible to argue for two opposing hypotheses. That is, first, that older adults may be less likely to engage in rescue and rescue-related activities, and second, that older adults may be more likely to engage in rescue than are younger adults.

In addition, even more than in the case of donation behavior, involvement in rescue may be affected by situational variables. Indeed, in contrast to the numerous studies indicating a linear relationship between age and generosity in the early years of life, even in studies limited to the years of childhood and adolescence, the relation between age and emergency intervention has been found to be complex, with diverse factors limiting helping at various ages. In adolescence, intervention on behalf of others may be limited by factors such as embarrassment, whereas fears of incompetence or inadequacy apparently limit helping among some young children (Midlarsky & Hannah, 1985). In old age, lessened physical competence or knowledge about how to intervene may serve as limiting factors. Furthermore, in many cases, deficits in financial resources and access to adequate transportation may limit participation in certain types of rescue work, even by the older adults characterized by very high levels of motivation.

In sum, the two plausible rival hypotheses are that (a) rescue behavior may increase with age, and (b) rescue behavior may decrease with age. We also anticipated that two situational variables—financial costs and transportation—may affect rates of participation.

Study B1

The first study was performed to determine the degree to which people of varying ages would attend classes designed to teach the fundamentals of emergency intervention, including first aid and cardiopulminary resuscitation (CPR), in a $3 \times 2 \times 6$ experimental design. Independent variables in the study were the fee for taking the course ($0, $3, or $10), provision of transportation (provided or not provided), and age of participant (18 to 24, 25 to 34, 35 to 44, 45 to 54, 55 to 64, and 65+).

Method

The study began when announcements were made of the availability of first aid classes throughout a large tri-county region in the Midwest. Six different regions were chosen as the sites for separate advertisements of the class, in order to recruit respondents for the six separate cells formed by the factorial combination of two of the independent variables—course fee and provision of transportation. That is, advertising campaigns were identical in each of the six regions, with the exception of variations in the fee announced and in the offer (or not) of free transportation to the class. Advertisements consisted of radio announcements and posters displayed in laundromats; supermarkets; hospitals; shopping malls; doctors', dentists', and chiropractors' offices; community centers; churches; and synagogues. Census data indicated that the six regions were comparable in socioeconomic status and age composition.

All announcements of the class provided a telephone number, and attached to all of the posters were ample numbers of reply postcards that required no postage. Classes began 1 month from the time that the advertising campaign began.

Everyone who contacted the project team was assigned to a class. On a random basis, one half were assigned to a class in which they received the CPR course. The other half were assigned to a class in which they were given "value clarification" sessions; they were told that they would receive the CPR course 4 weeks later. All participants in the classes filled out a questionnaire in which they provided information about their age, employment (or retirement) status, perceived financial resources (Liang, Dvorkin, Kahana, & Mazian, 1980), availability of transportation, perceptions about available time, and motives for participating in the course.

Results

The advertising campaign was very effective. Twelve hundred and seven people returned the reply card attached to the posters or telephoned to inquire about the class after hearing an announcement. A total of 1,163 men and women, or 96.8% of those making an initial contact, actually came to take the class. A series of chi-square analyses indicated that people attending the class were not significantly different from those not attending in age, sex, or in regard to the levels of the independent variables to which they were exposed.

Our first question was whether there was a significant association between participation and age level (consisting of ages 18 to 24, 25 to 34, 35 to 44, 45 to 54, 55 to 64, and 65+). A six-category chi-square was first calculated, and results indicated that rates of participation did indeed vary by age, $\chi^2(5, N = 1,163) = 57.05, p < .001$. The phi coefficient indicated that the relationship between age and participation accounted for 22% of the variance. As shown in Figure 4.1, numbers of participants increased from the youngest to the oldest age groups. Among the 18- to 24-year-olds there were 117 people (10%), and there were 146 people age 25 to 34 (13%). These were followed by a plateau across three age groups (35 to 44, 45 to 54, and 55 to 64)—similar to the plateau across the middle years in the donation studies reported above. Numbers of participants in these three age groups were 214, 216, and 215, which

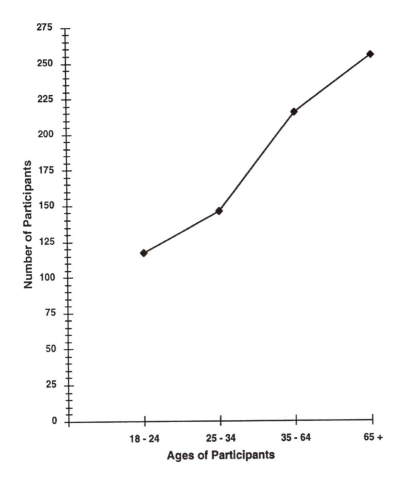

Figure 4.1 Graphic Representation of the Relationship Between Number of Participants and Age of Participant

represented 18%, 19%, and 18% of the participants, respectively. The largest number, $N = 255$, consisted of people age 65 years and older, and this group constituted 22% of the total sample. These data are graphically depicted in Figure 4.1.

Ryan's (1960) procedure was then used to test the pairwise significance of the observed differences among the age groups. Calculations
in accordance with this procedure yielded the finding that people age
65 and older were significantly more likely to attend the first aid
classes than were younger adults age 18 to 24, $\chi^2(1) = 46.1, p < .001$,
and 25 to 34, $\chi^2(1) = 19.03, p < .001$, but not significantly more apt to
participate than were people age 35 to 64, $\chi^2(1) = 1.07, p < .05$.

We then examined the relationship between the numbers of participants in the six age groups and the three levels of course fee ($0,
$3, and $10). A 3 × 6 chi-square indicated that, overall, the observed
variations in response to course fee by age were indeed significant,
$\chi^2(10, N = 1,163) = 42.81, p < .001$, accounting for 19% of the variance,
$Z = .188$. This relationship is depicted in Figure 4.2.

Findings from application of Ryan's procedure to pairwise comparisons were that, for the oldest participants, there were no
significant differences attributable to variations in course fee.
Percentages of older adults paying $0, $3, and $10 were, respec-
tively, 43%, 34%, and 23%. Statements by these older adults supported the interpretation that the knowledge expected as a result
of the course was considered important enough that there was
sufficient motivation to incur a cost—whether $3 or $10. Several
made such comments as "no cost is too high when health and life
are involved." For all other age groups, however, the course fee
did play a significant role—at least in some instances. In all three
of the age groups spanning the period from 35 to 64 (i.e., 35 to 44,
45 to 54, and 55 to 64), significantly more people attended the class
under the $0 fee condition, in comparison with the condition in
which a $10 fee was required, $p < .05$ for all comparisons. Among
25- to 34-year-old adults, there was a significant difference between the $0 and the $10 fee conditions, $\chi^2(1) = 9.69, p < .01$, and
between the $3 and $10 conditions, $\chi^2(1) = 7.11, p < .01$, but not
between the $0 and $3 conditions. For people age 18 to 24, all fee
conditions were significantly different from each other. The result for
$0 versus $10 was $\chi^2(1) = 16.5, p < .001$, for $0 and $3 it was $\chi^2(1)$
$= 0.95, p < .01$, and for $3 and $10, $\chi^2(1) = 8.45, p < .01$.

Did the provision of transportation versus no provision of transportation to the first aid class affect the numbers of people participating at the six age levels? According to the results of a 2 × 6 chi-

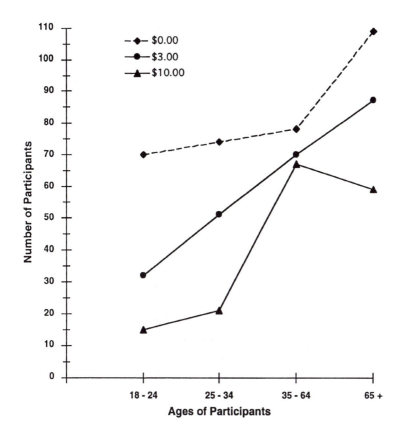

Figure 4.2 Graphic Representation of the Relationship Between Number of Participants and Age of Participant, Under Conditions of Three Levels of Course Fee

square, the relationship between number of participants and age of participants, under conditions of transportation provided versus no transportation provided, was significant, $\chi^2(5, N = 1{,}163) = 15.46$, $p < .01$, with $\phi = .11$. Figure 4.3 depicts this relationship.

Again employing Ryan's procedure for pairwise comparisons in chi-square, we found that older adults were significantly more

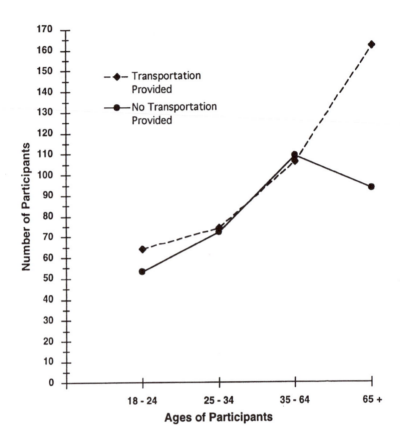

Figure 4.3 Graphic Representation of the Relationship Between Number of Participants and Age of Participant, Under Conditions of Transportation Provided Versus No Transportation Provided

likely to be represented in the condition in which transportation was provided, $\chi^2(1) = 11.08$, $p < .001$, $\phi = .21$. There were no significant effects found for transportation in any of the other age groups.

We then examined the responses of the study participants to the questionnaire. First, we found that 80% of the 18- to 24-year-olds were students, and 78% of the oldest adults were retired. All other individuals in the youngest and oldest age groups, and all participants age 25 to 64, reported that they were currently employed. There were no significant differences among the groups regarding perceptions about the discretionary time available to them. In response to open-ended queries, more than 75% of the respondents in each of the age groups spontaneously wrote that they perceived time to be "at a premium," that the expenditure of time was costly for them, and that they enrolled in the course because they perceived it as valuable.

In order to determine the degree to which the course fee was viewed as costly, we then examined the perceived financial resources and found that the older adults had significantly lower finances than did the other groups, $p < .001$ for all comparisons. Regarding transportation, 80% of the older adults, and 0% (or close to zero) of people in the other age groups had transportation-related problems and cited transportation as a significant potential limitation on their participation in diverse activities.

There was considerable variation in the reasons for participating in the course given by people in the varying age groups. Adults age 18 to 64 expressed motives of several types. Over half (54%) were curious about methods currently used in first aid, and more than a third (36%) took the class in order to determine whether they were interested enough in first aid to pursue further education or even careers in this domain. About 34% expressed a desire to learn first aid so that they would be in a better position to help others. Among the oldest adults, age 65 and older, the range of motives was far less varied. All said that they took the class because they felt that the information was critical. The preponderance (85%) said that they were taking the class to increase their capability to be of genuine assistance in the event of a health care emergency. About 62% spontaneously commented on the importance of CPR as a tool for saving lives and said that the inclusion of this component alone was enough to make the class worthwhile.

Study B2

The second study was conducted in order to determine the effects of participation in first aid classes on actual rescue behavior and on the effectiveness of the rescue behavior by adults of different ages. The independent variables in this study were preparation for emergency intervention (defined as training in first aid vs. no training) and age. In regard to age, the consistent finding across all of our studies—both of donation behavior and of rescue—of no significant differences in altruistic responses in the middle years led to the decision to categorize age somewhat differently in this experiment. That is, the three age groups ranging from 35 to 64, which were treated separately in the prior work, were treated as a single group, yielding a total of three age categories: younger adults (18 to 34), middle-aged adults (35 to 64), and older adults (65+). In sum, a 2 × 6 experimental design was used, wherein the six groups were formed by the factorial combination of the two levels of training and the six age categories. The dependent variables consisted of measures of the amount of helping and competence displayed in what appeared to be a health emergency.

Method

The method for obtaining participants for the first aid classes was identical to the procedure in Study B1. Everyone who contacted the project team was assigned to a class. On a random basis, 110 people in each of the three age groups (18 to 34, 35 to 64, and 65+) were assigned to a first aid class. Also on a random basis, 110 people in each of the three age groups were assigned to a class providing a series of communication and value clarification exercises, which were described to them as a prerequisite for the first aid classes (and they were given the standard instruction in first aid after the experiment was completed). A total of 660 people participated in the experiment. Any people not randomly selected, and consequently not accommodated within the six study groups, joined the "value-clarification" class participants in the first aid classes following the end of Study B2.

All study participants were asked to return on an individual basis at randomly determined times following the 2-month (eight-session) class, ostensibly to discuss the results of their participation and to fill out questionnaires. Appointments were scheduled in such a way that none of the participants saw any others during their appointment. Twelve different locations were used, corresponding to the locations in which the classes were held, in order to accommodate the large number of respondents in this study. Nevertheless, in all cases the scenarios were identical. In each, the respondent came to the building, and then, in order to arrive at the assigned room, had to walk down a corridor. In the corridor, a 30-year-old woman wearing a pantsuit and high heels was balancing on a stepladder so that she could change a fluorescent bulb high above her head. The corridor was empty except for the respondent and the woman on the stepladder. After the participant passed the place where the woman on the stepladder was seen, the young "accident victim" prepared for the staged emergency. She placed the stepladder on the floor (as if it had fallen), hid the fluorescent light and spread a bag of fine glass chips and fragments around the place where she had been standing to change the light, along with a pool of realistic-looking "blood." She changed to a pair of badly ripped slacks. On the leg with the rip, she applied a rather gruesome-looking bleeding wound; through attached tubing, she was able to continually pump additional theatrical blood to the wound site with a hand pump. To all appearances, then, she was sprawled on the floor, bleeding and too wounded to help herself.

When the participant came to the assigned room, he or she was told that the course instructor was running a bit late and to please fill out the questionnaire (containing the same questions as in Study B1) while waiting. Two minutes later, there was the sound of something heavy falling, glass shattering, and a high-pitched scream followed by a shout of "Help me, help me!"

During all of this, responses by the participant were observed through one-way mirrors extending from the room in which the questionnaire was filled out to the area in which the staged accident occurred. If, after 2 minutes, the participant remained seated, or if he or she rose to leave the situation entirely, then he or she was considered to be a nonhelper in this situation. In such cases, the course instructor came into the room (or stopped the respondent just outside the room), had the participant complete the questionnaire if not yet completed, and ended the experimental trial. For participants who left the room to help, the help was

Table 4.4   Numbers and Percentages of Attempts at Emergency
             Intervention by Age of Helper and Training Level

Age Group	Trained	Untrained
18 to 34		
Number	91	93
Percentage	83	85
35 to 64		
Number	97	95
Percentage	88	86
65+		
Number	87	67
Percentage	79	61

NOTE: Each of the six groups included 110 respondents.

coded as effective if direct pressure was applied to the wound and
ineffective if any other behavior occurred. Experimental trials
were terminated for participants attempting to provide help immediately after the initiation of any helping attempt. Responses
were separately recorded by two research assistants.

Results

As in Study B1, there was a sizable and enthusiastic response to
the advertisements of the first aid course, with well over 1,100
people responding. A series of chi-square analyses, comparing the
numbers of people of all ages responding to the advertisements,
yielded no significant age differences between the two studies. As
in Study B1, more than 95% of those making an initial contact with
the project team actually took the assigned class. Our first question
was whether the number of people attempting to help varied by
age and training. Table 4.4 presents the numbers and percentages
of people helping in the six cells of the research design.

Examination of Table 4.4 indicates that a smaller number of
older adults, age 65 and older, offered help in comparison with the
two younger age groups. Results of chi-square analyses revealed
that these differences were significant. Thus older adults were less

Table 4.5 Numbers and Percentages of People Intervening Who Gave Effective Help by Age of Helper and Training Level

Age Group	Trained	Untrained
18 to 34		
Number	45	14
Percentage	49	15
35 to 64		
Number	58	21
Percentage	60	22
65+		
Number	68	34
Percentage	78	51

NOTE: Helpers who did not apply pressure directly to the wound engaged in a variety of other behaviors. Among these were shouts or cries for help, queries to the accident victim (e.g., "Are you OK?"), attempts to find someone "in charge" or a telephone (to call 911), or requests that the experimenter help, when that individual returned.

apt to help than were both young adults, $\chi^2(1) = 10.73$, $p < .01$, and middle-aged adults, $\chi^2(1) = 18.52$, $p < .001$. In regard to the first aid training, there was no significant impact on the numbers of people helping, either among younger persons (age 18 to 34) or middle-aged persons (age 35 to 64), $\chi^2(1) < 1$ for both comparisons. Within the group of elderly participants, however, older people trained in first aid were more likely to help than those who had not taken the course, $\chi^2(1) = 7.81$, $p < 01$.

Our second question was whether the numbers of people helping effectively varied with age and training. For the analyses presented here, the dependent variable consisted of the number of people who gave help in the appropriate way, that is, by applying direct pressure to the wound. The numbers of people helping appropriately appear in Table 4.5.

Chi-squares performed on the data presented in Table 4.5 indicated that older people were more likely to be effective when trained in first aid than when no training had yet been received, $\chi^2(1) = 10.68$, $p < .01$. Furthermore, trained older people were significantly more effective than both trained and untrained younger adults, $p < .01$ for all comparisons.

Discussion

The studies on rescue behavior were designed to assess the generalizability of findings about age-related increases in altruism and helping in the form of donation behavior to an entirely different domain of action. That is, the goal was to determine whether older adults are motivated to help in the way variously designated as aiding under stress (Midlarsky, 1971; Midlarsky & Midlarsky, 1973), rescue, bystander intervention (Latané & Darley, 1969), and emergency intervention (Piliavin et al., 1981), as well as in the form of charitableness, donations (e.g., Barnett et al., 1979), or "sharing of the wealth" (e.g., money, time, resources) (Midlarsky, 1968). Results of the two studies on rescue suggest that many older people were indeed motivated and may be capable of providing care to others in health emergencies. In addition, their emergency intervention may be motivated primarily by the exocentric desire to be of genuine service to others in need. Among the age groups in the rescue studies, it was the oldest adults who were most likely to sign up for first aid classes—and to follow up by actually attending those classes.

In response to our first question in Study B1, about the relationship between age and helping, we found that the numbers of people signing up for first aid classes increased with age. We also found that their motives for participating may be altruistic to a greater extent than the motives of younger adults participating in this research. Thus older adults were more likely to express altruistic motives for taking the class, and they were more willing to participate in the course whatever the course fee ($0, $3, or $10). The greater willingness to incur a higher course fee was manifested despite significantly lower financial resources in the oldest age group. Although for many older people, the course was a costly activity, it was perceived as extremely valuable because of its potential link to the saving of lives. On the other hand, despite the strong motivation to participate, which even overcame financial considerations for many older participants, transportation apparently remained an obstacle to participation—in this case, solely for older adults. In contrast to younger people, for whom transportation was rarely, if ever, an issue, older people were less likely to participate if transportation was not provided.

Results of Study B2, designed to investigate the effects of age and training on actual helping, yielded lower rates of emergency intervention by the oldest adults. Why the apparent reticence by older adults, in the face of high motivation to learn first aid, apparently for the primary purpose of rescuing others in distress? In the absence of direct evidence, we can only speculate about possible reasons, but several possibilities come to mind. For example, in all cases the accident victim was a young woman—at least 35 years younger than the 65+ age group. In current American society, in which youth is equated with physical health and competence, the older adult may have felt relatively incompetent to help, despite the fact of an accident (Midlarsky, 1984). In dealing with relatively young people, it is possible that many older adults may perceive a role reversal if they attempt to provide help in a health emergency. Similarly, empathic arousal is an important predictor of altruistic helping, and empathy may be related in turn to perceptions of similarity with the victim. This perception of similarity—the "we-ness" or promotive tension that is related to helping (Hornstein, 1976, 1978)—may be curtailed among older adults confronted with need expressed by a person who is much younger and generally more physically able than they are. The effects on the age/altruism relationship of perceived competence and of similarity should be tested in future studies varying the characteristics of the potential help recipient.

Still another source of relative inhibition of helping by older adults may be the very fact that older adults put the welfare of the other foremost. They may desire an optimal outcome for the victim, whoever serves as the actual helper. Support for this speculation comes from the finding that participation in first aid training led to increased numbers of people helping only among the oldest adults. That is, similarly trained and untrained young and middle-aged adults offered help, whereas rates of help attempts were higher in the group of older adults who had received the first aid training. The possibility that the increase in helping associated with first aid training was attributable to altruistic motivation—the desire to intervene only if one can be certain that the recipient is helped and not harmed—was examined in Study B2. That study determined the effects of the factorial combination of age and training condition on numbers of people helping effectively.

The finding that there was a greater number of effective helpers in the group of older adults trained in first aid than in any other group has two implications. First, it contradicts the stereotype of older adults as poor learners. As memory researchers have found (Hartley, Harker, & Walsh, 1980; Hultsch, 1974; Light, 1991), the performance of older adults on tasks designed to assess memory is improved when the material is meaningful, when they are motivated, and when the tasks are performed in the context of a naturalistic situation rather than the artificial environment of the experimental laboratory. Second, this finding reinforces the notion that older adults only help when they know that their efforts will be effective. The apparent reticence observed in Study B2 may represent not only a cautiousness that may be characteristic of the older years of life but also an altruistic refusal to act unless one knows that action is likely to improve the victim's situation, rather than make things worse. The fact that there were more helping attempts by older adults who had taken the first aid class, whereas the instruction in first aid did not affect helping by younger adults, may reflect a lower level of pretraining confidence among the oldest participants. An important effect of the training may therefore have been a disinhibition of helping among the elderly.

In sum, the results of the naturalistic research on the two distinct types of helping reported in this chapter indicate that helping is a relatively frequent activity among older adults. Helping may be inhibited when there are critical barriers, such as transportation or, in the instance of monetary donations, disproportionately high financial costs. On the other hand, altruism in many older adults may be high enough to prompt participation even when costs are high. In order to more directly assess the motives of older helpers and the outcomes of the helping, a survey research study was conducted among community-dwelling older adults. This study is presented in Chapter 5.

NOTES

1. This section of the chapter, dealing with donation behavior in older adults, is derived from Midlarsky & Hannah, 1989, copyright 1989 by the American Psychological Association. Reprinted by permission of the publisher and authors.

2. Details of these analyses are available from the authors.

Predictors of Helping and Well-Being in Older Adults: A Cross-Sectional Survey Research Project

Experimental studies like the ones described in Chapter 4 have the great advantage of permitting the direct observation of behavior. However, issues of sampling may be less rigorously addressed in such studies, and a far narrower range of predictor variables can be considered than in surveys of broader populations. Encouraged by the experimental studies in naturalistic settings—which revealed the importance of helping for the elderly, and the likelihood that they engage in helping—a survey was undertaken to further explore the incidence, prevalence, and meaning of help giving in this age group.

The survey research described in this chapter was designed to explore personal and situational predictors, the nature, and the psychosocial sequelae of helping behavior for older persons within the social domains considered to be highly salient in their lives, that is, in the extended family, with neighbors/friends, and in the wider community (e.g., in volunteer activities). The study aimed to address three research questions:

1. What are the characteristics of helping behavior among the aged?

2. What are the personal, motivational, and situational predictors of helping by elderly persons?
3. What are the relationships among amount and type of helping, the proposed predictors of helping, and positive psychosocial outcomes?

As the literature on personal antecedents of altruism and helping has largely consisted of laboratory experiments investigating helping by children (Midlarsky, 1994), the study described herein was, to the best of our knowledge, the first to assess the generalizability of the experimental research to the self-reported, in vivo transactions of older adults. Helping was conceptualized as denoting a wide range and variety of behaviors, encompassing both normative, or extrinsically motivated, and altruistic, or intrinsically motivated, behaviors.

An important goal of this study was descriptive/exploratory in nature. There have been few studies directly focusing on altruistic or helping behaviors, broadly defined, in "real life" situations. A necessary and important first step in this area of research was, therefore, to deal with the identification of helping opportunities and a careful description of the types of help given. It was considered important to commence the investigation of helping in this fashion because of the paucity of information about the roles that older adults play as helpers and about their own definitions regarding their helping roles and functions.

In addition to the exploratory, descriptive aspects of the study, we investigated the relationships of the personal and situational predictors of helping, and of helping behavior itself, to outcomes of particular relevance to the mental health and psychosocial well-being of the elderly: morale, self-esteem, and the subjective sense of social integration (conceptually, the converse of loneliness).

Hence an important set of objectives involved the specification of a conceptual model directed toward understanding the relative importance of personal and situational antecedents on different types and dimensions of helping behavior and on positive psychosocial outcomes for the helper. Models that have been developed relating competence and helping in the field of altruism (Midlarsky, 1984), or role losses and competence in the field of

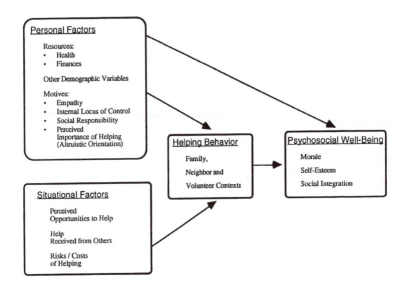

Figure 5.1 Contributory Model of Successful Aging

aging (Kuypers & Bengtson, 1973), all stress the circular nature of development, maintenance, and loss of competence. Thus better resources or greater competence are likely to result in performing meaningful social roles such as helping, which in turn results in a quasi-enforced sense of mastery, just as dependency results in learned helplessness (Seligman, 1975).

The study presented here was not designed to examine and test the complete models presented in these theoretical formulations. We focused only on selected personal and behavioral predictors and psychosocial sequelae of helping, without completing the cycle by examining the effects of positive outcomes as predictors. In our own conceptual model, the contributory model of successful aging, it is proposed that the elderly person may derive critical benefits by providing help to others. In addition to the knowledge that one has made an important and worthwhile contribution, it is proposed that effective helping leads to enhanced self-esteem, morale, and social integration. This model of successful aging in presented is Figure 5.1.

The adoption of a lifestyle in which the helping of others is an important focus may be predicted by personal factors, including resources (e.g., health and finances), motivational factors (e.g., empathy), and situational factors, such as perceptions that one has been the recipient of help. We also predicted that helping opportunities that exist in the normal ecological context of the aging person, including the family, the neighborhood, and the community context, are likely to provide major sources of social penetration for those older persons who engage in helping behavior. Our expectation of a positive relationship between helping, competence, and life satisfaction is sharply at variance with notions that aged persons must conserve their remaining energies and resources (e.g., Neugarten, 1964) and that more aggressive, irritating, or narcissistic lifestyles will characterize the aged who cope well with the stresses of the later years (Lieberman, 1975).

REVIEW OF THE LITERATURE

This section presents a brief review of the literature on helping that is relevant to the conceptual model depicted in Figure 5.1. Herein we discuss (a) the predisposition to help, (b) the nature of helping by older adults, (c) domains of helping, and (d) psychosocial outcomes of helping.

The Predisposition to Help

There is now considerable evidence that human beings are capable of behavior variously described as altruistic, prosocial, and helpful (Krebs & Miller, 1985; Rushton, 1982). In most of the literature, however, older persons have been generally viewed as helpless rather then helpful, and they have traditionally been viewed as help recipients rather than as help givers.

In contrast to this view of the elderly as "a handicapped population dangling at the end of the life span" (Ehrlich, 1979a, 1979b), recent research has indicated that elderly individuals are often competent persons who provide help to others (Midlarsky, 1991, 1992; Stewart & Smith, 1983).

Our review of theoretical perspectives (Chapter 3) and empirical evidence from our own studies and those of others (Chapters 3 and 4) suggest that older adults may indeed be motivated to help others. Thus, for example, a majority of aged residents of a Florida retirement community exhibited altruistic attitudes on a questionnaire measure of altruism (Midlarsky & Kahana, 1981). According to the 1975 Harris Poll (National Council on the Aging, 1975), 40% of Americans age 65 years of age and older saw themselves as "very useful" members of their community, and 39% saw themselves as "somewhat useful." Information provided by the respondents indicated that the criteria for usefulness comprised involvement in politics and organizational activities, helping others, doing volunteer charity work, and being a good neighbor and citizen. Lowenthal et al. (1975) found that older adults show increases in humanitarian purposes—with women emphasizing kindness to others and men expressing a desire to make a tangible contribution to society. Our own experiments provide evidence that older persons are highly motivated to help and may have the capacity to be highly competent helpers.

Among older adults, help giving is evident in diverse forms and contexts. Indeed, even older persons who need and obtain assistance from others reciprocate (Prohaska & McAuley, 1984), often giving more than they have received (Akiyama & Antonucci, 1986; Fairchild et al., 1978; Kahana & Felton, 1977).

In addition to the quest for meaning, the desire to be useful, and altruistic motives based on empathy and moral maturity (Midlarsky, 1968, 1984), older adults may desire to be of help precisely because they are themselves increasingly the recipients of help as they grow older. The very fact that one is frequently on the receiving end may have negative consequences for one's self-concept (Fisher, Nadler, & Whitcher-Alagna, 1983). As Mauss (1954) has pointed out, in human societies, the three predominant types of social obligation appear to be the obligation to receive, the obligation to give, and the obligation to repay. Thus it is likely that giving among the aged may be based, in part, on the desire to meet one's obligation to give to others and on the desire to pay past (or anticipated future) obligations. The desire to give may be strong among the elderly because of the desire to be productive and independent and because of the possibility of later ill health during which one may become dependent and unable to reciprocate fully. Furthermore the relative freedom from work and family obligations also allows older persons to channel their energies toward helping others to fulfill their need for meaning and enhance their "connectedness" to others in the community (Myerhoff, 1978). In considering those factors that enhance helping behavior, personal and situational variables were considered in this investigation. Personal antecedents of special relevance included health, financial resources, and motivational variables (e.g., empathy, social responsibility). Previous help received and opportunities to help were considered as potentially relevant situational factors.

The Nature of Helping by Older Adults

Helping behavior can be categorized in several ways. In one such schema (Midlarsky, 1968), helping is seen as consisting of giving (spontaneous gift or loan to another of anything over which one has legitimate control) and assistance (giving help so that another person can achieve a goal; this may include physical assistance, instructions, helping with a task, or giving advice). In Ehrlich's (1979a, 1979b) community service model, in which the elderly themselves become service providers for each other, the categories relevant to helping are:

1. group meetings (e.g., recruitment of new members, driving of others to and from meetings, helping to identify neighborhood needs)
2. neighborhood support services (e.g., telephone reassurance, checking on elderly neighbors for help, sharing, carpooling, and assistance to the handicapped)
3. civic activities (e.g., signing petitions, volunteering services beyond group activities, and donations to community projects)

Furthermore, Adams (1968) has developed a typology in which the types of helping may include (a) tangible items (money, gifts),

(b) intangibles (advice, emotional support, time), and (c) services (visiting, shopping, baby-sitting, household repairs).

Domains of Helping

Among the domains in which older adults can be of service are the extended family, one's own place of residence, and the organizational site of one's community/recreational activities. The older individual may have the opportunity to provide service to the extended family in his or her role as parent and grandparent; to neighbors in the place of residence; and to the wider community through the performance of volunteer and charity work.

Neighbors as Helpers. The publication of Sorokin's (1950) classic study on altruism among American "good neighbors" and the extensive media coverage of the failure by 38 witnesses to come to the aid of a young neighbor who was attacked (Midlarsky, 1968; Rosenthal, 1964) have focused considerable attention on the importance of helping relationships among neighbors. The existence and determinants of the wide range of possible responses by neighbors—from apathy or indifference to the plight of others to caring or altruistic helping—has been the subject of research by numerous investigators in the past 2 decades (Midlarsky, 1984; Rushton et al., 1981).

Although a prevalent myth is that the elderly reside largely in nursing homes or in their children's homes, data indicate that about 95 to 96% of the aged actually live in independent households. The residential milieu is likely to be of considerable importance in the life of the elderly in that many apparently spend 80 to 90% of their time there (Montgomery, 1972). Given the loss of earlier roles—marital, occupational, and the like—and the amount of time spent at home, it is probably no surprise that relationships with neighbors and friends increase in importance with age (Blau, 1973).

Members of the family, especially children (Kahana, 1972), serve as the primary foundation for the individual's support system. However, not all elderly individuals have living family members, and even those who do, as a rule, see their children no more than once or twice each week (Cantor, 1973). Relationships with neighbors and friends may thus become the primary means for fulfilling the need for intimate, daily contact with other human beings. For the elderly, relationships with neighbors have the potential to fulfill three types of needs—social and emotional needs, needs for socialization (through the provision of information about roles, role rehearsal, and insulation from stigma), and needs for assistance (e.g., help in an emergency, crisis intervention, and financial help) (Hess, 1972; Riley & Foner, 1968; Ward, 1977). Given the potential vulnerability of the elderly to victimization and their desire to continue an autonomous existence within the community, help by neighbors within the residential setting has particular importance. Probably for these reasons, investigations regarding age-segregated and age-integrated environments have found that many elderly individuals preferred age-segregated housing primarily because of the potential for increased interaction with age peers (Fishbein, 1975; Winiecke, 1973).

The importance of elderly helpers within the residential context was also underscored in a study by the authors (Midlarsky & Kahana, 1983a, 1983b) of 117 residents of senior citizens' housing sites. Its goal was to consider the nature and importance of helping among elderly residents. Helping was found to be a prevalent pattern of behavior, with 67% of respondents reporting that they provide a great deal of help to others, and only 7% reporting no helping behavior. Respondents frequently reported providing enduring and personally costly forms of assistance, such as taking care of an ill friend or relative for prolonged periods of time.

Helping Functions in the Family and Community. A considerable amount of helping is directed by elderly persons toward their spouses. Spouses are often the best source of help and support, and their one competing demand is their own health. Indeed, the existence of a living spouse often appears to be the single most important factor in the elderly person's ability to remain in the community (Johnson, 1980).

With the increasing recognition of the "myth of the nuclear family" (Sussman, 1965), and the prevalence of interactions and helping patterns within a broader family context, the helping role of grandparents in regard to both their grandchildren and their adult children is increasingly recognized, as well. Furthermore, as increasing numbers of young mothers return to the workforce (Smith & Midlarsky, 1985), there is also greater acceptance of interdependence rather then independence, with grandmothers frequently assuming the role of caretaker of children. Major helping roles are also often assumed by grandparents when there is divorce or widowhood among their adult children.

Although there is a widely held attitude about the importance of self-reliance and financial autonomy for adult children, numerous studies have in fact revealed that parents provide diverse forms of assistance to their adult and young married children. Thus, for example, Greenberg and Becker (1988) investigated the role of aging parents as resources to their children's families. They found that elderly family members play an important role in helping their adult children cope with major life stresses and changes. They also commented on the current tendency to focus on the older person's dependency, while ignoring the importance of older adults as resources, both to their families and to the communities in which they reside. Sanders (1988) found that within the context of the family, the elderly are more likely to give than to receive. Studies have also indicated that grandparents generally attribute a strong positive value to their grandparent roles and show affection for their grandchildren (Robertson, 1977).

In addition to the literature on older persons' helping neighbors and family members, there is growing evidence that the elderly provide services to the wider community through their donations of time, money, and energy, more notably through volunteer and charity work (Babic, 1972; Chambré, 1984; Dye et al., 1973; Harel & Linderberg, 1981). Payne's (1977) work yields estimates of regularly occurring volunteer work by 14 to 22% of the elderly. A survey by Harris and Associates (1975) indicated that the elderly are most frequently involved in service activities in health and mental health, transportation, civic affairs, psychological and social support services, give-away programs, and family, youth, and child-oriented services. The Harris survey indicated that 22% of the elderly engaged in organized volunteer work, and an additional 10% expressed interest in being so involved. As of 1975, approximately 4.5 million elderly persons were actively involved in volunteer work, and an additional 2.1 million expressed a desire to volunteer their services.

On a more concerted note, Petersen (1981) reported that the mean age of volunteers working with the elderly through an urban social service program was 68.9 years, indicating that those caring for the elderly are older persons themselves. Financial contributions to charitable organizations are also made by the elderly, both in response to solicitations (Midlarsky, Hannah, & Kahana, 1983, 1985) and in the form of bequests (Rosenfeld, 1979).

Which elderly provide help to the wider community, and what reasons do they cite for doing so? Research by Harris and Associates (1975) indicates that both men (20%) and women (23%) serve as volunteers, and persons who perceive themselves as healthier are more likely to help in this way. Volunteers are also distinguished from nonvolunteers on the basis of prior participation, with those having a history of service through organizations more likely to volunteer during the older years (Dye et al., 1973).

In regard to stated motives for volunteering, results of the Harris Poll suggest that prosocial impulses may guide the actions of a sizable number of older persons. When asked what makes someone a useful member of society, 50% of older persons cited helping and serving others, 43% cited involvement in community activities and organizations, and an additional 34% mentioned being a good neighbor. "Helping others" was also frequently noted as a basis for membership in voluntary organizations by group leaders and by persons involved in charity or volunteer work, in a study conducted by Ward (1979b).

Attitudes by older adults toward volunteer work appear to be quite positive. Far more than younger persons, they agreed that "doing volunteer work is a good way for people to keep themselves busy and active," "volunteer work is essential to meet the community's needs and everyone should do his share," and "people with unused skills and talents should make use of them doing volunteer work" (National Council on the Aging, 1975).

Psychosocial Outcomes of Helping by the Aged

Several lines of theory converge to support the position that involvement in altruistic activities may bring immense psychosocial benefits to the older person. From the perspective of humanistic/existential theory, old age is the time in which one becomes most acutely aware that time is finite, so that the final search for meaning is highly salient and even urgent at this time. In particular, the use of one's time in meaningful ways seems an important issue, at least to some (Chellam, 1977-1978; Kalish, 1979; Ward, 1981-1982). Atkinson (1985) also suggests that this search for meaning leads to a directed search for worthwhile ways to use the time remaining. Furthermore, in Atkinson's view, becoming a resource in one's community is one example of a creative and intrinsically satisfying way to achieve a sense of meaning.

In the literature of sociology, Kuypers and Bengtson (1973) point out that in contrast to their need for a sense of meaning, older people may develop negative self-concepts through interactions with an environment that labels them as deficient or incompetent—which may occur if they are in a primarily dependent position. Accepting this view of themselves as correct, older people may then reinforce these negative perceptions by performing in an increasingly incompetent manner. In order to break this pattern, the social reconstruction syndrome has been proposed (Kuypers & Bengtson, 1973); the first stage consists of defining meaningful participation differently than for the young. In place of a single ethic, the "ethic of doing," an alternative approach includes, among other items, "an ethic of sharing . . . an ethic of knowing, an ethic of enduring" (Fischer, 1977, p. 33).

Contributory roles can also be seen as an important route to well-being from the perspective of the developmental views of Erikson (1977), who emphasized intrinsic motives and satisfactions associated with caring and giving during the second half of the life cycle (see Chapter 3). The emphasis on satisfactions to be derived from contributory roles also fits with recent formulations (Gilligan, 1982) that question traditional hierarchies of values underlying theories of adult development for putting a greater premium on autonomy than on caring and a sense of responsibility or even sacrifice on behalf of others (Giele, 1980).

Empirical studies also provide evidence that prosocial behavior is associated with psychosocial well-being. For example, Rachman (1978) has noted that individuals who act in socially responsible ways during periods of stress appear to experience less fear and stress than those who are less active on behalf of others. Monk and Cryns (1974) made the suggestion that any activities that allow older people to provide help to others may allow for the resolution of Erikson's crisis of integrity versus despair. In a study by Fengler and Goodrich (1980), a group of disabled older men participating for one or more years in a sheltered workshop program told the investigators that one of the most important motives for them was being able to help others. The authors concluded that perhaps a vital ingredient in the program, for these men, consisted of the opportunity to gain awareness of their own competence and usefulness. In a further study of the elderly volunteer, Payne (1977) reported that "the personal satisfaction of helping others" was an important ingredient in volunteer satisfaction. Interestingly, men—many of whom were participating in direct service to others for the first time—found the volunteer role even more satisfying than women did. Studies of the effects of the foster grandparent program have also noted that psychological benefits accrue to the elderly helpers, as well as to the children for whom they care (Saltz, 1971).

One of the major psychological concomitants of helping among the aged appears to be that of higher morale. Hence Fairchild et al. (1978) found that a "giving only strategy" by the elderly yields higher morale than a "receiving only strategy." Akiyama and Antonucci (1986) wrote that elderly "overproviders"—defined as those who gave more support than they received—had the highest morale. In addition, Midlarsky and Kahana (1984) found that helping others was a significant predictor of morale among aged community-dwelling persons. In a study regarding friendship interactions among the elderly, Mancini (1980) found that older persons describing themselves as providing good company for their friends, being understanding of the friends' feelings and problems, and giving help when the friend was sick had higher morale scores as well.

Helping may also be an important predictor of subjective social integration—an important finding in light of the degree to which loneliness pervades the lives of some older people. Observational evidence from the fields of ethology and child development indicates that altruism may be critical in the formation and maintenance of social bonds (e.g., Eibl-Eibesfeldt, 1971; Midlarsky, 1994; Wilson, 1975, 1978). In Ward's (1979b) study of the meaning to older persons of participation in volunteer organizations, the most frequently cited reason for such participation (73%) was that the volunteer organizations brought the individual together with friends.

Also associated with helping are positive self-concepts and the sense of competence. In one of the few experiments regarding altruism among the elderly, Trimakas and Nicolay (1974) found that generosity was related to a positive self-concept. In a study of elderly residents of a retirement community, Midlarsky and Kahana (1981) found that individuals manifesting altruistic attitudes on a scale with good internal consistency were more likely to express positive feelings about themselves than those who did not. In addition, Riessman (1976) went beyond discerning a relationship between self-concept and helping to discover that helping may benefit the helper. In an article articulating the "helper-therapy principle," he notes that helping others benefits the helper—perhaps more than the recipient—by decreasing feelings of dependency while enhancing feelings of usefulness and self-worth. Press and McKool (1972) list as one of the four primary determinants of status and prestige in old age the extent to which one can contribute to the well-being of others.

There is also increasing evidence that the very fact that an individual is a recipient of help may lead to a decrease in other people's positive regard for him or her. It may be because the very fact of seeking help is likely to threaten the individual's social status and self-esteem that people are less likely to seek help when it has to be done publicly than when private help is available (Shapiro, 1978). In light of this evidence regarding probable links between interpersonal perceptions and the process of helping (combined with theory and data presented in prior chapters), it appears quite likely that the generalizations or stereotypes that aged individuals are helpless, vulnerable, incompetent individuals may be based, at least in part, on the expectation that they are, or are more likely to be found as, needy recipients rather than benefactors of the needy. On the other hand, should the elderly be viewed by others and by themselves as helpers, then this might enhance mental health and result in positive psychosocial outcomes. Thus it is our expectation, depicted in the conceptual model (Figure 5.1), that helpers portray higher morale, increased self-esteem, and a greater sense of social integration than nonhelpers.

METHOD

Sample

Rationale for Sample

Our interest in exploring helping in diverse social domains, or contexts, led to a decision to employ a replication design in which we chose two subsamples, each representing a prevalent lifestyle among older persons living in the community. One subsample was drawn from age-heterogeneous residential settings, such as single-family dwellings or apartments, and the second sample consisted of residents of senior citizens' apartments, representing age-homogeneous living arrangements. We chose these purposive strategic samples of older persons so as to obtain sufficient numbers of elderly helpers in conceptually differing areas of helping opportunities. To the extent that the present study sought to understand the nature, antecedents, and behavioral correlates of helping in natural social role situations, we felt that we must oversample for individuals who have opportunities to be of help.

The areas selected represent two of the social roles in which older persons are likely to be active following the loss of other social roles. The two proposed contexts for the study of helping also entail variation along other important dimensions. Older persons living in the community in which their children, grandchildren, and/or great-grandchildren reside are part of the informal context of the family, where a history of reciprocal help patterns is likely to exist (Pruchno, 1979). Elderly residents in retirement housing, in fact, are participants in semiformal organizations where more formal or normative expectations for helping may exist. Furthermore, these residences have been found to provide an atmosphere conducive to the formation of close relationships among neighbors (Nahemow & Lawton, 1975).

It is recognized that those individuals who are not identified as helpers in a given social context may nevertheless be helpers in other social role contexts or in other aspects of their lives. Similarly, it is also likely that persons identified in one social role area will exhibit varying degrees or levels of helping behavior in other areas or situations. For this reason, helping patterns as a family member, neighbor, and other roles (e.g., community volunteer) were determined for each respondent in both samples.

Sample Design

A total of 400 individuals served as respondents, 200 randomly chosen from the general community and 200 from senior housing sites. Respondents composing the two subsamples were selected from within the same communities to ensure that differences in helping patterns or in relationships between antecedents and outcomes of helping among samples were not due to differential demographic backgrounds of the respondents. A schematic representation of the sample design appears in Table 5.1.

All respondents also fulfilled some common criteria. Thus only those individuals age 65 or older were included so as to focus on persons of retirement age for whom helping roles outside of the work situation were particularly salient. In addition, only physically mobile residents (not homebound) were included in the community study. The residences for the elderly, of course, screened out individuals with incapacitating physical and/or mental impairments.

In order to ensure the appropriate representation of heterogeneous characteristics, we included four communities in the Detroit metropolitan area—Detroit, Clawson, Royal Oak, and Southfield, Michigan. An examination of the Housing Directory for Senior Citizens, prepared by the Detroit Public Library, revealed that

Table 5.1 Schematic Representation of Sample Design

	Source
Family helper sample, $N = 200$	Random sample of voter registration lists (screen for those with children, grandchildren, and/or great-grandchildren living in the area) in selected communities
Residential helper sample, $N = 200$	Random sample from voter registration lists of persons residing in senior citizen housing sites in selected communities

there were more than sufficient numbers of older adults in residences in those four communities to obtain the desired sample size. Furthermore, taken as a group, those communities provided an excellent cross section of demographic characteristics, ranging from urban to suburban demographic profiles.

Despite our care in choosing sampling sites, we are aware of the limitations on generalizability inherent in any project in which one employs anything other than a probability sample of the entire population of interest (cf. Raj, 1968; Yates, 1965). Thus, for example, excluded from our sample were the rural elderly and those residing in nursing homes or in other institutions. Within each of the two groups sampled, however, random sampling procedures were used so that data from each subsample could be generalizable to the population of helpers from which samples were drawn.

Senior Residences in the Detroit Metropolitan Area

Although the communities selected were diverse in regard to demographic characteristics, it is noteworthy that the communities had senior residences that had marked differences as well. Among the numerous housing sites in which study participants resided are Clawson Manor in Clawson, Michigan; Plymouth Towers and Boulevard Manor in Detroit; McDonnell Towers in Southfield; and Royal Oak Manor in Royal Oak.

Clawson Manor is a high-rise, senior citizen apartment building that was built in 1970 by the city of Clawson with the aid of federal

Housing and Urban Development (HUD) funding. It is currently owned and operated as a nonprofit, nonsectarian apartment project for people 62 years of age or older and people with disabilities of any age. At the time of the study, there were no residents under 55 years of age. The residence is a 15-story building comprising 280 units, most of which are efficiency apartments. Eligibility is based on annual income. The project has maintained full occupancy and a waiting list since its construction.

A visitor to Clawson Manor would probably first be struck by the way that the building easily merges with other residences, in a neighborhood containing one-story, single-family dwellings and other two-story apartment buildings. Upon entering the building, it seems very much like other apartment buildings of its type. Coming through the front door, one will often see one or more elderly persons sitting, chatting, and informally providing security for themselves and their neighbors by carefully scrutinizing newcomers. In addition to the presence of very small numbers of elderly residents—predominantly white females in their 70s and 80s in the lobby and walking outside—larger groupings of neighbors are scattered throughout the lounges on each floor, the pool room, and the community room. Clawson Manor is typical of the many senior citizen apartment complexes that are available to the upper-lower and middle-income retired person, who maintains a significant degree of independence, a secure and centrally located residence at a price commensurate with his or her fixed income.

Plymouth Towers, a 10-story apartment building for Detroit senior citizens, is part of the Medical Center Village, a complex of highrise apartments and town houses located in the city's "cultural center." The residence includes 194 one-bedroom units. At the time of the study there were 260 residents ranging in age from 60 to 90. Various services are provided through several area social service agencies, including a part-time social worker, nursing services one day a week, and a Food for Friendship program providing a free lunch to many of the residents several times a week. These two housing sites (one surburban—predominantly white; one urban—predominantly black) were only two of many in which our respondents lived.

Boulevard Temple. Consider the contrast provided by Boulevard Temple, a nonprofit residence privately sponsored by the Detroit Annual Conference of the United Methodist Church, in which elderly persons are housed in a building that once housed the Boulevard Temple United Methodist Church. This state-licensed facility houses 230 elderly in a three-level arrangement, each on a different floor of the building:

Fully Independent—from single rooms to 3 1/2-room apartments, all with their own bath.

Semi-Independent—for those who need limited assistance, such as daily "check-ins" by staff and help with medication. Residents have a private or shared room with kitchenette and bath.

Nursing Care Facility—a total care institution.

The rent, although somewhat higher than in Plymouth Towers, is far lower than in nonsubsidized, private housing. Rent subsidies are accessible to the residents and also available are laundry facilities, parking, a gift shop, a library, beauty parlor, barber shop, and medical clinic.

A visitor to Boulevard Temple should look for a large, older church in a commercial area of downtown Detroit, backed up against a residential area. Upon entering the outer door, the visitor must first stop at a glass-enclosed office and state the reason for entering. Once through the security door, one is struck above all by the dramatic architectural features, brought about by the extensive renovation of the inside of the building. This renovation, which resulted in what has been characterized as an "architectural showcase," has an entry-level area in which there are modern balconies overlooking a central dining area, a beautiful enclosed rooftop greenhouse (complete with hydroponic gardens), and patio. The entry-level story and, to some extent, the residential floors contain a variety of opulent touches—from fine paintings and prints that adorn the walls, to excellent and sometimes very valuable pieces of furniture, carpeting, pianos, and organs placed throughout the residence, to a library of finely bound books. These beautiful and unusual touches were donated by the small percentage of affluent Detroit Methodists who made Boulevard Temple their late-life home. Hence an atmosphere of elegance combining modern architecture and traditional opulence is present in many of the public areas. In the various common rooms, the beauty shop, and the dining area, one sees numerous elderly individuals, including a higher proportion of black residents, more disabled persons, and a higher average of older residents than in suburban facilities. The atmosphere is generally a quiet one and usually lacks any sense of hurry or bustle.

McDonnell Towers, on the other hand, consists of two modern, high-rise towers with balconies, connected in an H-like fashion by a public senior activities center. Each tower contains close to 200 one-bedroom apartments for persons 62 years of age and older. Rental in this city-sponsored residence, restricted to residents of the city of Southfield, is priced quite reasonably, and rent supplements are available. The McDonnell Towers are about 15 years old, are always fully occupied, and are located in a relatively commercial area near shopping and restaurants. Amenities include provision for security through intercoms and TV surveillance, ready access to public transportation, parking facilities, a laundry, air conditioning, many recreational features within the building, and facilities for dining at nominal cost (government subsidized).

The visitor to McDonnell Towers is likely to be impressed by a bustling feeling in and around the buildings. In warmer weather, there are always some people out on their balconies. The parking lots are typically well filled, and people pull in and out with a good deal of frequency. The bustling quality is due to not only the activities of the residents but also the elderly residents of the city of Southfield who frequent the senior activities' center connecting the towers. Upon entering either tower, one would see many elderly people and an admixture of younger staff, moving about and appearing quite active. The towers appear to be a warm, comfortable, and vibrant place. Residents with disabilities are apparent—one sees a gentleman with a walker, a lady in a wheelchair—but even these who have manifest disabilities seem otherwise healthy. Residents seem to know one another; they greet one another and generally exhibit an upbeat quality. Although this residence is among the most heterogeneous on several dimensions,

including race, age, and ethnic background, one senses a predomi-
nance of middle-class, American-born older people, with a larger
number of females than males—exhibiting a pride in their milieu
and a sense of autonomy and a friendliness.

Royal Oak Manor consists of a single high-rise building with a total
of 247 efficiencies and one-bedroom apartments. The rent range is
exceptionally low, and rent supplements are available. The building is an older apartment house, approximately 30 years old,
which was converted to use as a residence for the elderly through
primarily federal funds (HUD). Features include carpeting and
drapes, an elevator, parking, laundry facilities, and a beauty shop.
It is well integrated into downtown Royal Oak, a small well-
established city in the Detroit metropolitan area, which has a very
urban character. Hence it is an easy matter for residents who are
physically mobile to take short walks to recreational facilities,
banks, doctors, and the like. Royal Oak Manor is one of a sizable
number of residences run by Cooperative Services, Inc., a nonprofit organization with the philosophy that residences for the
elderly should be run by the elderly—through an elected board of
residents—with the only staff consisting of a custodian in each
building. This is in marked contrast to the other residences, in
which there is an obvious presence of younger people who staff
the building.

Unlike most of the other residences, Royal Oak Manor looks and
feels like an apartment building—not a recreation center (McDonnell)
or a showplace (Boulevard Temple). The entry is smaller than
those in the other residences. The visitor walks first into a narrow
hall leading to the elevator and stairs. Another first-floor hall
contains a small sitting room and library, designed to accommodate about 15 people; it includes a small counter displaying handi-
crafts made by the residents, which are available for purchase.

It becomes quickly obvious that this building is staffed by an
elected leadership of healthy, vibrant older residents. Their presence is felt, along with the sense of pride and personal control and
proprietorship. The newcomer to the building may meet Joe, who
will proudly tell you about the drive by the board, which he
implemented, to get flowers and then plant them to beautify the

residence. "Too bad you didn't come when the flowers were in bloom," he may remark. Even though there's a custodian, the board has its own "fix-it committee," so you may come upon men fixing hinges or light fixtures in the hallways. Although there are security locks, people volunteer for 8-hour shifts in the lobby to monitor the entryway. When the custodian was ill, Mike took over the vacuuming. "We're used to caring for our own homes," residents remark, "so there's pleasure in keeping up our joint home."

Procedures for Sampling

Respondents were randomly selected from separate voter registration lists maintained by each of the four communities. These lists contain information about the age and address of each respondent, so that our staff was able to develop separate lists of elderly (65+) persons by community and by residence (i.e., standard community residence vs. senior citizens residence). Thus we had lists of all community elderly living in each of the four communities and lists of elderly persons living in senior residences in each of the four communities. We chose to use voter registration lists because although they do not comprise the total universe of older adults in a given community, they provide a useful way to identify the vast majority of elderly—due to the high levels of voting by this segment of the population (98% in the communities under investigation).

For the 200 family helpers, we drew our sample from the lists of community elderly in the four communities. From each of the four lists, we first selected approximately 100 names of older persons by using a table of random numbers (excluding, as noted above, names of persons residing in senior residences). We chose the number 100 for each community, although our final goal was to obtain 50 persons from each of the four communities (200 total). This was because of the expectation, based on our own prior experience, that at least 50% would meet the sampling criteria (see above) and would be both willing and able to participate. Telephone numbers were obtained, and potential respondents were called and asked a brief screening question, regarding whether they had any children, grandchildren, and/or great-grandchil-dren residing within the Detroit metropolitan area. As expected, approximately 70% of the elderly had family members living nearby. All who responded in the affirmative, up to 50 per community, were asked to participate. Telephone calls (up to five callbacks) were made until a sufficient number of respondents were obtained.

In a similar manner, residential helpers were randomly selected from lists of older persons living in senior citizens housing sites located within the communities under study. From lists of registered voters in each of the four communities, 100 randomly selected elderly persons residing in senior residences comprised the initial pool. Telephone calls were then made until we located approximately 50 persons in each community who had resided in a given residence for at least 6 months and who were also willing to participate. Only those persons living in a given residence for at least 6 months were included, so as to allow for helping networks to emerge. We considered the inclusion of neighbor pairs. However, considering that the emphasis was on the helper rather than on the helper-recipient dyad, the advantages of adherence to random sampling seemed to outweigh the potential advantages of obtaining data on neighbor pairs. By not imposing additional constraints on the residential sample, more parallelism could be maintained with the sample of family helpers.

The final sampling plan was further augmented. In order to include people who might not have fallen into the original sample because they were not represented in the voter registration lists, we also did a door-to-door screening of a subset of potential respondents. By employing this technique, we feel that we had the opportunity to include persons who might be nonvoters, who had no telephones, or had unlisted telephone numbers. In addition, we made every effort to include as many males as possible in each of the study subsamples.

These techniques, although somewhat cumbersome and time-consuming, were effective. Because of our willingness to call potential respondents back up to five times, we were able to obtain the cooperation of the vast preponderance of individuals through our random sampling procedures. The employment of screening questions by empathic and well-trained interviewers resulted in an exceptionally small number of interviews that were "broken off" by respondents (a total of 8 in a sample of 400).

Interview Procedures

Once respondents were contacted and agreed to be interviewed, an appointment was made to conduct the interview in the respondents' own home. An effort was made to complete the interview in one session. However, on very rare occasions, it was necessary to schedule return visits. The interviewing staff attempted to get as high a completed response rate as possible. Nevertheless, they were instructed to be considerate and attentive to the respondent's situation and to respect the wishes of those not willing to participate in the study.

Upon arriving at the home of a respondent, interviewers had the task of introducing themselves, showing their identification, and establishing a private place to conduct the interview. In setting appointments, interviewers made it clear that only the respondent, and not other family members or friends, would be included in the interview situation.

Introductory remarks were then made in accordance with the informed consent procedures and included (a) who the interviewer was and who she or he represented, and (b) what he or she was doing. It was important that the respondent understand that he or she was part of a "random sample" and that the interview was anonymous. Major goals were to obtain consent that was truly informed and, if consent was given (which it almost always was), to obtain and maintain rapport.

The interviewer's first job was to start by setting up a friendly relationship because the participant's response to him or her as a person would be important. Interviewers were trained to behave in a warm and understanding manner and to express genuine interest in each respondent as a person—not just as an "answerer of questions." It was the interviewer's job to respect the participant's confidences completely. A common barrier in interviewing the elderly is their fear that they will be embarrassed by what they think may be difficult questions. Here, it was considered important and necessary to let respondents know that they had worth as individuals and that their opinions, whatever they might be, were of interest. Respondents were also told that the interview questions had no wrong answers.

Although most people went through the interview without any questions, some asked questions either during the introduction or after the interview began. Material presented in training sessions and conferences with the interviewer's supervisor provided information that could be used in answering respondents. Before leaving the home of the respondent, each interviewer expressed appreciation for being permitted into the respondent's home. The respondent was given a card with the name, address, and telephone number of the project office and investigators. Respondents were encouraged to call if they had further questions. At the end of the interview, each respondent was also presented with a small gift and a Certificate of Appreciation for his or her participation.

The Variables and Their Measurement

Because of the multidimensional nature of this investigation, the individual interviews were designed to include multiple measures to determine exogenous factors, helping behavior, and outcome variables. An extensive analysis and careful selection of the "best" measures and instruments, as well as the construction of numerous additional indices, preceded implementation of the study. A list of the measures, and average times to complete each one, appears in Table 5.2.

Health/Finances/Demographic Variables

Health status was measured by a version of Rosow's (1967) standard Health Scale, which had been revised and modified in earlier investigations (Kahana, 1974). Cronbach's alpha for this scale, in the current study, was .73. Also examined were self-reports regarding a variety of specific disabilities and physical problems. In addition, health was measured by items assessing the individual's

Table 5.2   Actual Time to Complete Each Measure

Measure	Number of Minutes
Health Measures	2
Evaluation of Financial Adequacy	2
General Demographic Information	3
Empathy	6
Locus of Control	4
Social Responsibility	2
Moral Judgment	7
Closed- and Open-Ended Questions on Situational Variables and Helping	24
Philadelphia Geriatric Morale Scale	3
Measures of Self-Esteem	6
Subjective Social Integration	3
Average Total Time	62

perception of his or her health (e.g., "In general, how is your health now?") with answers on a scale from *excellent* to *very poor.* Participants also responded to other Likert-type items in which they compared their current health and energy with others their own age and with their own health at an earlier stage in their lives (cf. Sechrest & Cohen, 1983). Our decision to employ self-reports of health was based on the widespread acceptance of self-reports as valid indications of health status among older adults. This acceptance is based on findings of strong associations between self-assessed health and ratings by physicians or such objective measures as numbers of hospitalizations and visits to physicians (Costa & McCrae, 1985; Kermis, 1984; LaRue, Bank, Jarvik, & Hetland, 1979; Linn & Linn, 1980).

Respondents' self-reports served as the primary subjective measure of subjective financial adequacy. The five-point Evaluation of Financial Adequacy employed in this study is a modification of a scale that has been successfully employed in numerous gerontological studies as an index of finances (Liang et al., 1980). Cronbach's alpha for the scale was .84.

We also collected and employed data on age, education, marital status, religion, and race. Occupation and education were coded in accordance with categories derived from Hollingshead and Redlich (1958), and the Hollingshead two-factor index was the measure of socioeconomic status (SES).

Personality Variables

Research on psychological/motivational predictors of altruism has been rather sparse. This is primarily because much of the psychological research has consisted of experimental studies performed in the context of social learning theory. As such, it has primarily emphasized situational determinants rather than the role of personality factors. Only recently has attention been focused on the role that personality variables may play as predictors of prosocial action (e.g., Eisenberg, 1983; LeMare & Krebs, 1983). In cross-sectional research of this type, it it not possible to provide a direct test of the degree to which interpersonal variables are antecedent to self-reported helping. Instead, a goal is to see whether motivational variables found to be related to prosocial action during the earlier years of life are also related during the later years. On the basis of our own prior work, and that of others, we predicted that four personality/motivational variables would predict helping—and in some cases, well-being as well: These were empathy, locus of control, social responsibility, and altruistic moral judgment. In regard to all of the variables except locus of control, prior work has focused on younger individuals; hence work was needed to further develop and refine instruments for use with the elderly.

Our measure of empathy was adapted from a scale developed by Mehrabian and Epstein (1972). This measure primarily taps empathic arousal—or emotional empathy—rather than the cognitive aspect of empathy, as do measures of perspective-taking (cf. Underwood & Moore, 1982). This 33-item scale was reduced in length for certain of the items, as a sizable number of our respondents were foreign-born—in contrast to the college-student sample whose responses the measure was originally scaled to suit. As in the original scale, the discriminant validity of our adapted scale was excellent. For example, we obtained a .02 correlation with the Crowne and Marlowe (1960) Social Desirability Scale. Coefficient alpha for the scale in the current study was .78. Results of a principal components analysis of the empathy items yielded a first factor with an eiginvalue of 3.25, explaining 54.2% of the variance. Varimax rotation indicated three nonoverlapping factors, accounting for a total of 80% of the variance. These consisted of:

1. adverse reaction to the neediness of others (e.g., "I get angry when I see someone hurt," or "It upsets me to see helpless people.")
2. matching of moods to those of others (e.g., "Seeing people cry upsets me.")
3. responsiveness to emotional imagery (e.g., "The feelings of people in books affect me.")

Locus of control was measured by an adaptation of Rotter's (1966) original scale, modified for use with the elderly (Midlarsky & Kahana, 1981; Midlarsky, Kahana, & Corley, 1987). Cronbach's alpha in our present sample was .68.

Social responsibility, defined as the tendency to engage in socially responsible action on behalf of others, was measured by means of the eight-item Likert-type scale developed by Berkowitz & Lutterman (1968). The alpha for this scale was .64.

The measure of altruistic moral judgment contained three stories, each of which described a conflict between the desires and needs of a story protagonist (described as male or female in accordance with the respondent's sex) and those of a needy other. Following each story, participants were asked to indicate what the story character should do and why. All open-ended responses to the stories were coded by two research assistants, who were blind to the respondents regarding other study variables. The classification of moral judgment in our investigation was based on a priori classifications used by other investigators (Eisenberg-Berg & Hand, 1979; Kohlberg, 1969), modified by a close examination of the data from a subsample of our respondents (Midlarsky, Kahana, & Corley, 1987). The interrater reliabilities across categories of moral reasoning by study respondents were very high, ranging upwards from .90.

In addition, the study included our own Altruistic Orientation Scale (AOS), wherein participants were queried regarding their altruistic values. The AOS consists of a series of 5-point Likert-type items. Coefficient alpha for the measure was .70.

Situational Variables

Prior research—consisting of experimental studies of helping by younger persons—has found that the costs or risks associated with helping, the perceived dependency or need of the recipient, and the degree of help previously received by the potential helper are determinants of help giving. Our original plan in this study was to use 5-point Likert scales to assess these situational factors in relation to each helping transaction reported by respondents. However, as we developed our measures and our plan for this research, we realized that the nonindependence of the data on situational variables and helping collected in this way would pose methodological difficulties. For example, individuals perceiving that help giving is a costly activity may report less helping—hence reporting fewer costs of helping. Such data would be misleading.

Our approach, therefore, was to develop separate sets of Likert items designed to assess facets of the situation that could be expected—on the basis of theory and prior research—to be associated with helping and, in some cases, with well-being among the elderly. These variables included perceived costs of helping, perceived opportunities to help others, help previously received, and the convenience of access to facilities outside of one's residence (e.g., shops, doctors' offices, recreational facilities). Alphas for these subscales were .68, .60, .73, and .79, respectively. For perceived opportunities, to cite one example, respondents were asked to what extent there are people who need their help and to what degree volunteer helping activities seem to be available for their participation.

Helping Behavior

Helping behavior was, of course, the central component of this investigation. Furthermore, much of the research on prosocial behavior has been performed by social learning theorists, who employ experimental and observational studies and deemphasize the use of survey or paper-and-pencil methodologies. Hence within this investigation we had the challenging task of developing a means for obtaining both quantitative and qualitative self-reports of helping in domains most salient to the elderly—in a psychometrically sound manner.

Qualitative data were obtained by means of several open-ended questions, such as, "What is a typical helping activity in which you have engaged during the past year?" A number of Likert-type items were developed to facilitate inquiries about such facets as the degree to which our elderly respondents saw themselves as helping more or less now than they did in the past, the degree to which they viewed their help giving as spontaneous versus planned, and the like. In order to obtain quantitative data that would have the potential to be maximally useful in the multivariate analyses, we included (a) our own modification, for use with the elderly (Midlarsky & Kahana, 1983a), of the Self-Report Altruism Scale developed by Rushton and his collaborators (Rushton et al., 1981) and (b) a measure developed by us for this investigation, which inquired about the amount of various types of help given by the elderly to their children, grandchildren, and/or great-grandchildren, spouse, other family, friends, neighbors, as a member of an organization, and "other"; this has been called the Domains of Helping Scale. Results of factor analysis and other scaling procedures have indicated that our measurement strategy was a satisfactory one.

Analysis of the entire set of quantitatively scored items, across the two scales, yielded evidence that there may be a unitary trait determining the self-reported actions (Kahana & Midlarsky, 1983; Midlarsky & Kahana, 1984). Both the subscale measuring overall amount of helping, based largely on the Rushton items, and subscales corresponding to the four primary domains—children, other family, neighbors, and member helping—were internally consistent. Alphas were, respectively, .90, .91., .87, and .92.

Four measures of well-being were considered in this study. Enhanced self-esteem, morale, current happiness, and subjective sense of social integration are the psychological indicators of well-being that were hypothesized to be affected by involvement by aged respondents in helping behavior. Prior work done in these areas streamlined the measurement of these variables.

The measure of self-esteem was Rosenberg's (1965) scale, which has been found to be inversely related to depression, neurosis, and self-criticalness. Originally developed for use with adolescents, the scale in our own studies with the aged, had a convergent and predictive validity that far exceeded those for other measures. One example of an item on the Rosenberg scale is, "I feel that I'm a person of worth, at least on an equal plane with others, Strongly Agree . . . Strongly Disagree." An alpha of .85 was obtained for Rosenberg's measure in this study.

The measure of morale was the Philadelphia Geriatric Morale Scale. This scale was developed by Lawton (1975a) to measure morale, or "inner adjustment," among the aged. Lawton obtained a validity coefficient of .47 when the test was correlated with judgments of morale on a Q-sort. Test-retest reliabilities have been quite high, ranging from .75 to .90. The total scale is considered a measure of the older person's perception of his or her adjustment and mood. This scale had an alpha coefficient of .85 in the present investigation.

In addition to assessing morale, which reflects mood over a span of time, we were also interested in determining present—and potentially more transient—affect. For this purpose, we employed the Affect-Balance Scale (Bradburn, 1969).

Subjective social integration was examined by adding items to the measure originally developed by Liang et al. (1980). Cronbach's alpha for the full scale was .71. For two primary additional subscales that emerged in a factor analysis—emotional integration and loneliness—alphas were .66 and .76, respectively.

RESULTS:
DESCRIPTIVE DATA

In understanding the nature of the interrelationships among variables in this study, knowledge of the background characteristics of the sample is critical. This section presents the distribution of personal characteristics of the respondents, starting first with the data based on frequency of occurrence in the total sample of 400 persons, and the results of selected cross tabulations.

The Sample: Demographic Characteristics

In the total sample of 400 respondents, the age range was from 64 to 110, with a mean of 77.6 and a standard deviation of 9 years. Over two thirds (70.5%) were females, and 29.5% were male. Racially, 82.5% were white, 15.5% were black, and 2% fell into neither category. Results of χ^2 analyses indicated that there were no significant relationships between age and sex, race, place of birth, occupation, education, or religion. The religious preference of 44.5% of the respondents was Protestant, 23.3% were Catholic, 19.3% were Jewish, and 13.9% did not fall into any of these three categories. The largest group of respondents consisted of native Michiganians (32%), followed by those born outside of the United States (22.5%), then those born in the Northeast (14.5%) and other places in the Midwest (11.7%). Smaller percentages came from such regions as the South (10.5%), Southeast (7%), Northwest (1.2%), and West (.5%). Educationally, 21.7% of the elderly respondents had 0 to 8 years of grammar school training, 53% had some high school or a high school diploma (9 to 12 years), 19.5% had some college or a college degree, and 3.7% had at least some postbaccalaureate graduate or professional training. The most prevalent type of preretirement occupation consisted of sales or technical work (20%), followed by employment as a skilled worker (19.3%) or homemaker (18%). Administrators/semiprofessionals constituted 10% of the sample, 9.7% were semiskilled, 9.7% were unskilled workers, 7.5% were managers, and 2.8% were top executives.

In regard to marital status, 55.7% were widowed, 34.7% were married, 4.7% divorced, 1.7% separated, and 3.4% were never married. Just over a third of the respondents (34.2%) were currently living with their spouse. Most respondents (70%) had one, two, or three children, whereas 22% had four or more and 7.5% had no children. Modal number of living children was two (31.3%); 21% had fewer than two living children, and 41% had three or more.

Close to a quarter of the study participants (24.2%) preferred not to report their approximate income in the past year. Of those providing a dollar figure, 19.8% reported a yearly income of less than $5,000, 32.7% earned from $5,000 to $10,000, and 47.5% earned over $10,000. In regard to perceived financial adequacy, the largest single group of respondents viewed the level of their income as more than adequate (46%), 41.5% saw it as "just enough," 12% expressed the feeling that their incomes were "not quite enough," and only .5% saw their incomes as "not at all adequate." Results of statistical analyses employing measures of association indicated that these variables were significantly related to one another and to certain other demographic factors. Finances measured in the two separate ways had a Pearson correlation of .58, df = 303, $p < .001$. Reports of actual income were significantly related to chronological age, $r = -.17$, $df = 303$, $p < .001$, with older persons having lower incomes, and to sex, $r = -.25$, $df = 303$, $p < .001$, with females having significantly less income than males. Higher incomes were also reported by individuals with higher amounts of formal education, $r = .49$, $df = 293$, $p < .001$, and by individuals with higher self-ratings of health, in regard to both Rosow's (1967) measure, $r = .25$, $df = 303$, $p < .001$, and a Likert measure of global health, $r = .21$, $df = 303$, $p < .001$. Similarly, perceived financial adequacy was found to be significantly related to sex, $r = .34$, $df = 309$, $p < .001$, educational attainment, $r = .33$, $df = 388$, $p < .001$, perceived health, $r = .30$, $df = 398$, $p < .001$, and Rosow's (1967) functional health status, $r = .33$, $df = 398$, $p < .001$. In contrast to reports of actual income, perceived financial adequacy was not significantly related to sex of respondent.

The preponderance of respondents (74.5%) felt that their health was either fair or good, 15.5% felt that it was excellent, 8.8% rated it as poor, and 1.2% felt that it was very poor. In addition, many viewed their health as either the same as (29.5%) or better than (49%) that of others of their age, with 13.7% reporting it as much better; 7% viewed their health as worse (6.5%) or much worse (.5%). A full 45% spent not a single day in bed due to illness, with 75.7% spending less than two weeks in bed. Although 80% reported that they did have chronic health problems, only 18% reported much or very much trouble from these problems, and 16% indicated that their health problems interfered with their desires to a great extent. Regarding specific physical problems, 93% noted no orthopedic problems of any kind (e.g., paralysis, missing limbs, or broken bones), 88% reported fair, good, or excellent eyesight, and 91.5% reported fair, good, or excellent hearing. When asked to characterize their health status, 3% informed the interviewers that they were currently suffering from a life-threatening illness, 23.8% from one or more painful problems, and 40% from minor problems; 33% reported having no serious problems at this time.

Respondents' self-reported health was significantly related to educational attainment, $r = .15$, $df = 390$, $p < .01$. Furthermore, as reported above, a significant relationship was found between self-reported health and perceived financial adequacy, $r = .33$, $df = 398$, $p < .001$, in that those reporting more satisfaction with their current finances were significantly more likely to report better health.

Men and women in the current study were comparable in regard to the nature of the residential environment in which they currently lived (senior residence vs. independent house or apartment), household composition, race, and place of birth. In regard to significant differences between the sexes, in the current sample, the preponderance of women were living alone (72.3%), with only 17.7% living with their spouses, and 20% living with others. In contrast, 63.6% of the men were living with their spouses, with 30.5% living alone, and 5.9% with others. Results of a χ^2 analysis indicated that this difference is significant, $\chi^2 = 82.10$, $df = 3$, $p < .0001$. Husbands of those women still having a living spouse were significantly older than male respondents whose wives were still living. Among the women, 7.4% had spouses aged 46 to 60, 57.4% had spouses age 61 to 75, and 35.2% had spouses age 76 and older. The preponderance of the spouses of the male respondents were 61 to 75 years of age (73.6%), with 17.6% age 46 to 60, and 8.8% age 76 and older, $\chi^2 = 90.68$, $df = 11$, $p < .001$. As anticipated, significant differences were found between the sexes in regard to marital status, $\chi^2 = 95.79$, $df = 4$, p < .0001, with the majority of women reporting that they were widowed (69.1%), and the majority of men stating that they were married (69.5%).

The men and women interviewed in this study did not differ in regard to educational attainment. On the other hand, differences in preretirement occupation were found. Thus, for example, the most prevalent occupation reported by females was homemaking (25.5%), followed by 23.4% involved in sales or technical work, and 12.4% previously employed as skilled laborers; only 2.1% were top executives, and 5.7% were managers. Among the males, skilled labor was the most prevalent occupation (35.6%), followed by 11.9% each in sales/technical work, management, and unskilled labor; 4.2% reported that they were top executives prior to retirement, $\chi^2 = 68.47$, $df = 10$, $p < .0001$.

As noted above, reports of actual income were related to sex, with females reporting less current income than males, $r = .25$, $df = 303$, $p < .001$. In contrast to responses about actual income, males and females did not differ significantly in the degree to which they perceived their finances as adequate to meet their needs. No significant differences were found between the sexes on several of our measures of health—including perceived functional health (Rosow, 1967), global ratings of health, or such facets as time spent in bed due to illness, or the presence of chronic or acute health problems of various types. On the other hand, men were less likely to report that they were currently limited in their ability to work, $\chi^2 = 10.55$, $df = 4$, $p < .05$, and men reported leaving their residence with a higher frequency than did women, $\chi^2 = 26.65$, $df = 6$, $p < .001$.

In addition to examining sex differences, we investigated variations in characteristics of respondents in the two study subsamples—that is, the sample drawn from age-homogeneous residences and the sample drawn from those elderly living in "standard," independent, or homogeneous residences. Our rationale for including these subsamples was to ensure the inclusion of individuals certain to have opportunities to help children, grandchildren, and/or great-grandchildren, because of their relative geographic proximity to such individuals (independent community sample) and the inclusion of those with high probability of having opportunities to help neighbors, due to the proximity of such older neighbors (senior residence sample). In addition, we anticipated that these individuals might differ in other respects as well. To cite one example, on the basis of our own research and that of others, we expected that individuals living in senior citizens residences would be older as a group and likely to perceive themselves as having more health-related problems—as these are included among the factors that often appear to motivate elderly persons to give up their former homes and move to such residences (e.g., Midlarsky & Kahana, 1984).

Results indicated that whereas 100% of seniors living independently had at least one child, grandchild, or great-grandchild living in the Detroit metropolitan area, this was true of only 77% of those living in the senior residences. As anticipated, those living in senior residences were indeed older as a group, with 42% between the ages of 64 and 75 (versus 77% among the independent sample), 41.5% between 76 and 85 years of age (versus 19.5%), and 14% age 86 and older (versus 3.5%), $\chi^2 = 49.04$, $df = 4$, $p < .001$.

Differences in perceived health were found, as well, with elderly persons living independently perceiving their health as generally better in a global sense, $\chi^2 = 11.94$, $df = 2$, $p < .01$, and reporting a higher level of functional health on our adapted health scale, $\chi^2 = 90.30$, $df = 44$, $p < .001$. No significant differences were found when respondents were asked to compare their health to their own age cohort in regard to time spent in bed due to illness, presence of chronic health problems, hearing difficulties, or orthopedic problems. On the other hand, elderly persons living in age-homogeneous residences were more likely to report problems with their eyesight, $\chi^2 = 35.72$, $df = 15$, $p < .01$, and were less likely to leave their residence on a frequent basis, $\chi^2 = 69.24$, $df = 30$, $p < .0001$.

In addition, over half of those living in independent residences (53.5%) were still living with their spouses, in contrast to only 15% of those in senior residences, a highly significant difference, $\chi^2 = 5,929$, $df = 2$, $p < .0001$. This finding, in combination with qualitative interview data, indicates that the loss of one's spouse was one of the determinants of the decision to live in a senior residence in the current sample. No differences were found between the two subsamples in regard to sex, SES, race, religion, place of birth, perceived financial adequacy, or reports of actual income.

In general, these data indicate consistency between the characteristics of the current sample and those found in prior studies of community-dwelling elderly persons (e.g., Lawton, 1989). The significant relationships observed between education, finances, and health are also consistent with previous reports in the field of gerontology (Riley & Foner, 1978). The finding that 100% of those living independently in the community had children, grandchildren, or great-grandchildren living nearby indicates that our screening procedures effectively led to the inclusion of appropriate subsamples in this regard. In addition, the range of differences between the two subsamples—for example, in regard to age, health, and marital status—suggests the desirability of testing our causal model separately in regard to the two subgroups, as originally planned.

Personality Variables

Issues of personal control have captured considerable interest as a motivational variable of potential importance in the lives of the elderly (Langer, 1980; Midlarsky & Kahana, 1985a), and work on measures of this variable was conducted prior to the initiation of the current investigation. In regard to the other personality variables studied here—empathy, perceived importance of helping (termed *importance* here), social responsibility, and moral judgment—little or no prior work addressed the presence or interrelationship among these variables or their relationship with the other factors investigated here.

As we have indicated above, in the section on the personality variables and their measurement, the locus of control measure appeared appropriate (e.g., alpha of .65), and we were successful in developing measures of empathy, importance, and social responsibility that were at least moderately internally consistent (alphas of .78, .68, and .64, respectively). In regard to altruistic moral judgment, interrater reliabilities across categories of moral reasoning ranged from .97 to 1.00.

In accordance with prior research, it seemed reasonable that the personality variables included in this study could potentially be combined into a single measure of "orientation toward prosocial behavior," in a manner similar to the analytic strategy employed by Staub (1974) for data obtained from younger individuals. However, results of a factor analysis performed on our four measures of altruistic motivation yielded no evidence supporting the construc-

tion of such a composite measure. Hence the separate relationship of
each personality variable both to helping and to the facets of well-being
was investigated throughout the course of the analysis of project data.

In addition to our interest in discerning the nature of helping
among the elderly, and in specifying and testing a causal model, we
had the goal of investigating prosocial orientations of diverse types
among the elderly and their relationships to other personal factors.
Results of this study indicated that all but 4 of the 400 respondents
in this survey (99%) felt that helping others is an important activity
in their lives. The largest single group (50%) described helping as
important, 39% deemed it very important, and only 9% described it
as somewhat important. The tendency to view helping as an important and valued activity was inversely related to age, $r = -.15, p < .01$,
and positively related to global perceptions about one's health, $r =
.11, p < .05$. Another personality variable, empathic tendency, is
inversely related to age, $r = -.18, p < .001$, and is positively related to
both functional health, $r = .10, p < .05$, and perceived financial
adequacy, $r = .11, p < .05$. Furthermore, women were more apt than
men to express an empathic orientation, $\chi^2 = 21.21, df = 3, p < .001$.
Women were more likely than men to express the view that helping
is an important and valued activity, $\chi^2 = 11.27, df = 5, p < .05$, and
importance was both positively related to global perception of health,
$r = .15, p < .05$, and inversely related to age, $r = -.15, p < .01$. Social
responsibility was inversely related to age, $r = -.11, p < .05$, but
positively associated with the Hollingshead two-factor index of SES,
$r = .26, p < .001$, to both global perceptions of health, $r = .15, p < .001$,
and functional health, $r = .20, p < .001$, to actual income, $r = .29, p <
.001$, and to perceived financial adequacy; no sex difference was
found. In regard to locus of control, men were more likely than
women to be internal controllers, $\chi^2 = 41.72, df = 15, p < .001$. Whereas
this variable was found to be unrelated to age of respondent, significant findings were obtained for its association with SES, $r = .16, p <
.001$, both global perceptions of health and functional health, $r = .19,
p < .001$ (for both), and with actual income and perceived financial
adequacy, $r = .22, p < .001$ (for both).

Particular attention was paid to altruistic moral judgment, as
manifested within our sample of elderly respondents. Results of our
analyses indicate that six categories of moral reasoning were used

among our sample of elderly persons. Of these six, the categories used most frequently were, in descending order of frequency:

1. reasons based on a needs-oriented approach, and nonhedonistic pragmatism (Level 3)
2. empathic orientation/internalized affect (Level 5)
3. abstract and/or firmly internalized reasons (Level 6)
4. hedonistic concerns (Level 2)

No significant differences in reasoning based on age, gender, or functional health status were obtained.

Only moral reasoning at the highest level—Level 6—was significantly related to self-reported helping. Hence relationships between the degree to which respondents employed Level 6 reasoning and other study variables were separately calculated for the two residential subsamples. Results indicated that global perceptions of health (but not functional health) were related to Level 6 morality, $r = .13$, $p < .001$, and that this relationship was significant for those living in independent housing, $r = .16$, $p < .001$, but not for those living in senior residences (possibly due, in part, to the greater homogeneity in perceived health among the latter). On the other hand, SES was significantly related to principled reasoning among residents of senior housing, $r = .19$, $p < .001$. Interestingly, individuals in senior residences who reasoned at the highest level reported lower perceived financial adequacy and lower actual incomes, $r = -.20, p < .001$ (for both), findings that held for the total sample as well, $r = .13, p < .001$. This lends a modicum of support to the notion that adherence to high moral principles may be somewhat in opposition to an orientation toward the accumulation of material wealth, with financial pursuits more highly related to a hedonistic orientation (Level 2). These data are considered important because they are among the first systematic analyses of moral judgment among a sample of older adults residing in noninstitutional contexts.

Situational Variables

As noted above, the situational variables employed in the investigation were costs/risks of helping, opportunities to help others, help previously received, and the convenience of access to facilities outside of one's residence.

Following the development of internally consistent measures, we assessed the relationship of these variables to demographic characteristics of the respondents and also to the residential context in which they lived. Results indicated that age of respondent had significant zero-order correlations with all four of the situational variables. Older individuals appeared significantly less likely to perceive opportunities to help others, $r = -.15$, $p < .001$, and to evaluate their environments as having convenient (for them) access to diverse facilities, $r = .25$, $p < .001$, and they were less likely to incur costs or risks in order to help others. Older persons were also more likely to report higher levels of help received within the past year. In a similar vein, individuals rating their global health as lower were significantly less likely to assess facilities (e.g., doctors, shops) as convenient, $r = .29$, $p < .001$, and more likely to have received help from others in the past year, $r = -.23$, $p < .001$. Functional health as measured by the Health Scale was also significantly related to amount of help received from others, $r = -.34$, $p < .001$, and to perceived convenience, $r = .32$, $p < .001$. In addition, individuals with higher functional health noted more opportunities to help within their environments, $r = -.10$, $p < .05$. Elderly persons reporting higher incomes were less likely to have recently been help recipients, $r = -.18$, $p < .001$, and they saw facilities as more convenient, $r = .34$, $p < .001$. Similar results were obtained when finances were assessed with the Perceived Financial Adequacy Scale, such that the correlations with both help received, $r = -.10$, $p < .05$, and convenience of facilities, $r = .42$, $p < .001$, were significant.

Another finding of this study is that women reported receiving help to a higher degree than did men, $\chi^2 = 30.75$, $df = 8$, p $< .001$, and people residing in senior residences reported receiving higher amounts of help than did those living in their houses or apartments in nonhomogeneous contexts, $\chi^2 = 67.81$, $df = 32$, $p < .001$.

Also examined were the relationships among the situational variables. We found that those older persons perceiving more opportunities to help others were more willing to incur costs when helping others, $r = .17$, $p < .001$, and they described facilities of various types as more convenient, $r = .18$, $p < .001$. On the other hand, elderly individuals receiving more help from others during the past year saw needed facilities as less convenient than did those receiving less help, $r = -.19$, $p < .001$.

Helping Behavior

A major goal of this study was to discern the nature and manifestations of helping among the elderly. In this section, we present a brief overview of some of the results regarding helping in our study sample.

Quantitative Descriptive Data on Helping

In response to the question about how much they had helped others during the past year, 53% of our elderly respondents reported helping very much or much, 29% helped somewhat, and 17.5% helped little or very little. Amounts helped also varied with age, with older respondents helping significantly less than younger respondents, $r = -.230$, $p < .001$. Amount of self-reported helping did not vary with sex or place of residence.

The largest single group of respondents, 44%, reported that helping in the past year was about the same as it had been throughout their lives. The next largest group, 41%, stated that they used to help more (16.2%) or much more (27%), whereas 15% reported that they used to help less or much less. Change in helping varied with neither sex nor place of residence.

Respondents were asked about the three types of helping in which they engaged most frequently. These types of helping were then categorized in accordance with the Adams (1968) typology as provision of tangibles, intangibles, service, or a combination of intangibles and service. In all cases, the largest sample group provided services—consisting of instrumental help of some kind (45%)—followed by both tangibles (23%) and intangibles (19%), with the remainder (13%) a combination of two or more types of help. About 36% of the respondents described the type of help given now as similar to that given in the past, in contrast to 21%

describing it as somewhat similar and 43% for whom it was different or very different.

Respondents were also asked about the degree to which their helping was planned in advance or provided on the spur of the moment. Help giving was described as usually spontaneous for 59% of the sample, planned for 18%, and sometimes planned for 23%.

The largest number of individuals who were interviewed (45%) indicated that they spent some of their time helping others, followed by 39.8% reporting that they spent much or very much of their time in this way.

Most of the aged respondents reported that the person that they helped most frequently was a child, grandchild, or great-grandchild, followed, in descending order, by a parent or a sibling and then a stranger. Of persons responding to the question, "Is this recipient the person that helps you most frequently?" about half (47%) said yes, and half (53%) said no. The degree of reciprocity implied in responses to this latter question did not vary across respondents either by sex or by residence.

On the other hand, men and women in the sample did respond differently to the question regarding the recipient of their helping efforts, $\chi^2 = 49.40$, $df = 10$, $p < .0001$. That is, men most frequently cited their spouse as recipient of their efforts (42%), followed by a child (32%), friend or neighbor (16%), other relative (7%), and stranger (3%). The largest single group of women cited a child (29%), followed by other relatives (22%), friends (13%), neighbors (17%), spouse (12%), and strangers (2%). The difference between the percentages of men and women who referred to their spouse as the individual whom they helped the most may be attributable to the fact that fewer women than men reported having living spouses, and male spouses of women tended to be younger than female spouses of men. However, it is also likely that retired men who take on even light household chores may characterize this as helping. Women, on the other hand, may see much of their daily family service as a continuation of an obligatory lifelong role, so that only extraordinary service—as to a sick or disabled spouse—may be referred to as a helping behavior. These data are presented in Table 5.3.

Interestingly, when asked about the degree to which their spouse helps them, many men also reported higher degrees of help re-

Table 5.3 Percentages of Females and Males Helping Diverse Recipients

Recipient	Male (%)	Female (%)
Spouse	42	12
Child	32	28
Parent	0	2
Sibling	4	14
Other relative	3	8
Friend	12	17
Neighbor	4	17
Stranger	3	2

Table 5.4 Percentages of Males and Females Judging Spouses as Helpful

Response	Male (%)	Female (%)
Very helpful	68.0	38.9
Moderately helpful	24.0	16.7
Neither helpful nor unhelpful	0.0	38.9
Moderately unhelpful	4.0	0.0
Very unhelpful	4.0	5.6

ceived from their spouse then did women. Taken together, these data may indicate that retired men are more sensitive to (and satisfied with) helping transactions with their spouses than are women, $\chi^2 = 12.33$, $p < .01$. These data appear in Table 5.4.

As anticipated, recipients of help by older people differed significantly in the two study subsamples, $\chi^2 = 114.06$, $df = 50$, $p < .0001$. The very nature of the residential environment made it likely that our "senior residence" subsample would include more persons with opportunities to help their neighbors. Concomitantly, 23% of those in the age-homogeneous apartment dwellings said that they help neighbors more than any other type of recipient, in contrast to 7.8% of those living in age-heterogeneous situations. We then looked at the relative frequencies of individuals in the two subsamples reporting that they mostly helped neighbors in combination with those saying that they mostly helped friends—as the terms *friend* and *neighbor* were used interchangeably within this survey (per reports by 70% of respondents). Whereas 17% of those living within independent, age-heterogeneous residences reported helping a friend or neighbor most frequently, 43% of those living in senior residences helped a friend or neighbor most frequently of all.

Just as the subsample living in senior residences was chosen because of their proximity to elderly neighbors who might benefit from the respondents' help, the "independent" subsample was selected partly on the basis of proximity to children. Not surprisingly, the largest single group of individuals within that subsample (36%) reported that they most frequently helped their child (36%), followed by a spouse (27%), other family, or friend/neighbor (17% for each category), with the smallest percentage helping strangers (3%). As noted previously, the largest percentage of older persons living in senior residences reported helping a neighbor or friend (43%). In descending order of frequency, others helped were a child (22%), other family (19%), a spouse (14%), and least frequently, a stranger (2%).

In addition to asking who were the most frequent recipients of help by our aged sample, we also asked who received the greatest magnitude of help. We learned that 27% gave most help to their children, followed by friends/neighbors (26%), spouse (20%), other relatives (12%), grandchildren (7%), recipients of volunteer efforts (7%), and strangers (1%). Amounts given varied with both sex, $\chi^2 = 40.05$, $df = 6$, p < .0001, and residence, $\chi^2 = 50.51$, $df = 7$, $p < .0001$. In regard to differences among people living in the two residential contexts, 42% reported giving the most help to children or grandchildren and only 12% to friends and neighbors. Those living in senior residences gave the greatest amounts of help to friends and neighbors (40%), with 25% giving most generously to children and grandchildren. Fewer respondents in senior residences do volunteer work than those in other residential contexts (5% vs. 9%), and both groups give relatively little help to strangers (1% each).

Similar numbers of men and women reported giving the highest amounts of help to their children and grandchildren (32% and 34%, respectively), to strangers (1% vs. 2%), and in the context of volunteer activities (6% in each group), but men and women differed in regard to other recipients. Among men, 39% reported giving the greatest magnitude of help to their wives, 17% to friends and neighbors, and 5% to other relatives. In contrast, 30% of the women interviewed reported giving most of their help to friends and neighbors, 15% to other relatives, and only 13% to their husbands.

Regarding special obstacles to helping, 83% reported that there were none. Most respondents (71%) also stated that helping has its own special rewards. Neither sex nor residence was significantly related to responses to these questions. The obstacles and rewards cited are presented below, along with other data from the open-ended questions.

Respondents were queried about their behaviors and preferences about giving versus receiving help. The largest single group (38.6%) felt that they received and gave help about equally, 26.2% said they usually gave more, and 23.2% said they always gave more. Only 9.5% reported that they usually received more than they gave, and 2.5% said that they always received more. Thus 88% said either their giving and receiving were in balance or that they gave more, at least "usually." Concomitantly, most of these respondents (84%) indicated that they always or more often were most comfortable when they gave more, and 12.2% liked their giving and receiving to be about equal. Only 2.8% more often preferred to receive than to give, and 1% said that they always preferred to receive. An age-related difference was found, wherein from the youngest ages in this sample through ages 75 to 80, increasingly more comfort was experienced in giving than in receiving. After the age of 79, the degree of comfort in giving versus receiving dropped. The great majority of respondents (78.5%) felt that they gave just the right amount, with 7% saying that their amount of giving was far too much or too little, and 13.7% saying that it was somewhat more or less than the most comfortable amount. Most (84.7%) indicated that they received far too much or too little, and 11.5% said that they received a bit more or less than was desired.

In several questions, respondents were asked to specify the total number of persons helped and then to answer questions about their helping interactions with up to five recipients. The preponderance of respondents (78%) named from one to five people, whereas 16% helped 6 to 11 people, and 12 respondents (.3%) named none. Number of persons helped varied with residence. More people living in senior residences gave no names of persons helped during the past year (5% vs. 1%), and fewer named more than five help recipients (13.5% vs. 22.5%). On the other hand, more residents of such apartment houses named between one and five people whom they had helped (81.5% vs. 76.5%). In the case of each of the first five recipients, the largest percentages of respondents provided aid every day (25%). Only 8% said that they provided help less than several times a year, and 16% provided aid once or twice a month.

We also examined responses to the Modified Self-Report Altruism Scale (a modification of the scale by Rushton et al., 1981), which presents diverse types of helping acts and asks respondents about the frequency with which they were emitted during the past year. Table 5.5 presents percentages and frequencies of responses to these items. An examination of Table 5.5 reveals that the three helping acts in which the largest percentages of respondents engaged once or more than once during the year are holding the elevator for someone (91.4%), giving emotional support (90.5%), and donating money to charity (88%). The three helping acts engaged in by the smallest percentages of respondents are donating blood (2.6%), lending a stranger an item of value (16.3%), and helping an acquaintance move households (27.4%).

In sum, based on our data, helping emerges as a highly significant, extensively engaged in, and personally meaningful form of behavior among our respondents. The findings regarding patterns of helping by older persons reveal a great deal of spontaneity rather than deliberation in providing help; 59% provide assistance to others on the spur of the moment. Helping others represents a significant effort in terms of time commitment for many of the respondents. About a quarter of the sample (23.1%) reported spending a considerable amount of time helping others. There is also a broad spectrum of persons helped by these senior citizen housing dwellers. Hence fully two thirds of the respondents provided some form of assistance to various family members, and one

Table 5.5 Percentages of Older Adults Engaging in Diverse Helping Acts

		Response			Summary	
			More Than		Very	Once or
Item	Never	Once	Once	Often	Often	More
Gave blood	97.4	1.7	0.9	—	—	2.6
Carried belongings	31.6	5.1	35.9	18.8	8.5	68.3
Held elevator	8.5	1.7	14.5	44.4	30.8	91.4
Let ahead on line	24.8	0.9	39.8	20.4	14.2	75.3
Gave lift in car	42.9	3.8	12.4	21.9	19.0	57.1
Pointed out undercharge	67.3	11.5	17.7	3.5	—	32.7
Lent stranger item of value	83.6	1.7	9.5	3.4	1.7	16.3
Bought card from charity	39.3	18.8	25.6	9.4	6.8	60.6
Helped with chores	69.8	6.0	17.2	2.6	4.3	30.1
Looked after things	54.3	11.2	18.1	11.2	5.2	45.7
Helped handicapped cross street	40.5	4.3	30.2	16.4	8.6	59.5
Offered seat	58.8	7.0	26.3	4.4	3.5	72.7
Helped acquaintance move	72.6	9.7	17.7	—	—	27.4
Looked in on sick	17.1	0.0	34.2	24.8	23.9	82.9
Gave directions	17.9	2.6	35.0	27.4	17.1	82.1
Made change	26.5	0.9	35.0	29.1	8.5	73.0
Money to charity	12.0	6.8	31.6	30.8	18.8	88.0
Money to someone	40.9	11.3	37.4	8.7	1.7	59.1
Goods to charity	25.6	15.4	35.9	11.1	12.0	74.4
Volunteer work for charity	51.3	3.4	19.7	6.8	18.8	48.7
Looked in on friend or neighbor	18.1	4.3	23.3	24.1	30.2	81.9
Gave advice to friend	25.9	5.2	31.0	19.8	18.1	74.1
Picked up things at store	25.2	2.6	27.8	27.0	17.4	74.8
Baby-sat free	67.5	2.6	17.1	6.0	6.8	32.5
Helped neighbor with chores	56.9	5.2	19.8	9.5	8.6	43.1
Gave emotional support	9.5	5.2	33.6	29.3	22.4	90.5

third help neighbors and friends. Confirming the importance of the residential context for assistance provided to neighbors, the highest percentage of assistance provided by residents of age-homogeneous dwellings was given to friends and neighbors. For those living in other contexts, helping of family members was clearly most prevalent.

The social role of the helper appears to be both socially desirable and important for elderly individuals. Thus there appear to be far more respondents describing themselves as primarily providers than as primarily recipients of assistance. Although responses indicate that there may be some degree of reciprocity in helping, the role of provider of assistance appears to be most salient for the majority. This may in part be explained by the high value placed on independence versus dependency by older persons. Being in the position of helping others generally underscores the older person's competence and ability to function independently.

Responses to Open-Ended
Questions About Helping

In addition to the quantitative data obtained from the closed-ended questions on helping, each respondent also provided information in several open-ended questions. In this section, we present results of responses to questions regarding changes in patterns of helping in comparison with earlier life, rewards of helping, and a special act of helping in which the respondents engaged. Finally, we provide several case examples that may serve to illustrate self-reported helping by our older respondents.

Changes in Patterns of Helping

For most of the elderly interviewed, the amount of helping that they reported providing to others either remained unchanged or decreased over time. Nevertheless, a significant minority (15%) increased the amount of help that they provided to others in their late life.

Many of the individuals reporting no change in their helping behavior offered comments indicating that they continued to maintain high levels of helping behavior.

Those whose helping had declined over time most frequently cited problems with their own physical health as the reason for providing less assistance ($N = 45$). In addition, some respondents ($N = 4$) noted financial or social limitations, which curtailed the help they could provide to others. A second set of reasons responsible for providing less assistance in late life related to the presence of fewer opportunities to help others ($N = 12$). In addition to making general comments about lack of opportunity, some respondents ($N = 3$) said that they rarely came in contact with people needing assistance, and still others ($N = 5$) cited diminished obligations especially in terms of family responsibilities. These older people expressed the view of themselves as free from family obligations, which necessitate extensive helping behavior.

Although the number of respondents who increased their helping in late life was small, they represent a group of particular interest in this project ($N = 60$). The major reason provided for increased help offered to others was greater availability of free time after retirement ($N = 24$). This finding confirms expectations based on the gerontological literature that retirees may be able to devote more time to volunteering and helping activities than persons still in the workforce. Several respondents indicated changes in their own personality and outlook on life ($N = 17$) that enabled them to perform more helping behaviors. In some cases, increased help provided reflects greater need for assistance by a spouse or other family member ($N = 4$) or increased environmental opportunities for providing assistance, such as being in close proximity to neighbors ($N = 15$).

Obstacles to Providing Help

In considering special obstacles encountered by respondents in their efforts to provide assistance to others, the vast majority ($N = 292$) did not report any special obstacles to helping others. Among the 108 respondents reporting some type of obstacle, the most important problem cited was that of personal limitations of the helper ($N = 52$). Twenty-four individuals referred to health-related limitations. Six respondents referred to financial problems or limitations. Thus over half of those reporting obstacles referred to obstacles related to competencies of the helper.

The remainder reported various obstacles related to the recipients of assistance or to environmental obstacles to providing assistance ($N = 56$). Environmental obstacles were exemplified by uncooperative management of the senior residence or problems encountered at an emergency room. Lack of cooperation by others involved, lack of appreciation, or lack of necessary instrumental support by other family or neighbors of the recipient were also cited. Lack of receptiveness by the recipients (e.g., refusal to accept help), the extensiveness of their problems, and their emotional reaction or unwillingness to admit to needing assistance represented major obstacles related to recipients of help.

Rewards of Helping

One hundred-eighty respondents, 45% of the sample, reported no special rewards of helping. The absence of any response may be considered using two alternative interpretations. On one hand, it is possible that many respondents could not articulate what, if any, the rewards of helping were. On the other hand, their statement that helping has no special rewards may reflect their belief that helping is its own reward—that is, it requires or possesses no external rewards.

The majority of respondents considered the rewards of giving to be intrinsic in nature. In response to the question, "What do you consider to be the special rewards of helping?" the preponderance of those who viewed helping as especially rewarding (192 of 220) cited rewards that are intrinsic in nature. These included a sense of inner satisfaction ($N = 120$), an enhanced sense of usefulness or competence ($N = 26$), increased self-esteem ($N = 21$), a sense of fulfilling religious obligations ($N = 11$), and the lessening of inner pain after one has alleviated the suffering of another ($N = 4$). As one 88-year-old respondent said, "Even though there are things I can no longer do, I can still bring a smile to my neighbor's face." In the words of an 86-year-old respondent, "Helping others confirms one's own existence and integration."

A small group of respondents ($N = 37$) reported extrinsic rewards as the salient ones in helping behavior. Specific forms of reciprocal help were mentioned by six respondents. Material payments, acknowledgment by others, gratitude, and a good reputation were noted by 27 respondents as rewards of helping others.

These findings provide a strong indication of the importance of altruistic motives for self-reported helping behavior by older persons. Thus it appears that the majority engage in helping others primarily because of the psychological benefits they derive for so doing, rather than because of specific and tangible forms of assistance, or even recognition that they may anticipate in return. These findings raise questions about the applicability of an exchange model of helping to elderly providers of help (cf. Kahana & Midlarsky, 1982; Kahana, Midlarsky, & Kahana, 1987).

In considering specific extrinsic rewards noted by respondents, it is also interesting to note that the majority of these were given by older respondents who appeared more needy and less independent. For example, they might say "Since I've started helping my friend with his chores, he now takes me for rides in his car—it gets me out of here" or "When I help, people in my apartment house know my name."

Special Acts of Helping

Each respondent was asked to describe a helping act that he or she considered "special." Of the 400 respondents, 343 were able to describe such an act. In response to the Likert-scale item, "How similar was that (special helping act) to daily helping?" 46% characterized their special helping behavior as *dissimilar* or *very dissimilar.*

Those aspects of helping identified by the elderly as having special significance to them provide important data on dimensions of helping by the aged. When elderly respondents were asked to recall special help that they provided to others and personally valued, a rich and interesting portrayal of the personal salience of helping became available.

The types of special help provided spanned a broad range, from heroic rescue to daily acts of assistance or courtesies. Most respondents, however, referred to enduring and personally costly forms of help, such as helping care for an ill relative in one's own home for several months to several years. This is a generation that has had a great deal of experience as major providers of informal support to others. Frequently the special forms of help respondents provided referred to assistance given to parents or siblings early in their lives. Some mentioned assisting family members during the Depression of the 1930s. It is especially interesting to note that respondents vividly recalled these acts of altruism and that they held great salience for them even in their old age. These findings are consistent with evidence from earlier work that suggests that the elderly often engage in a life review (Butler, 1975) and refer to early relations with parents as a salient aspect of their self-concepts (Kahana & Coe, 1969).

Among those describing helping behaviors in which they engaged during their postretirement years, about half referred to help with a chronic, or long-standing problem, whereas half gave assistance during an acute crisis, or emergency situation. Whereas about one third described helping in a situation that entailed considerable threat and potential harm or costs, two thirds spoke of situations entailing serious or extreme threat. Also, although recipients of diverse ages were mentioned, the largest single group of our respondents (27%) reported special acts in which they helped other elderly respondents. Twice as many reported helping females, in comparison with those helping males. In regard to the latter, however, the fact that the preponderance of our respondents were female, reflecting the presence of a higher proportion of females especially at the higher reaches of the life span, may account for this finding.

Overall, assisting others in times of illness—whether chronic or acute—seemed the most salient and highly valued type of assistance. In such cases, the recipients are particularly needy, presenting an opportunity for helping. Qualitative findings of this type also support our quantitative data regarding the importance of situational determinants of helping.

Fifty-six noted instances of assuming total responsibility for the care and/or welfare of another individual as the special help that they provided. In the majority of these instances, care was given to a member of their family who was undergoing a lengthy illness. Examples included "taking care of an ill sister-in-law after moving her into my home," "moving in with a daughter who had cancer and assuming her family responsibilities," and "giving up all outside activities to stay home caring for an ill wife." These responses also underscore findings by Shanas (1967) about the important role that family members play in caring for one another during times of illness or other family crises.

The second and related form of special assistance cited by a large proportion of respondents referred to provision of assistance during times of illness or medical emergency, wherein the helper did not live with the recipient while providing help. Fifty respondents provided examples of assisting ill persons with chores and medical treatments on an ongoing basis. An additional 24 provided household assistance to others who were ill. These examples often referred to current involvement in assisting neighbors or friends. Yet another 81 respondents related single instances of assistance in a health crisis or illness. These included rescue behaviors—for example, calling an ambulance or doctor—obtaining medication, or calling the family of an ill resident, and they often referred to assistance provided by an older person to other elderly persons. Accordingly, illness represents the most important stimulus for special helping acts by older persons, who compose a very significant informal support network for one another when illness strikes. When all four aspects of caretaking and helping during times of illness and crisis are combined, close to two thirds of the sample ($N = 211$) was accounted for.

Fifty-seven individuals did not report providing any remarkable or special forms of help to others. This is a very small proportion of the total sample (14%), attesting to the fact that the vast majority of elderly persons view themselves as at least occasional providers of special assistance to others.

Salient forms of special assistance provided to others also included volunteer activities ($N = 17$), provision of financial assistance ($N = 37$), baby-sitting or child care activities ($N = 28$), emotional, spiritual, or religious help ($N = 20$), heroic rescue ($N = 15$), as well as other forms of assistance. With very few exceptions, the examples provided by respondents attested to risk, courage, self-sacrifice, or other special costs to providers of assistance clearly going beyond trivial, routine, or normative forms of helping activity.

One respondent cited driving disabled neighbors around; another purchased life insurance policies for 13 family members. One reported activities as an alcohol crisis worker, and another advised a doctor friend to seek psychiatric assistance.

The recipients of special forms of assistance included family members, friends, neighbors, and strangers. Thirty-five respondents provided special assistance to the spouse, 23 noted helping their own parents, and 18 assisted sons or daughters. It is interesting and somewhat surprising to note that the proportion of those noting special assistance to their parents exceeds those citing examples of assisting their children. Sisters, brothers, and cousins were assisted by 14 persons and in-laws were helped by 6 people, attesting to the importance of the extended family. The remarkable absence of assistance given to grandchildren ($N = 10$) deserves mention and supports the contention by some gerontologists that caretaking functions of grandparents have diminished in modern U.S. society (Kahana & Kahana, 1971). Help was provided to friends and neighbors by 59 persons, to colleagues by 3, and to employees or clients by 9, with 58 assisting strangers. In the remainder of cases, either there was some other relation to the recipient or the nature of the recipient's relationship was not specified.

CASE EXAMPLES OF OLDER HELPERS

Portraits of some of the older helpers interviewed may provide additional insights into the nature of helping in this age group. John B. is an 80-year-old man who looks as if he is in his 60s. He said that his most important and valuable activity is caring for his wife, who has a bad back and is immobilized. He helps her get around, buys all the groceries and other necessities, and cleans their apartment. Because he has a car, he frequently takes neighbors in his senior apartment complex out for dinner or for entertainment.

Sara L. is a 69-year-old woman who said that her greatest pleasures come from the hours she spends reading to county school children, making sure that poor people get the health care they deserve, or counseling teenagers about pregnancy and safe sex. A retired psychiatric nurse, Sara said that her greatest reward is seeing people get the help that they need.

Leona C., 91, who is a very skilled seamstress, has been altering clothes for other residents of her senior apartment complex, free of charge. She and other residents have also donated their crafts to hospitals. "We first started making crafts for ourselves," she said, "but then we just decided to start doing them for others." More recently, she hurt her hip, and although she still donates crafts, she has stopped doing alterations because she cannot measure people. "I'd love to go to the hospital and read to the blind, or write letters for them," she said. Leona C. is always smiling or laughing: "I've had such a good life. And anyway I go around with a cheerful face because that encourages people a lot—knowing you don't have to go around with a sad face. I figure if you can't help somebody, what's the use of living?"

Sam B. went to college for 2 years and quit to start his own small business. During his career, his primary involvements were with family and his job. Now that he is 68, he feels that he has the time to devote to charitable causes. In addition to helping his wife and children, and making financial contributions to charity, last year Sam agreed to go from door to door in his neighborhood and collect for a charitable cause. Sam hated every minute of this activity. He said that some of his neighbors were upset at being asked to contribute because they felt unable to give, and he felt bad about putting them on the spot. Others were very rude and unpleasant or put him off on several occasions, only to later shut the door in his face. Several neighbors began to ignore him after being thus approached. Yet Sam stated that despite the unpleasantness of the experience, he continues to collect for this charity and for others. "After all," he said, "I believe in these causes and someone has to do the unpleasant work of getting the money that is so sorely needed."

May H., 64, is involved in a social network within her residence. However, in addition to the daily favors and courtesies exchanged with neighbors, she had agreed within the past 6 months to make daily visits to Joe, a double amputee who lives upstairs. Joe is nothing like her other neighbor friends or like her husband, Sam. Whereas they are cheerful and gregarious, he was best characterized when she first met him as a surly isolate filled with self-pity. Somehow, she got into the habit of dropping in to visit Joe every day, saying a few cheerful words and often bringing him something handmade. For the first month of her visits, he seemed surlier than ever and never thanked her in word or deed. However, she noticed that he began to come out of his apartment and mingle with the other residents more than he ever had. He also seemed more relaxed and even smiled on occasion. The change in Joe, and her conviction that her visits and gifts were benefiting him were enough to keep Sara's visits going for several months, until she felt he was comfortable enough with others not to need her anymore. May seldom mentioned her visits to Joe, even when people started to comment about the change in him.

Lester R. has been living in Detroit for years; it's over 60 years since he left the farm on which he spent his boyhood. Nevertheless, he never stopped growing everything from apples to zucchini in his backyard. He now says that retirement—which first left him feeling useless—gave him an opportunity to feed others. It all started when he and his wife grew and cooked food to help their divorced daughter feed herself and her children. Now that their daughter is back on her feet, Lester and his wife spend at least an hour a day telephoning local agencies that may need food or food-related services. For about 5 years they have been providing their own produce—and the surplus from nearby farms—to shelters for the homeless, and they welcome five or more homeless families into their house every Sunday, providing a home-cooked meal.

John L. is an 83-year-old retired engineer who always seems to be in the thick of activities within his family—many of whom live in his neighborhood. He is a warm and extroverted person, self-confident and interested in everything around him. He is alert to problems that may arise and eager to be involved in their amelioration. When something simple needs to be fixed in his own apartment, that of a neighbor, in a hallway or common area, or in the home of a family member, John will be quick to offer to fix it. If it is more technical or complex, he will offer to help to get the job done. In discussions with his son-in-law and several of his friends, he found that many of them were losing money on taxes. Because he is good at preparing tax forms, he prepares tax returns for an ever-increasing number of family members and friends, free of charge.

Mary A., 78 years of age, is a warm, extroverted woman who said that helping others makes her feel good. She currently cleans a disabled man's apartment, volunteers to pass out coffee each day to residents, brings lunch to a neighbor who might otherwise miss that meal, and volunteers to run the reception desk. "I help because I can," she said. "I might as well help as sit here." Mary also mentions that once she befriended a person who had personal problems. She came in one day and found that a suicide attempt was in progress. She immediately called the police, and the woman was saved. She now visits her and tries to provide emotional support on a daily basis.

Val is a 72-year-old man who has a small and a cheerful greeting for everyone. "I like to make people feel good," he said. Val said that he does not like to live among "old folks," so he walks around downtown Royal Oak a good deal and knows many of his neighbors outside of the Manor. Within his own home, Val is frequently seen fixing things, whether hammering or painting. He initiated and implemented the planting of flowers around the residence and has taken on the responsibility for the Meals-on-Wheels program at the residence.

Leona H., age 76, said that helping others is very important for her. When her husband was still alive, she primarily took care of him. These days, she has more time and energy to devote to friends and neighbors. "My group were all aging," she said, "so I took a CPR course, just in case." Sure enough about a year ago, a man that she was with started having a heart seizure. She called 911, but began CPR, and kept it up even in the ambulance all the way to the hospital. She said, "all the time I was determined I would do everything I could for him. I felt wonderful when I knew that I had saved his life. Helping helps the helper," Leona insisted.

In summary, these case studies—and the data on helping—confirm the variety and significance of special assistance provided to others by elderly persons. During later life there appear to be numerous individuals who engage in helping acts that benefit a wide range of recipients in the three primary helping domains.

MULTIVARIATE ANALYSES OF SURVEY DATA

Preliminary Analysis

In assessing relationships among the study variables presented in Figure 5.1, we first calculated zero-order intercorrelations among them. These results appear in Table 5.6.

Table 5.6 Zero-Order Correlations of Study Variables

	1	2	3	4	5	6	7	8	9	10	11	12	13
Exogenous Variables													
1. Sex													
2. Age	-.02												
3. Health	-.04	-.41***											
4. Finances	-.05	.00	.31***										
5. Importance of helping	-.04	-.16***	.04	.03									
6. Empathy	.25***	-.18***	.10	.12*	.23***								
7. Internal locus	-.15**	-.01	.17***	.12*	.21***	-.06							
8. Social responsibility	-.03	-.09	.16***	.31***	.21***	.13*	.25***						
9. Opportunity to help	-.02	-.14**	.06	.03	.24***	.07	.12*	.19***					
10. Former help received	.23***	.21***	-.35***	-.08	.06	.06	.05	.03	.10*				
Concomitant													
11. Helping behavior	-.01	-.34***	.33***	.22***	.54***	.26***	.21***	.31***	.32***	.11*			
Endogenous Variables													
12. Morale	-.04	-.09	.33***	.27***	.11*	-.20***	.32***	.26***	.05	-.13*	.28***		
13. Self-esteem	-.05	-.13*	.35***	.35***	.17***	-.03	.34***	.36***	.06	-.20***	.37***	.62***	
14. Subjective integration	.01	-.14**	.16***	.16***	.31***	.04	.27***	.24***	.14**	-.01	.39***	.49***	.47***

NOTE: $N = 398$-400 for all table entries.
*$p < .05$; **$p < .01$; ***$p < .001$.

182

Table 5.7 Predictors of Helping

Predictor Variable	R^2 Increment	Standardized Regression Coefficient	F to Enter or Remove
Importance/value of helping	.29	.38	150.23**
Perceived health	.09	.26	54.00**
Opportunity to help	.09	.12	19.80**
Age	.02	.61	10.56**
Finances	.02	.14	11.40**
Social responsibility	.01	.12	5.77*
Empathy	.01	.55	4.08*

NOTE: The adjusted R^2 = .46. The order of entry for each variable was determined by the magnitude of the relevant zero-order correlation.
*$p < .05$; **$p < .01$.

Multiple Regression Analysis

In order to provide an initial test of the contributory model of successful aging (Figure 5.1), we performed hierarchical multiple regression analyses. In these analyses, the order of entry was based on the magnitude of each zero-order correlation between an independent variable and the appropriate dependent variable. First we examined the relative influences of the proposed personal and situational predictors to helping. Then we investigated the effects of those predictors and of helping on psychosocial well-being. Tables 5.7 through 5.10 present the results of the analyses.

As Table 5.7 indicates, the primary predictors of helping in this analysis were the importance/value attributed to helping, followed by perceived health, opportunities, age, finances, social responsibility, perceived health, and empathy. The four personality variables had some ability to predict helping, even after controlling for health, finances, age, sex, and the like.

As Table 5.8 shows, the most powerful predictor of subjective social integration was self-reported helping, followed by locus of control, perceived health, the importance or value attributed to helping, and social responsibility. Hence, as predicted, helping is inversely related to an important problem for many elderly: the sense of isolation from others, including loneliness.

Table 5.8 Predictors of Subjective Social Integration

Predictor Variable	R^2 Increment	Standardized Regression Coefficient	F to Enter or Remove
Helping	.15	.20	64.73**
Locus of control	.04	.58	17.41**
Perceived health	.01	.20	5.94*
Importance/value of helping	.01	.17	5.52*
Social responsibility	.01	.47	3.14*

NOTE: The adjusted R^2 = .21. The order of entry for each variable was determined by the magnitude of the relevant zero-order correlation.
*$p < .05$; **$p < .001$.

In accordance with the results presented in Table 5.9, six variables had significant impacts on morale: perceived health, locus of control, empathy, social responsibility, helping, and finances. It appears that among the elderly surveyed in this study, morale was affected first and most powerfully by perceived health, and finances also played a role (cf. Back, 1982). Of interest is that even after controlling for those factors, two of the personality variables—social responsibility and internal locus of control—were significant predictors, as was helping. An inverse relationship was also found between empathy and morale. In an age group in which health problems and death are prevalent, sensitivity to the feelings and experiences of others may well be a two-edged sword. It may lead to prosocial action but also to emotional pain and a decrease in morale.

In Table 5.10, we note that among the predictors of self-esteem were perceived health, social responsibility, locus of control, empathy, and finances. In addition, as predicted, being a recipient of help was associated with lower self-esteem, whereas being a helper was associated with higher levels of self-esteem.

Path Analyses

The relationships among the variables included in the causal model presented in Figure 5.1 were analyzed next, by means of

Table 5.9 Predictors of Morale

Predictor Variable	R^2 Increment	Standardized Regression Coefficient	F to Enter or Remove
Perceived health	.28	.23	138.09***
Locus of control	.05	.68	29.52***
Empathy	.04	.26	24.24***
Social responsibility	.03	.55	16.70***
Helping	.01	.24	8.43**
Finances	.01	.62	4.17*

NOTE: The adjusted R^2 = .46. The order of entry for each variable was determined by the magnitude of the relevant zero-order correlation.
*$p < .05$; **$p < .01$; ***$p < .001$.

Table 5.10 Predictors of Self-Esteem

Predictor Variable	R^2 Increment	Standardized Regression Coefficient	F to Enter or Remove
Perceived health	.15	.44	63.94***
Social responsibility	.09	.10	142.57***
Locus of control	.09	.13	23.62***
Helping	.03	.45	15.36**
Finances	.02	.12	12.40***
Empathy	.01	.48	7.13***
Former help received	.01	.16	5.27*

NOTE: The adjusted R^2 = .35. The order of entry for each variable was determined by the magnitude of the relevant zero-order correlation.
*$p < .05$; **$p < .01$; ***$p < .001$.

multiple regression-based path analyses. In these analyses, the variables were viewed as links in a causal chain—using a technique originally designed as a means for assessing the plausibility of causal inferences from cross-sectional data (Blalock, 1971).

Our project was planned using a replication design, wherein the two subsamples of community-dwelling older persons, (a) those living in standard houses and apartments and (b) those living in senior citizens residences, served as two replicates. Hence we were able to perform path analyses on each of the separate subsamples, each comprising 200 individuals, and on the overall sample as well. In the analyses presented here, the measure of helping was the principal component derived from the factor analysis of the helping measures. Table 5.11 presents the path coefficients, significance levels, and R^2 values for the path analyses conducted—first on Subsample A, then on Subsample B, and finally on the overall sample of 400 elderly persons.

As the data in Table 5.11 indicate, support was derived for the central hypothesis of this investigation, that is, that helping would be linked to positive psychosocial outcomes for the elderly helper. Indeed, the most consistent finding across these analyses is that, as predicted, the direct effect of helping on the outcome variables is significant across all analyses, even after controlling for the relatively strong effect of health. Also notable is the magnitude of the R^2 values, demonstrating proportions of variance explained by our study variables ranging from .15 to .51.

As anticipated, for the total study population, significant predictors of helping behavior were age, health, certain motivational variables—empathy, social responsibility, and moral judgment—and two situational variables, opportunities to help and costs/risks of helping. Perceived costs of helping were positively related to helping, with those sensitive to costs or risks also emitting more helping responses; this is contrary to our prediction that those perceiving higher costs would help less. The relationships predicted between helping and one of the motivational variables, locus of control, were not obtained in this analysis. However, in separate analyses in which the predictors of helping in the separate domains were determined (i.e., helping of children, other family, neighbors, as volunteer), locus of control was found to be a significant predictor of help given to one's children but not of help proferred to others.

In addition to variations in predictors of helping in the diverse domains, differences were also perceived in regard to variables predictive of helping in Subsamples A and B. Both empathy and moral judgment predicted helping in Subsample B, the sample of older persons living in age-homogeneous senior residences, whereas none of the motivational variables predicted Subsample A helping.

In addition to findings in support of our initial predictions, certain findings were intriguing because they were unexpected and shed new light on facets of interpersonal functioning among

Table 5.11 Relationships Between Personal and Situational Variables, Helping, and Psychosocial Well-Being in Subsamples A and B and the Total Sample: Path Analysis

							Dependent Variables								
	Helping			Morale			Affect-Balance			Self-Esteem			Subjective Social Integration		
Independent Variables	A	B	Total	A	B	Total	A	B	Total	A	B	Total	A	B	Total
Socioeconomic status	.09	.10	.09	.06	-.02	.03	.06	.06	.06	.02	.04	-.02	.01	.02	.08
Age	.07	.08	.11*	.06	-.04	-.03	.09	.04	.04	.06	-.09	-.01	.10	-.01	-.01
Health	.18*	.23**	.13*	.27*	.41****	.39****	.21*	.23**	.20**	.12	.32****	.12*	.01	.14	.11
Finance	.09	.06	.06	.08	.11	.12	.16	.10	.16*	.13	.24**	.16**	.05	.04	.09
Empathy	.12	.23**	.16***	-.30****	-.28***	-.29***	-.19**	-.15*	-.18**	.02	-.07	.00	-.06	-.04	-.06
Social responsibility	.16	.08	.11*	.14	.06	.10*	.16*	.03	.09	.16**	.25***	.24***	.07	.16*	.09
Internal locus of control	.12	.05	.08	.10	.21**	.16**	.03	.30***	.16**	.07	.16*	.14**	.03	.20*	.09
Moral judgment	.11	.17*	.14**	.07	.08	.04	-.06	.05	-.01	.05	-.08	-.02	.03	.16*	.10
Opportunity to help	.17*	.20**	.17***	-.02	-.03	-.02	-.09	.04	-.01	-.03	.00	-.03	.10	-.07	-.02
Costs/risks of helping	.27***	.21**	.24****	-.16*	-.12	-.17**	.10	.04	.01	-.15*	-.11	-.13*	-.08	-.09	-.10
Help received from others	-.05	.04	-.01	-.04	.08	.02	.01	.07	.04	-.13	-.04	-.05	.04	.09	-.04
Helping				.17*	.17*	.17***	.18*	.26**	.21***	.23**	.22**	.21***	.28**	.31***	.24**
R²	.40***	.43***	.43***	.43***	.46***	.47***	.33	.40***	.33***	.40***	.51***	.44***	.15**	.33***	.21**

NOTE: Table entries are path coefficients (P) for A (N = 200 in own house, apartment), B (N = 200 in senior residence), and T (Total sample, N = 400).
*p < .05; **p < .01; ***p < .001; ****p < .0001.

187

the aged. Of interest, for example, is the finding that people who help more perceive higher costs of helping and that individuals reporting higher costs of helping also have significantly lower morale and self-esteem. When we combine this finding of our path analysis with qualitative data, there is some indication that people perceiving higher costs are currently being challenged by life events that may be perceived as threats to their well-being (e.g., decrements in strength and health) and that may particularly challenge them to cope by providing help to others (e.g., children of theirs are in dire need). Although aged persons in situations of that type may indeed help despite the costs, the same factors eliciting helping responses may also lead to decrements in morale and well-being. That is, recognition of their own difficulties in facing an important but demanding opportunity may adversely affect their perceptions in some cases. This set of relationships may well be important subjects for future investigation.

As noted above, the significance of empathy with the plight of others as a determinant of helping was predicted, but its negative impact on facets of psychosocial well-being was unanticipated. What this set of relationships well may indicate is that the sensitive, empathetic elderly may undergo considerable vicarious pain when exposed to situations in which helping is a natural response. In the younger years, one often feels that even when one is called upon to help others under highly stressful circumstances, one is vigorous enough to make a difference for the suffering other. However, it is possible that for the elderly person who has an altruistic orientation to others in which empathy is a salient factor, and who is aware of the dimensions of personal resources (e.g., health, strength, power), even the most ardent helping efforts may not have consequences as beneficial as they might have been during the younger years. Added to that is the fact that as one ages, one may be more frequently confronted with pain and suffering for which there is simply no ready cure—so that, for example, after years of helping a dying spouse in every way imaginable, death does occur. Special attention to the needs of such specially empathic individuals may indeed be warranted.

Helping and Volunteering in Late Life: The Results of an Experimental Intervention

In this chapter, we describe an experiment investigating the impact of an intervention that provided older adults with information about volunteer opportunities within their communities. We hypothesized that this intervention would lead to increased volunteering and helping and to concomitant enhancements of psychosocial well-being.

This study was planned as a natural elaboration and outgrowth of the survey research project presented in Chapter 5. Although the results of the survey research—based on the application of path analyses and hierarchical multiple regression analyses to cross-sectional data—generally supported our conceptual model (see Figure 5.1), further research with an experimental methodology was needed to clarify the direction of causation.

Of the types of helping domains that we have considered (family, friendship/neighborhood, wider community/volunteer), why the choice of volunteer activity in the current investigation? This choice was based, first of all, on our recognition of the importance of volunteering by this numerically expanding age group. Older adults are acutely needed now, particularly in the face of the dwindling of the younger corps of volunteers as larger numbers of women are employed outside of the home and as the high divorce rate impels both men and women to assume dual responsibilities—as both employed persons and caregivers (e.g., of children, especially in single-parent homes, and as caregivers to frail older parents).

Second, in addition to the community's need for older volunteers, participation in community volunteerism has the potential to be meaningful to and valuable for older adults, even more than for the often overcommitted younger individuals. To the extent that older adults are visibly supplying care to others in volunteer roles, their activities as caregivers may counteract the stereotype that all elderly persons are unilaterally care recipients.

A third factor prompting this study was the relative paucity of older adults participating in volunteer activities. Although respondents to our own surveys have indicated that helping others is a valued activity in which many older people engage, others have found that relatively few provide help within the context of voluntary service organizations (e.g., Harris & Associates, 1975). Those who do volunteer report that their helping fills a role vacuum (cf. Chambré, 1984) and that they are now helping more than they ever have, in response to the perceived need for their help within the context of voluntary service organizations. They report that as a result of responding to perceived helping opportunities, they feel that their lives are very meaningful and that they themselves are good and valuable individuals.

What, we may ask, can encourage volunteering at the outset? For the elderly whom we surveyed, perceived opportunities were an important determinant of helping behavior. Not surprisingly, the influence of perceived opportunities on helping was particularly salient for the volunteers. When help is needed by one's neighbor, friend, or family member, that need may become readily apparent through cues and transactions within the interpersonal domain. However, the need for volunteers to meet important societal needs is likely to be less apparent, particularly to elderly individuals no longer engaged in paid employment—or in other roles in which one routinely comes in contact with diverse requests for volunteers (e.g., appeals for blood donors in employment settings; cf. Foss, 1983). Indeed, a great many participants in our survey research, whose participation apparently sensitized them to this issue, have made requests for information about ways in which they could become involved in community helping activities.

The need to involve older persons in community service programs, both to take advantage of the competencies and skills of this often underutilized group and to help provide meaningful and constructive new roles for the aged, has been apparent for several years (Uhlenberg, 1979). In response, a variety of volunteer programs have been developed and funded through a national agency, ACTION; these include Foster Grandparents, the Retired Senior Volunteer Program, and Senior Companions. Furthermore, younger persons initiating small-business ventures may make use of talents available through the Senior Corps of Retired Executives. In the private sector, organizations such as the National Council on Aging and AARP/NRTA have sponsored diverse community programs for older persons. At the local level, hospitals, nursing homes, associations for persons with disabilities, and charitable organizations urgently need volunteers (Volunteer Action Center, 1986).

In general, those elderly individuals who do volunteer have many opportunities to be of service and are likely to feel particularly needed in the current climate (Cherry, Benest, Gates, & White, 1985).

Despite the existence of these opportunities, however, our own research indicates that many older persons are not fully aware of community service options. Although some individuals may take the initiative to seek out such opportunities, many do not have the skills to do so or even the awareness that such a search may be warranted. Hence a need may exist to provide information to older individuals about the full range of community helping opportunities available to them, in a maximally useful way.

The project that we conducted had three goals:

1. To evaluate the impact on helping behavior by fully informing elderly persons about volunteer opportunities, in contrast to not fully informing them.

The hypothesis was that because of the sensitization effect of exposure to information about helping, even experimental group participants not volunteering through formal agencies would give higher amounts of help in other domains (e.g., neighbor, family contexts), in comparison with subjects in the control group.

2. To investigate the impact on psychosocial well-being of self-reported helping.

The hypothesis was that individuals engaging in higher rates of helping would also manifest higher levels of well-being. This study was also designed to ascertain whether helping of different kinds—for example, volunteer activities versus helping one's friends or neighbors—differentially affects the indices of well-being.

3. To determine the best ways to inform older persons of volunteer activities.

In order to achieve this goal, we investigated the views of older respondents and also measured the impact of the intervention on their motivation to participate, on attempts to engage in new volunteer activities, and on their perceptions of the results of their attempts to volunteer.

A basic premise of the current research was that the provision of information about volunteer opportunities may result in an increase in helping behavior and that important benefits would then accrue not only to the recipient of services by the elderly but to the elderly helpers as well.

RESEARCH DESIGN

The study was designed to capitalize on the fact that we had already surveyed 400 elderly persons (see Chapter 5) to ascertain their helping and well-being and that the preponderance of these people were available and willing to participate in the proposed study.[1] Because of the availability of the "pretested" group, we were in an excellent position to employ the powerful Solomon Four-Group Design, which has the advantage of controlling for both internal and external validity (Campbell & Stanley, 1963). The design for this study was as follows:

Group 1	R	0_1	X	0_2
Group 2	R	0_3		0_4
Group 3	R		X	0_5
Group 4	R			0_6

where R refers to the randomization of elderly participants, 0 refers to the interview (pretest and/or posttest), and X refers to the intervention.

In this study, Groups 1 and 2 were randomly selected from the 400 individuals interviewed 4 years earlier in our prior study (i.e., pretested), as indicated in 0_1 and 0_3. Participants in Group 1 received the intervention and information about volunteering (X), and Group 2 did not; both groups were then interviewed subsequent to the intervention (0_2 and 0_4), as described below. Groups 3 and 4 were randomly chosen from the same population from which Groups 1 and 2 were selected and represented groups for which no "pretest" data existed. Group 3 received the intervention (X), and both groups were interviewed subsequent to the intervention period (0_5 and 0_6).

Because this design has an experimental and a control group, both of which were pretested (Groups 1 and 2), it permitted us to evaluate the effects of the intervention, and of subsequent helping, on psychosocial well-being. It has the potential, therefore, to make a powerful contribution to the literature on the effects of such altruistic inductions on psychosocial well-being (cf. Stewart & Smith, 1983). In our prior survey research projects, the elderly respondents made self-reports about perceived opportunities to help, helping, and well-being, and path analysis was employed to test a model regarding causal relationships among those variables; however, all of the data were collected at one time. Our findings based on applying path analysis to the cross-sectional data indicated that the model has a good degree of explanatory power. However, because neither longitudinal nor experimental components were included in that research, no definitive statement could be made about the direction of causation. Thus, for example, we had reasoned that although correlation between perceived opportunities and helping may imply that perceiving opportunities prompts helping, the converse may be true. People who are helpers may perceive helping opportunities more readily than nonhelpers (or create their own opportunities). By employing an experimental design, we felt that we would be in a better position to directly examine the effect of information about opportunities on helping and well-being. It would also be possible to ascertain changes in helpfulness subsequent to the intervention (in cases for which pretest data exist).

There were two purposes for including Groups 3 and 4 in the design. First, the use of four groups increases the power of the design. That is, through this design, the effect of X is replicated in four different fashions: $O_2 > O_1$, $O_2 > O_4$, $O_5 > O_6$, and $O_5 > O_3$. The actual instabilities of experimentation are such that if these comparisons are in agreement, the strength of the inference is greatly increased (Campbell & Stanley, 1963, p. 25).

A second purpose was to increase external validity, or generalizability. That is, if we had used the two-group design—and concluded that information about helping opportunities increases helping and well-being— then it could be argued that the observed set of relationships occurred only because the respondents had been sensitized to the role and importance of helping in the course of undergoing the pretest. However, it could further be argued that the intervention might not have a significant effect among those not so sensitized. Indeed it is the very evidence of interest invoked among participants in our survey research study that spurred the present application, that is, that many respondents questioned the interviewers about helping opportunities in their communities.

In sum, then, we chose to employ a Solomon Four-Group Design in this study in order to gain important advantages. First, we gained power. Second, we gained external generalizability. Thus if the main effect of the intervention were significant, and in the absence of a significant interaction with exposure to the pretest, we could have evidence that an intervention of this type may encourage helping by other older persons with similar demographic characteristics. Of course, the finding of a significant main or interactive effect of exposure to the pretest would have utility as well. Specifically, it would lead us to recommend to any volunteer action programs seeking older volunteers that their efforts may be more effective if they sensitize potential volunteers by employing pretests (or other sensitization strategies) before conveying information about opportunities to serve the needs of others.

METHOD

Sample

Participants consisted of 120 older adults who resided in the Detroit metropolitan area outside of institutional settings. Thirty of these people were assigned to each of the two pretest-posttest groups (i.e., Groups 1 and 2) in the four-group study design. These 60 were randomly selected from a list of 372 participants[2] in the survey research project presented in Chapter 5. All had agreed to participate prior to the initiation of the project.

Of the 28 people (7% of the prior sample of 400) unable or unwilling to participate, 5 had died since the completion of the survey, 4 had become too ill to seriously consider helping others, and 8 had moved and could not be located. Only 11 of the original 400 (3%) refused to participate in a second research project. Examination of the protocols of the 28 individuals unable or unwilling to participate revealed no systematic differences from the total sample with one exception. The average age of the 5 who died was higher than the average age of the current sample: 89 versus 77.6 years.

The additional 60 people who were assigned to the no-pretest groups (Groups 3 and 4) were selected from the Detroit metropolitan area in the same manner in which the 400 respondents were selected for the original survey research project.

Prior to choosing Groups 3 and 4, we first selected four communities in the Detroit area as sampling sites: Detroit, Southfield, Clawson, and Royal Oak. These communities were chosen because they provide an excellent cross section of demographic characteristics, ranging from urban to suburban profiles. As we noted in presenting the survey research project in Chapter 5, each of the four communities maintains a separate voter registration list. Our primary means for drawing the sample was to randomly select potential respondents from the separate voter registration lists maintained by each community, each of which contains information about the age and address of each voter. Furthermore, special cluster directories available through the telephone company permitted us to develop lists that excluded seniors living in institutional settings. Once the lists were compiled, we had the information necessary to call potential respondents and to ask our brief screening questions, which could later be supplemented with a face-to-face screening.

All respondents were chosen to fulfill certain criteria in common. In the initial study only individuals age 65 and older were included, so as to focus on persons of retirement age for whom helping roles outside of work situations would be particularly salient. We included 60 persons from that initial sample, all of whom were 68 years of age and older. Hence one criterion was that all respondents in the four experimental groups should be 68 years of age or older. In addition, only physically mobile persons (not homebound) were included, to allow for the possibility that helping may be given within the context of service organizations.

The overall study procedures encompassed three phases. Phase 1, the pretest phase, consisted of participation in the survey research project. In Phase 2, the intervention phase, respondents were exposed to the experimental treatment. In Phase 3, the posttest was administered. The following two sections describe the intervention and the posttest, respectively.

Phases of the Study

The Intervention Phase

The cooperation of respondents chosen through our random procedures was obtained by means of letters followed by telephone calls. As anticipated, the elderly persons contacted expressed interest in the project, and the great preponderance did, indeed, agree to participate.

The intervention was administered to each respondent in his or her home, when he or she was there alone. In a telephone contact prior to the intervention, a staff member obtained sufficient information to enable preparation of an individualized brochure, designed in accordance with demographic facets, interests, and educational and preretirement occupational characteristics of the individual. The staff member making the appointment arrived at the respondent's home carrying a card clearly identifying herself. Each respondent was first told, in a carefully standardized manner, that he or she was one of a group of older persons randomly selected to be given information about volunteer opportunities—designed as ways that community members of all ages can provide sorely needed help to other individuals and to charitable organizations.

Each participant heard a standardized message in which his or her help was solicited. This standardized means for soliciting help by elderly persons was based on research regarding ways in which verbalizations to potential benefactors can elicit helping responses (Midlarsky et al., 1973). Exhortations to the older respondent about the need for older community volunteers and helpers emphasized that because of pressing needs at this time, the help of every able older person is meaningful. By making such a statement, and by virtue of the fact that the interview was administered individually rather than in groups, we attempted to put into practice the empirical finding that focusing responsibility on the individual increases the probability of prosocial action (Krebs & Miller, 1985). Following the introductory remarks and verbal exhortations about helping, each older person was given information about prosocial volunteer opportunities. Information was given both verbally and in the form of the individually prepared brochure, which was read to and with the elderly respondents.

The individualized brochures were prepared with the help of personal information obtained from the individual during the initial telephone contact and also with the aid of volunteer guidebooks and extensive contacts with volunteer coordinators in the four communities chosen. Information in the brochures was very specific, containing names and telephone numbers of contact persons, types of persons and skills specifically being requested, the nature of the tasks and duties, why the help is needed, and what people are expected to benefit, as well as suggestions for transportation to the volunteer site(s). Illustrative examples were given of older men and women who had made a difference in the lives of others through their volunteer activities.

Each brochure had a printed cover, containing the title: "Expand Your Horizons: Volunteer Opportunities for Older Americans," followed by a standardized page of information, outlining the benefits of volunteering (headed: Older Adults: Helping Others Helps You, Too). The body of the brochure designed, for example, for a woman living in Royal Oak, Michigan, who was a school-teacher prior to retirement might have several pages of information about church organizations needing the help of a volunteer with her background (e.g., "Help needy children who have never had their own toys learn to play with the toys donated to them"; "Help potential donors decide on age-appropriate educational toys for children") and about volunteer opportunities with the Royal Oak Parks & Recreation Department ("Do you have some kind of recreational skill that you would be willing to teach others?" "Would you be willing to assist in a social program, or an arts and crafts workshop? . . . If you don't want to be so active, how about becoming a volunteer program coordinator?"). The former owner of a small retail business who resides in Detroit might be informed that "food and clothing donations are needed," and "people are needed to serve as clerks—or to train clerks—to distribute toys and food to needy people," both at a nearby shelter for the homeless. He might additionally read that "people are needed to help with fund raising for a local charity, maybe by approaching local businesses," and "young businessmen need your help. Will you share your experience and knowledge with them?"

Our original plan was to limit the intervention to a 35- to 60-minute session with each respondent. In the vast preponderance of cases (97%), however, because of the interest and curiosity of the respondents themselves, sessions required 75 to 90 minutes. After presentation of the intervention, each respondent was given the individualized brochure, a card with the name, address, and telephone number of the research center, and the name of a staff person who could be contacted with additional questions.

The Postintervention Phase

Six months after the experimental treatment (i.e., administered to Groups 1 and 3), the postintervention interview was conducted with all study respondents. This interview included, first of all, the measures employed in the prior survey research and described in Chapter 5 in the section on "The Variables and Their Measurement." In the current experiment, the postintervention measure queried all 120 respondents about helping in the past 6 months—

Table 6.1 Actual Time to Complete Each Measure

	Number of Minutes
Demographic information	6
Empathy	6
Locus of control	4
Social responsibility	2
Moral judgment	7
Altruistic orientation	2
Closed- and open-ended questions on helping behavior	22
Morale and positive affect	5
Self-esteem	6
Social integration/loneliness	4
Postintervention Questionnaire	18
Average length of interview	82

the period directly subsequent to the intervention (at least for participants in Groups 1 and 3, who received the intervention). Participants in Groups 1 and 3 were additionally interviewed with what we herein call the Postintervention Questionnaire. This questionnaire was not administered to participants in Groups 2 and 4, who did not experience the intervention. This measure, described below, inquired about reactions to the intervention. Average amounts of time for respondents to complete each measure—including the Postintervention Questionnaire—are given in Table 6.1.

In response to interview procedures, once respondents were contacted and agreed to be interviewed, an appointment was made to conduct the interviews in the respondents' own homes. Upon arriving at the home of a respondent, interviewers had the task of introducing themselves, showing their identification, and establishing a private place to conduct the interview. In setting up appointments, interviewers made it clear that only the respondent, and not other family members or friends, would be included in the interview situation.

Introductory remarks were then made in accordance with the informed consent procedures and included (a) who the interviewer was and whom she or he represented, and (b) what she or he was doing. It was important that respondents understand that they were part of a "random sample," and that the interview was anonymous. Major goals were to obtain consent that was truly informed and, when consent was given, to obtain and maintain rapport. Questions were asked in the exact order presented in the interview schedule, and every question specified was asked.

Before leaving the home of the respondent, each interviewer expressed appreciation for being permitted into the respondent's home. Each respondent was also presented at the end of the posttest with a small gift and a Certificate of Appreciation for his or her participation.

Postintervention Questionnaire

All respondents exposed to the experimental intervention were interviewed with the Postintervention Questionnaire. This instrument was designed to assess a variety of attitudes and perceptions about volunteer activities by the elderly and about the intervention used in this project to inform and motivate older persons to participate in volunteer activities. Each Likert-type item employed consisted of a stem followed by a 5-point scale. For each item, one attitude was represented by one of the extreme points, and its opposite was represented by the other extreme. Respondents answered by pointing to the one number of the five that best represented their attitude or feeling.

The items included in the postintervention measure resulted in six separate variables: satisfaction (with the intervention), importance (perceived importance of volunteering), motivation (perceived influence of the intervention on volunteer motivation), knowledge (perception that the intervention increased knowledge of opportunities), action (intervention resulted in concrete action taken), and contact (the intervention led to a contact by the respondent with a voluntary agency). The items and alphas for each of these indices appear in Table 6.2.

In addition to the inclusion of items that could be scaled and entered into quantitative analyses for the purpose of hypothesis testing, questions were also asked for an additional purpose. That is, numerous open- and closed-ended questions were asked to determine the respondents' suggestions and opinions about what aspects of an intervention of this type are most likely to engender satisfactory involvement in volunteering and helping activities.

Table 6.2 Indices of Intervention Efficacy Derived From the
Postintervention Interview

Satisfaction[a] (Alpha = .84)

How useful is it to tell older people about volunteer opportunities face-to-face
and in brochures, as in this study?

About the brochure that we left with you, how much did you like:

the size of the brochure?

the size of the print?

the pictures?

How interesting is the brochure?

How much did it remind you about volunteering?

How much did it remind you about helping in general?

Importance (Alpha = .90)

How much do you feel that volunteer activities help

society as a whole?[a]

your community?[a]

the volunteer himself or herself?[a]

How much do you feel that volunteering *by older adults* helps

society as a whole?[a]

your community?[a]

the volunteer himself or herself?[a]

How much do you feel that *your own participation* helps

society as a whole?[a]

your community?[a]

the volunteer himself or herself?[a]

After hearing about volunteer opportunities for older people, and seeing the
brochure, I felt more than ever that it is important that older people be
volunteers.[b]

I felt, more than ever, that it was important that I volunteer.[b]

Motivation (Alpha = .89)

Hearing the talk and seeing the brochure made me want to volunteer.[b]

After participating in this project, I want to volunteer more than I have in the
past.[b]

Knowledge (Alpha = .89)

The information presented to me increased my knowledge about volunteering.[b]

I feel that now I know a great deal about volunteer activities in my community.[b]

Action (Alpha = .91)

It made me do something about being a volunteer.[b]

It made me participate in new volunteer activities.[b]

Contact (Alpha = .88)

To what extent did you attempt to contact an agency, or agencies, listed in the
brochure?[a]

To what extent did you attempt to contact other volunteer agencies (not in the
brochure) since we spoke to you?[a]

a. Items were rated on a 5-point scale, from 1 = *not much at all* to 5 = *very much*.
b. Items were rated on a 5-point scale from 1 = *strongly disagree* to 5 = *strongly agree*.

RESULTS

Sample Characteristics

In the total sample of 120 respondents, the age range was from 68 to 104, with a mean of 80.5 and a standard deviation of 9 years. Close to three quarters (72.9%) were females, and 27.1% were male. About 80.5% were white, 15% were black, and 1.5% fell into neither category. Results of χ^2 analyses indicated that, as in our survey research study, there were no significant relationships between age, on the one hand, and sex, race, place of birth, occupation, education, or religion on the other.

The religious preference of 44.2% of the respondents was Protestant, 23.6% were Catholic, 19.7% were Jewish, and 13.5% did not fall into any of these three categories. In regard to marital status, the largest single group (59.9%) was widowed, 30.8% were married, 5.1% divorced, 1% separated, and 3.2% never married. The mean income was $15,900. The preponderance of respondents (74%) felt that their health was good or fair, 15% felt that it was excellent, and 11% felt that it was poor or very poor. In regard to place of residence, 52% lived in an age-homogeneous apartment complex for older persons, and 48% lived independently in age-heterogeneous settings. These results are summarized in Table 6.3, along with the demographic characteristics of the sample in the original survey research project.

As Table 6.3 indicates, the demographic characteristics of the current sample were quite comparable to those of the original sample, indicating that our sampling procedures were apparently efficacious. In addition, it appears that attrition was not a significant problem in regard to either size of the original group available for the project (93% of the original 400 were available) or characteristics of those who were available. Of course, differences occurred in mean age, with the current sample older, as planned. Variables correlated with age also showed expected changes. Hence the gap between the percentage of females and the percentage of males had widened still further, which is not surprising based on average life expectancies for the two sexes. However, all of our prior and current work indicates that sex is significantly associated

Table 6.3 Demographic Characteristics for the Current Sample in Comparison With the Original Survey Sample

	Original Sample N = 400	Current Sample N = 120
Age		
Range	64-110	68-104
Mean	77.6	80.5
SD	9 years	9 years
Sex		
Male	29.5%	27.1%
Female	70.5%	72.9%
Race		
White	82.5%	83.5%
Black	15.5%	15%
Other	2%	1.5%
Religion		
Protestant	44.5%	44.2%
Catholic	23.2%	23.6%
Jewish	19.3%	19.7%
Other	13.9%	13.5%
Income		
Mean	$15,600.00	$15,900.00
SD (in categories)	2.1	2.3
Marital status		
Married	34.7%	30.8%
Widowed	55.7%	59.9%
Divorced	4.7%	5.1%
Separated	1.7%	1.0%
Never married	3.2%	3.2%
General health		
Excellent	15.5%	15%
Good or fair	74.5%	74%
Poor or very poor	10%	11%
Residence type		
Age homogeneous	50%	52%
Age heterogeneous	50%	48%

with none of the personality or helping variables considered in this investigation. Also, as anticipated, there were fewer married individuals and more who were widowed.

Also of importance were the distributions of both demographic and personality characteristics across the four experimental groups. Among the demographic factors of particular interest were possible group differences in perceived health, as this variable is one that tends to be a significant predictor of both health and psychosocial well-being. Because all the personality variables included have been found to be significant predictors of helping, and most predict well-being, their variation across groups was critical. However, our analyses revealed that the four groups in our Solomon Four-Group Design differed neither in regard to the demographic nor in regard to the personality factors investigated here.

Reactions to the Intervention

Reactions to the intervention by the 60 participants who were exposed to it were generally positive. That is, 62.4% indicated that their knowledge increased much or very much, 83.6% agreed or strongly agreed that following the intervention they now know a great deal about volunteer opportunities for older adults, and 47.3% said that the intervention made them do something about volunteering. In addition, two thirds of the participants (66.5%) expressed the opinion that the preferred way to receive information about volunteer opportunities was the approach used in this study—face-to-face and in brochures.

A range of choices was given about other manners in which information about volunteering could be distributed—for example, in churches or synagogues, in apartment complexes, by mail, by telephone, on radio and television, on bulletin boards, in senior centers, or in the newspaper. The preferred locus for information dissemination by far (after the one used in this study) consisted of the context of the senior center. On the other hand, information received by mail, by telephone, or posted on bulletin boards was likely to be ignored or disregarded, according to our respondents: The frequency with which announcements of volunteer opportunities are posted on bulletin boards or disseminated by mail and by telephone points up the practical significance of this finding.

The brochures employed as part of the intervention included several distinguishable elements. These included stories about older helpers, detailed information about volunteer agencies, people in need of assistance, specific information about persons in need of assistance, specific information about contact persons and their telephone numbers, and diverse photographs. In addition, a large number of opportunities were depicted and described. Of these elements, the inclusion of highly specific information about agencies and how (particularly with whom) contact was to be made was cited by respondents as the most important and valuable facet of the brochure. This element was followed most closely by the provision of a large range of helping opportunities from which to choose.

Of the 60 persons receiving the intervention, 30 were in the pretest group, and 30 were in the no-pretest group. Of interest in the investigation was the question of whether the pretest sensitized respondents to the intervention, as reflected in their reactions to the intervention.

In order to determine whether pretesting did make a difference, a one-way multivariate analysis of variance (MANOVA) (pretest vs. no-pretest) was performed on the postintervention interview data. The dependent variables in this analysis were satisfaction (with the intervention), importance (perceived importance of volunteering), motive (perceived influence of the intervention on volunteer motivation), knowledge (intervention increased knowledge of opportunities), action (intervention made me do something), and contact (intervention resulted in contact with volunteer agencies). The MANOVA yielded a significant effect for pretesting, $F(7,53) = 2.18, p < .05$.

In order to examine these results with greater precision, univariate analyses of variance (ANOVAS) were performed. Significant effects were found for exposure to the pretest versus no exposure on three of the dependent variables: importance, $F(1,53) = 5.55, p < .05$; satisfaction, $F(1,53), p < .05$; and knowledge, $F(1,53) = 13.33, p < .001$.

Thus older persons who were exposed to the "pretest" prior to the intervention were apparently sensitized to the intervention in several ways. They reported significantly higher satisfaction with volunteering following the intervention and agreed significantly more that the intervention made them feel that volunteering is a critical activity, compared to those who were not exposed to the

Table 6.4 Intervention Efficacy: Cell Means and SDs for Significant
             Effects

Variable	Factor	Mean	SD
Importance	Pretest	48.93	6.99
	No pretest	44.56	5.95
Satisfaction	Pretest	30.76	4.64
	No pretest	27.47	5.56
Knowledge	Pretest	4.00	.76
	No pretest	3.00	1.19

pretest. The Motive factor, measuring perceived influence of the
intervention to increase volunteer motivation, approached significance as well, $F(1,53) = 3.79$, $p < .057$, as did Contact, measuring
perceived increases in the likelihood of contacting agencies, $F(1,53) =
3.33$, $p < .07$. Table 6.4 presents means and standard deviations for
the variables for which significance was obtained (importance,
satisfaction, and knowledge).

Effects of Primary Study Variables on Perceived Opportunity

In prior investigations, perceived opportunity to help or volunteer has emerged as a significant predictor of altruism in diverse
contexts. Hence an important goal of this study was to develop
and assess the effects of the intervention on perceived opportunity,
both in comparison with and in its interaction with prior exposure
to the in-depth pretest interview.

A 2×2 factorial analysis of variance (ANOVA) was performed,
wherein independent variables were intervention and pretest and
the dependent variable was perceived opportunity. Results of this
analysis are presented in Table 6.5. Perceived opportunity was
significantly affected by both the pretest, $p < .001$, and the intervention, $p < .01$. Etas squared calculated on the main effects
indicated that they accounted for 9% and 6%, respectively. The
interaction between the pretest and the intervention was significant as well, $p < .05$, accounting for 5% of the variance. Cell means
for the significant interactions are presented in Table 6.6.

Table 6.5 Summary of Analysis of Variance of Perceived Opportunity

Source	SS	df	MS	F	p	n^2
A. Pretest	45.89	1	45.89	13.74	.001	.09
B. Intervention	29.10	1	29.10	8.71	.01	.06
A × B	25.19	1	25.19	7.54	.01	.05
Error	387.65	116	3.34			
Total	489.11	119	4.11			

Table 6.6 Cell Means for the Significant Interactive Effect of Pretest × Intervention on Perceived Opportunity

	B1 No Intervention	B2 Intervention
A1 No pretest	6.15	6.19
A2 Pretest	6.46	8.40

NOTE: All means are based on $n = 30$.

Newman-Keuls revealed that the mean for the pretest/intervention group was significantly different from the means for the other three groups, $p < .01$. No other differences were statistically significant. Examination of the means reveals a multiplicative effect indicating that the intervention, albeit significantly affecting perceived opportunity taken alone, was significantly strengthened when respondents had been sensitized previously by the initial interview conducted 4 years earlier. A graph of the function appears in Figure 6.1.

Relationships Among Responses to the Intervention,
Perceived Opportunity, Helping, and Well-Being

Table 6.7 presents the correlations among six variables reflecting reactions to the intervention as well as the measures of perceived opportunity, four indices of helping, and an index of well-being.

Three of the measures of reactions to the intervention— Satisfaction, Importance, and Motive—are discussed above. Three others—

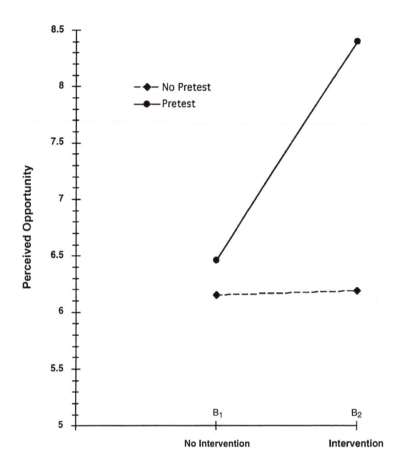

Figure 6.1 Graphic Representation of the Interactive Effect of Pretest – Intervention on Perceived Opportunity

Volunteer Resp. (the extent to which volunteer behavior was viewed as increasing following the intervention), Broch. Made Vol. (the extent to which the brochure is viewed as a cause of subsequent volunteering), and Reminded (the extent to which the brochure served to remind respondents to consider volunteering) all consisted of single-item indices derived from the postintervention questions.

Table 6.7 Intercorrelations Among Responses to the Intervention, Perceived Opportunity, Helping, and Well-Being

	1	2	3	4	5	6	7	8	9	10	11
1. Satisfaction with the intervention	.45****	.52****	.55****	.72****	.79****	.39***	.57****	.53****	.52****	.26*	.23*
2. Perceived importance of volunteering		.45****	.25*	.27*	.22*	.32*	.40***	.37**	.38***	.04	.38***
3. Motive			.59****	.58****	.54****	.44****	.45****	.43****	.42****	.02	.28*
4. Volunteer Resp.				.54****	.51****	.24*	.41***	.52****	.33***	.10	.13
5. Broch. Made Vol.					.92****	.28**	.39**	.44****	.40***	.07	.09
6. Reminded						.32*	.43****	.40***	.42***	.17	.08
7. Opportunity							.52****	.34****	.42****	.41****	.13
8. Helping (Princ. Comp.)								.65****	.80****	.51****	.46****
9. Volunteer									.43****	.23**	.29***
10. Neighbor										.51****	.32****
11. Totfam											.18*
12. Well-Being											

NOTE: Motive = perceived influence of the intervention on volunteer motivation; Volunteer Resp. = the extent to which volunteer behavior was viewed as increasing following the intervention; Broch. Made Vol. = the extent to which the brochure is viewed as a cause of subsequent volunteering; Reminded = the extent to which the brochure served to remind respondents to consider volunteering; Helping = the first principal component derived from several scales of helping behavior; Volunteer = degree of help given as a volunteer; Neighbor = help given to neighbors; and Totfam = help given to children and/or grandchildren, spouse, and any other family members.
*p < .05; **p < .01; ***p < .001; ****p < .0001.

Indices of helping consisted of the three subscales of the Domains of Helping measure discussed in Chapter 5—Volunteer (degree of help given as a volunteer), Neighbor (help given to neighbors), and Totfam (help given to children and/or grandchildren, spouse, and any other family members). Also included is the measure of helping consisting of the first principal component derived from several scales of helping behavior. This index of overall helping was represented by the first principal component, which accounted for 50% of the variance in helping in the present study.

In regard to psychosocial well-being, a principal component analysis of the measures employed here (i.e., of morale, affect, social integration, and self-esteem) resulted in a single-factor solution wherein the first factor accounted for 58.5% of the variance. The principal component of well-being emerging from that analysis was the index of well-being employed in the correlational analysis.

As examination of Table 6.7 indicates, the measures of reactions to the intervention were all significantly related to one another. The strongest associations were between Reminded and both Motive and Satisfaction. That is, respondents who said the brochure designed for them and left in their homes was the strongest reminder to volunteer also expressed the greatest degree of satisfaction with the intervention, $r = .79$, $p < .0001$, and were the most highly motivated to volunteer following the intervention, $r = .92$, $p < .0001$.

Each of the measures of reaction to the intervention was also significantly related to perceived opportunities to help, with the strongest relationships obtained between Opportunities on the one hand, and on the other, Satisfaction (with the intervention), $r = .39$, $p < .0001$, and Motive, $r = .44$, $p < .0001$. In regard to the latter, although the correlation is based on cross-sectional data, from a logical perspective it appears more likely that in this instance, the motive to help led to perceived opportunities rather than the converse.

All indices of reaction to the intervention were also related to the measures of helping. Those expressing the highest degree of satisfaction with the intervention were most likely to report the highest amount of helping overall, $r = .53$, $p < .0001$, to help in the context of volunteer agencies, $r = .53$, $p < .0001$, to help their neighbors, $r = .52$, $p < .0001$, and to a somewhat lesser degree, to help their families, $r = .23$, $p < .05$. None of the other variables assessing the intervention were significantly related to helping within the family domain, although all were significantly associated with both neighborly helping and volunteer participation.

All measures of helping were significantly related to well-being. However, the strongest relationships were obtained between well-being and the overall index of helping, the principal component, $p < .0001$, and both volunteering, $p < .001$, and neighborly help, $p < .0001$. The relationship to well-being of helping one's family was less strongly, albeit significantly, related to well-being, $p < .05$. Perceived opportunities to help (Opportunity), although significantly related to all measures of helping, were not significantly related to psychosocial well-being.

The Effects of Primary Study Variables on Helping and Volunteering

The analyses reported in this section were designed to determine whether elderly persons exposed to the experimental intervention, in which they were fully informed about volunteer opportunities, would be significantly more helpful than persons not so informed. In addition to assessing the effects of the intervention on subsequent helping, the design also permitted us to examine the effects of prior sensitization on helping through a pretest and of the interaction between the pretest and the intervention. We anticipated that because of the overall sensitization effect on helping opportunities by pretest, intervention, and their interaction, even experimental group participants who did not volunteer through formal agencies would give higher amounts of help in other domains (e.g., neighbor, family contexts) in comparison with participants in the control group.

In order to assess the effects of the experimental treatment on volunteering, we performed a 2 × 2 ANOVA. Independent variables in the analysis were pretest and intervention, and the dependent variable was the volunteering subscale of the domains of

Table 6.8 Cell Means for the Significant Interactive Effect of Pretest ×
Intervention on Overall Helping

	B1 *No Intervention*	B2 *Intervention*
A1 No pretest	−.53	.02
A2 Pretest	−.51	.97

NOTE: All means are based on $n = 30$.

helping measure ($\alpha = .89$). Results of the analysis revealed that there were significant main effects of the pretest, $F(1,116) = 4.53$, $p < .05$, $F(1,116) = 20.95$, $p < .0001$. Calculation of etas squared indicated that these effects explained 3% and 14% of the variance, respectively. As predicted, elderly persons who were pretested, $M = 20.87$, were significantly more likely to volunteer than were those who were not pretested, $M = 17.79$. Furthermore, those experiencing the intervention, $M = 22.38$, were significantly more likely to volunteer than those not experiencing it, $M = 16.04$. The interaction between pretest and intervention failed to reach significance.

A 2×2 ANOVA was next performed to determine the effects of pretest and intervention on overall or generalized helping, as measured by the helping principal component. Helping was significantly affected by both the pretest, $F(1,116) = 10.78$, $p < .01$, and the intervention, $F(1,116) = 43.78$, $p < .0001$. Etas squared indicated that the main effects accounted for 6% and 24% of the variance, respectively. There was a significant interaction between pretest and intervention as well, $F(1,116) = 9.30$, $p < .01$, which accounted for 5% of the variance. Cell means for the interaction are presented in Table 6.8.

Newman-Keuls calculated on the significant interaction indicated that the pretest/intervention mean was significantly greater than the means for the other three groups, $p < .01$. No other differences among the means were statistically significant. The functional form of the effect replicates the interactive effect of the same two independent variables on perceived opportunity (see Figure 6.1).

In order to further examine the differential effects of the independent variables on the diverse types of helping, a 2×2 (Pretest × Intervention) multivariate analysis of variance (MANOVA) was

Table 6.9 Effects of Experimental Variables on Helping Domains: Cell Means and SDs

Variable	Factor	Mean	SD
Child help	Pretest no		
	Intervention no	16.97	5.99
	Intervention yes	21.63	10.24
	Pretest yes		
	Intervention no	16.42	5.03
	Intervention yes	24.40	9.56
Family help	Pretest no		
	Intervention no	17.23	5.86
	Intervention yes	23.30	9.18
	Pretest yes		
	Intervention no	17.81	7.06
	Intervention yes	26.73	9.20
Volunteering	Pretest no		
	Intervention no	15.93	4.98
	Intervention yes	19.67	7.32
	Pretest yes		
	Intervention no	16.16	5.82
	Intervention yes	25.10	10.56
Neighbor help	Pretest no		
	Intervention no	17.63	6.10
	Intervention yes	22.87	8.87
	Pretest yes		
	Intervention no	16.24	4.41
	Intervention yes	29.27	7.00
Rushton et al. Scale	Pretest no		
	Intervention no	66.91	12.38
	Intervention yes	70.00	19.62
	Pretest yes		
	Intervention no	67.93	14.63
	Intervention yes	87.50	15.71

performed on the helping data. Dependent measures were scores on the self-reported helping of (a) children, (b) other family, and (c) neighbors as well as (d) volunteer helping. Also included as a dependent variable, for comparative purposes, was (e) our modification of the Self-Report Altruism Scale (Rushton et al., 1981), which taps normative helping, primarily of strangers and acquaintances. Cell means and SDs employed in this analysis are in Table 6.9.

The MANOVA revealed significant effects for the intervention, $F(5,116) = 14.77$, $p < .0001$, and for the pretest × intervention interaction, $F(5,116) = 2.26$, $p < .05$. The effect of the pretest variable approached significance, $F(5,116) = 2.13$, $p < .067$.

In order to inspect these findings, univariate ANOVAS were then conducted. In the ANOVAs in which the effects of the intervention on helping were investigated, significant effects were found on all five helping measures. Thus older persons exposed to the intervention, in contrast to those not exposed, reported increased helping of their children, $F(1,116) = 17.80$, $p < .0001$; family, $F(1,116) = 25.63$, $p < .0001$; neighbors, $F(1,116) = 51.91$, $p < .0001$; and helping as a volunteer, $F(1,116) = 20.58$, $p < .0001$. Generalized helping on the scale by Rushton et al. (1981) was significantly affected as well, $F(1,116) = 14.90$, $p < .001$. Etas squared for the significant main effects were, in ascending order of magnitude, generalized helping, .12; children, .14; volunteering, .16; family, .19; and helping of neighbors, .32. Hence, as predicted, the intervention employed in this study resulted in an augmentation of helping both in the context of voluntary agencies and in other domains.

Univariate analyses of variance investigating the pretest × intervention interaction indicated that this interaction affected generalized helping, $F(1,116) = 7.87$, $p < .01$, and the helping of neighbors, $F(1,116) = 9.46$, $p < .01$. Effects of volunteering approached significance, $F(1,116) = 3.46$, $p < .07$, and the effects of helping of children and other family members failed to reach significance. Etas squared for the significant effects indicated 8% of the variance explained for neighbor and 7% for generalized helping; the eta squared for volunteering was .03.

As reported above, the MANOVA results for the effect of the pretest on helping approached but failed to reach significance, $p < .067$. Nevertheless, univariate ANOVAs were performed to determine whether the pretest affected any of the individual domains of helping. Indeed, results indicated significant effects of the pretest on generalized helping, $F(1,116) = 9.95$, $p < .01$; volunteering, $F(1,116) = 4.09$, $p < .05$; and neighborly helping, $F(1,116) = 3.90$, $p < .05$. Etas squared for these effects were .08 for generalized helping, .04 for volunteering, and .03 for helping neighbors.

Effects of Primary Study Variables
on Psychosocial Well-Being

In developing the hypotheses for this investigation, we found no reason to predict, on an a priori basis, that either the administration of a pretest or the exposure to the intervention should directly affect well-being or its components. Instead, we anticipated that the independent variables—intervention and/or pretest—would affect helping, which would then have a direct effect upon well-being.

For the sake of thoroughness, however, we performed a MANOVA to determine the effects of the primary independent variables, intervention and pretest, on four of the measures of well-being described above: positive affect (affect-balance), loneliness (a component of subjective integration), self-esteem, and morale.

Results of the MANOVA indicated, as expected, that the effect on well-being of the pretest and the Pretest × Intervention interaction failed to reach significance. Contrary to prediction, the MANOVA revealed a significant effect for the interaction, $F(1,116) = 13.11$, $p < .0001$.

The univariate ANOVAs investigating the effect of the intervention on well-being yielded a significant effect only for Self-Esteem. The cell means and standard deviations for this effect are presented in Table 6.10.

As Table 6.10 reveals, persons exposed to the intervention manifested higher self-esteem on the posttest measure of self-esteem than did those not so exposed. Qualitative data, reflecting opinions expressed by the respondents, may shed some light on this finding. In the course of the intervention session, many of the respondents spontaneously expressed surprise and pleasure that "so much trouble" was taken to give them individually designed information about volunteering, face-to-face and in their own homes. They were assured, in a standardized way, that this intervention was developed precisely because volunteering and helping by elderly persons in general—and people just like them, in particular—was potentially so important in fulfilling societal needs. As feelings of usefulness appear to be an integral part of self-esteem (Rosenberg, 1965), then the reinforcement of perceptions

Table 6.10   Effects of Experimental Intervention on Self-Esteem: Cell
                 Means and SDs

Factor	Mean	SD
No intervention	24.21	2.08
Intervention	27.28	3.10

NOTE: Each mean is based on $N = 60$.

of oneself as useful, based on the very fact that the intervention
was offered, may have led to the observed effect.

Effects of Helping on Psychosocial Well-Being

Results of this investigation support the hypothesis that the
experimental treatment affects helping and volunteering, as does
pretesting. Furthermore, the intervention affected a component of
well-being—self-esteem. Another question that we asked was
whether helping affects psychosocial well-being. In particular, the
study design permitted determination of whether self-reported
helping of different types—for example, volunteer participation
versus helping of one's friends, neighbors, or family—differentially affects the separate indices of well-being.

In order to determine how the domains of helping and the facets
of well-being variables are related, we first calculated zero-order
correlations among them. These results appear in Table 6.11.

Hierarchical multiple regression analyses were then performed,
in each of which the order of entry was based on the magnitude
of each zero-order correlation between any individual variable
and the appropriate dependent variable. Regression analyses for
four dependent variables—positive affect (affect-balance), morale, self-esteem, and subjective social integration— are presented
in Tables 6.12 to 6.15.

As results depicted in Table 6.12 indicate, helping in all four
domains—child, family, neighbor, and the volunteer context—led
to significant increases in positive affect. Helping one's neighbors
was most strongly associated with current happiness. As Table

Table 6.11 Zero-Order Correlations Among Measures of Helping and Well-Being

	1	2	3	4	5	6	7	8
Helping variable								
1. Child								
2. Family	.67****							
3. Neighbor	.42****	.52****						
4. Member	.22**	.21**	.43****					
Well-being variable								
5. Positive affect								
(affect-balance)	.23**	.17*	.29***	.16*				
6. Morale	.17*	.05	.09	.22**	.67****			
7. Self-esteem	.18*	.18*	.43****	.45****	.25***	.42****		
8. Subjective social								
integration	−.03	−.02	.21	.30**	.43****	.43****	.41***	

$*p < .05$; $**p < .01$; $***p < .001$; $****p < .0001$.

Table 6.12 Predictors of Positive Affect

Predictor Variable	R^2 Increment	Standardized Regression Coefficient	F
Neighbor help	.08	.24	10.19**
Child help	.02	.19	6.12**
Family help	.00	−.09	4.26**
Volunteering	.00	.04	3.21*

NOTE: $R^2 = .10$.
$*p < .05$; $**p < .01$.

Table 6.13 Predictors of Morale

Predictor Variable	R^2 Increment	Standardized Regression Coefficient	F
Volunteering	.05	.21	5.89*
Child help	.02	.22	3.87*
Family help	.01	−.13	3.04*
Neighbor help	.00	−.02	2.27

NOTE: $R^2 = .08$.
$*p < .05$.

Table 6.14 Predictors of Self-Esteem

Predictor Variable	R^2 Increment	Standardized Regression Coefficient	F
Volunteering	.21	.33	29.41****
Neighbor help	.07	.31	21.19****
Family help	.00	−.05	14.14****

NOTE: $R^2 = .28$.
****$p < .0001$.

Table 6.15 Predictors of Subjective Social Integration

Predictor Variable	R^2 Increment	Standardized Regression Coefficient	F
Volunteering	.09	.26	5.27*
Child help	.01	−.09	2.91
Neighbor help	.02	.20	2.30
Family help	.01	−.11	1.80

NOTE: $R^2 = .12$.
*$p < .05$.

6.12 also shows, of the four domains of helping, volunteering had the lowest impact on affect.

The converse is true, however, when the impact of helping on the three other indices of well-being was considered. Examination of Tables 6.13, 6.14, and 6.15 shows that volunteering emerged as the strongest predictor of morale, self-esteem, and subjective social integration. Hence, as predicted, helping emerged in this study as a predictor of several indices of well-being. Of the types of helping considered, volunteering appears to have the most widespread and potent impact.

SUMMARY AND CONCLUSIONS

Results of this study indicated that individuals who are presented with information about volunteering in a face-to-face session and are left with a personalized brochure are more likely to become cognizant of helping opportunities than are those not receiving the intervention. Furthermore, those previously interviewed in-depth about their help giving (i.e., during the pretest) perceived more opportunities to help, both by virtue of the pretest and due to the interactive effect of the pretest and the intervention.

The two primary independent variables—pretest and intervention—also significantly affected overall helping and volunteering. Of the forms of helping being studied—family helping, child helping, neighborly helping, and volunteering—all were significantly increased as a result of exposure to the experimental intervention. However, volunteering had the most prevalent effects on psychosocial well-being. That is, whereas neighborly helping was the primary predictor of one index of well-being, current positive affect, volunteer behavior emerged as the primary predictor of morale, self-esteem, and subjective social integration.

This study also explored the attitudes and opinions of the elderly respondents both about what aspects of the current brochure were most satisfying and about what their preferences were in regard to interventions designed to increase volunteer behavior.

The preponderance of respondents in this study indicated that the intervention employed in the current work did a good job in augmenting their knowledge about opportunities. They stated that their preferred way to learn about volunteer opportunities is to have a face-to-face session in their homes and to receive a personalized brochure (as in the current investigation). Next in preference would be a group or individualized session within a senior center. Information received by mail and telephone or posted on a bulletin board was cited as most likely to be ignored or disregarded. Respondents noted that a brochure of the type used in our study can be very helpful. Specifically helpful aspects were the reminder value of the brochure (it tended to remind them, whenever they saw it, that their services to volunteer agencies were considered valuable) and the concrete information about agencies, contact persons, and telephone numbers.

When responses by study participants who were pretested were compared with those not pretested, the pretested individuals were more likely than those not pretested to express satisfaction with the intervention and to report that the intervention increased their knowledge about volunteer activities and augmented their view of volunteering as an important activity.

Results of this study indicate that interventions designed to increase volunteering and helping behavior may be effective, particularly when concrete information is provided in a face-to-face format, in combination with prosocial exhortations. Prior sensitization in a manner designed to provoke introspection about one's own prosocial behavior may also affect helping behavior, both by itself and in combination with the intervention. However, effects of the intervention were found to have a significant impact, even when no presensitization occurred. In addition, the effect of the intervention considerably outweighed that of the pretest. Another interesting finding is that when elderly persons received an intervention in which they were given personalized information and were left with an individually designed brochure, the intervention taken by itself led to significant increases in self-esteem. Apparently, respondents felt honored that so much trouble was taken to draw them into activities that could benefit others. One of the items on the widely used self-esteem scale by Rosenberg (1965) inquires about whether respondents "feel useless at times." A personalized intervention designed to woo elderly people into volunteering may be a mechanism for persuading them that society views their efforts as forming the basis for vital contributions.

NOTES

1. Although participation in the survey had occurred 4 years earlier, we characterize this survey as a pretest for two reasons. The first is that it prompted intense introspection about helping and well-being, according to informal self-reports by many (over 50%) of our respondents. Second, phone inquiries about the study by respondents throughout the intervening 4-year period attested to its continued salience.

2. Of the original sample of 400 persons, 372 agreed to participate. This constitutes a total of 93% agreeing, with a 7% attrition rate.

SEVEN

Conclusions and Implications

When asked what they would like to be remembered for, most people mention something beneficial to humanity. . . . Beethoven's music and Mill's humanitarian philosophy are expressions of that sentiment. The greater the benefit to the greater number of lives, the greater the significance to our own. —Irving Singer

It is one of the most beautiful compensations in life that no man can help another without helping himself. —Ralph Waldo Emerson

This book on helping by older adults began with the statement that it represents the union of two literatures that have heretofore been disparate—the literatures of altruism and of gerontology. As we complete the writing of this volume, the social and developmental psychologies of altruism (or *prosocial behavior*) still primarily focus on the early years of life, and the preponderance of gerontologists continue viewing older adults through the lenses of dependency, autonomy, and exchange theories. Nevertheless, a paradigm shift favoring investigations of meaningful behavior among older populations is becoming apparent. Practical realities, as well as the evolution of theories and new empirical findings, may well be prompting this shift. As a result, in this last decade of the 20th century and beyond, studies of helping in late life may have great pragmatic as well as theoretical significance.

Our goal in this final chapter is, first of all, to provide an overview of the evolution of theories in the field of social gerontology, emphasizing current thinking on personal meaning and its creation. Next, we briefly summarize our findings, and those of others, regarding late life helping and its outcomes. Finally, the implications of our contributory model of late life helping for policy, research, and practice will be discussed.

ALTRUISM AND PERSONAL MEANING

An historical overview of the literature of gerontology reveals that much of the early work was based on the debate over whether successful aging is associated with disengagement (and passivity) or, conversely, with activity. Maddox (1970), for example, argued that in order to maintain physical and psychological well-being, and to adapt to the many losses associated with aging, engagement with the world through activity is essential.

When activity failed to serve as a panacea, the spotlight shifted to the role of personal control. Control makes life feel more predictable, and when events can be predicted, they are less likely to evoke feelings of helplessness. Control reduces stress at the physiological level by diminishing reactions by the autonomic nervous system. In addition to having diminished physiological reactions to stress, people who believe that they have the power to control events may take action to enhance their lives and to avoid difficulties. They may also engage in health-promoting behaviors (e.g., moderate exercise), succeed in omitting unhealthy patterns (e.g., overeating, smoking), and obtain appropriate health care. Nevertheless, despite the enormous appeal of control theory, particularly in a society that promotes and values autonomy and individualism (Waterman, 1981), a growing number of investigators have found that internal control, like activity, is limited as a means for promoting successful aging (Karuza, Rabinowitz, & Zevon, 1986; Schulz, 1986; Wong & Sproule, 1984). In contrast to the original belief in "the more control the better" (Schulz, 1986), recent findings indicate that the extreme of internality may have negative ramifications for well-being.

In accordance with this finding, recent theories emphasize the need for flexible responding, in place of the assumption that people must always maintain control over their environments. Kahana and Kahana (1993), for example, have presented a model of preventive-corrective proactivity, in which successful aging is associated with the individual's ability to modify his or her behavior in response to changing internal and external conditions, such as losses and stresses. Similarly, Lawton's proactivity-docility model (1989), a revision of an earlier, ecological model (Lawton & Nahemow, 1973), portrays a mix of reactive (docile) and proactive behaviors.

Limitations on the capacity of any unidimensional theory to determine successful aging (disengagement, activity, personal control) have raised the possibility that there may be no single behavioral route to successful adaptation in later life. More important, perhaps, the imposition of values (e.g., the more control, or activity, the better) may be unwarranted (Aldwin, 1986). Aging is a personal matter, as are the derivation and attribution of meaning and value. Indeed, it may be argued that it is the derivation of personal meaning that may be a critical factor in late-life adaptation (Midlarsky & Kahana, 1986; Wong, 1989).

Definition of Personal Meaning

Many philosophers and literary figures have long been preoccupied with the definition and discovery of "the meaning of life." Indeed, part of our humanity may be our perpetual concern with questions of meaning (Singer, 1992).

For some, there is a unitary answer to all such questions. Tolstoy (1983), for example, found meaning in the simple life and faith in the Almighty, expressed best by the Russian peasants. For Mishima, the Japanese novelist, meaning inheres in beauty. On the other hand, questions about meaning have also been dismissed as extrascientific or unscientific by many 20th-century social scientists. Sigmund Freud, for example, wrote: "The moment that one inquires about the sense or value of life one is sick, since objectively, neither of them has any existence" (from Freud's late-life letter to

Marie Bonaparte, quoted in Jones, 1953-1957, p. 3). In contrast with
Freud, however, Frankl (1963) argued that there is indeed a meaning to be discovered, and Weisskopf-Joelson (1968) views this
meaning to be each individual's interpretation of life.

The Creation of Meaning in Life

However human the search for meaning, incessant preoccupation with metaphysical solutions to the puzzle of existence seems
to be associated with depression (Tolstoy, 1983) or with the after-
math of extreme stress or trauma (Frankl, 1963; Lifton, 1988).
However, one alternative to what may be an unending and often
futile search for an established, unambiguous purpose for human
existence is the decision to create meaning in life. Maddi (1970),
for example, wrote that each person must create his or her own
personal meaning. For those fortunate enough to have their fundamental survival needs met, it becomes possible to strive for
goals in accordance with their personal values.

Some may seek meaning in the contentment that results from
one's own gratifications or achievements. For others, pleasure is
associated with *il dolce far niente* (doing nothing). Still others search
for meaning in peak experiences of joy. Indeed, a favorite outcome
variable in gerontological studies (including those reported in this
volume) is personal happiness. In contrast to the focus on happiness as the solitary standard of value (George, 1981), one may
argue, as did Wittgenstein (1979), that a more appropriate standard of value is, in Dostoyevsky's words, "fulfilling the purpose of
existence" through the creation of meaning.

Involvement in tasks that are significant to us because of our
personal values results in the generation of personal meaning.
Thus some older people may choose to dedicate themselves to the
attainment of "successful aging" by engaging in pleasurable pursuits. Others, limited by physical disabilities or chronic illness,
may create meaning primarily through engaging in life review, the
conscious use of reminiscence. Still others may choose to be gain-
fully employed as long as they are able, to cultivate their creativity,
or to pursue philanthropic goals.

The pursuit of humanitarian, or philanthropic ideals, as noted above, supports a dedication to the welfare of others or to social causes and is likely to be based on an identification with others. The sense of shared humanity, common fate, and significance that the dedication to others represents may lead to compassion and concern with the welfare of the other. Also inherent in the recognition of the significance of other lives is the recognition that one's own life and life in general are significant. Particularly for older adults, for whom mortality is imminent, humanitarian concerns may, therefore, reflect a commitment to life itself.

HELPING IN LATER LIFE: EMPIRICAL RESULTS

A number of recent surveys have revealed a growing involvement by Americans in charitable donations and in helping and volunteering. Thus, for example, according to the 1990 Gallup Poll, there was a sharp increase in donations between 1987 and 1989, and many survey respondents indicated that they had given money to charity for the first time during the prior year (Independent Sector, 1990).

If developmental theorists are indeed correct (Midlarsky, 1994), then the motivation and capacity for altruism should increase with age. Results of studies presented in this volume and elsewhere provide support for the prediction of increases in humanitarian concern in later life (Herzog & House, 1991; Lowenthal et al., 1975; Schaie & Parham, 1976; Weiner & Graham, 1989). In our study entitled "The Generous Elderly" (Chapter 4 of this volume), the highest percentage (92%) of donors was in the 65- to 74-year age group. Significantly fewer of the oldest respondents (75+ years; 88%) donated than did those in the 65- to 74-year age group. However, more of the people in the oldest age groups donated than did any in the under-65 age groups.

The drop-off in amounts donated, in contrast to the numbers of people donating, was attributable in our research to the disproportionate monetary cost of donations experienced by the older adults, many of whom reportedly have barely enough money to cover the necessities of life (Kieffer, 1986). Still, according to the 1987 Gallup Poll (Independent Sector, 1988), among those worried about their future financial prospects, only older adults gave 2% or more of their annual income to charity. In our experiment on donation behavior (see Chapter 4), when financial barriers were removed, older adults were significantly more generous than were members of younger age cohorts.

In contrast to the findings from research on donations, the results of research on helping that requires expenditures of time and effort (rather than money) generally indicate that the relationship between age and helping is curvilinear, with the lowest amounts of help given by the young and the old (Herzog et al., 1989; Independent Sector, 1988). Although the age at which the drop-off in helping occurs has increased over time—from age 55 in the 1970s, to age 75 or older in recent surveys (Chambré, 1993)—nevertheless, a drop-off is reported, at least in studies of "volunteer" behavior.

Despite the relative consistency in studies reporting late-life decreases in helping, however, two questions may be raised. First, if we consider helping across all domains available to potential helpers, are there actual decreases in helping behavior? Second, if helping does, in fact, decrease in late life, then why does this decrease occur? Cessation or diminution in helping behavior because of decrements in personal resources such as health has a decidedly different implication than decrements based on a growing lack of interest in the plight of others.

The lack of clarity about the meaning of life-span trends in helping, reported in the national surveys, has several roots. To begin with, help giving falls into at least two categories—informal helping (e.g., giving to one's family, friends, neighbors, strangers), and formal helping (in the form of "volunteering," arranged through organizations). For the most part, studies of formal and informal helping are found in separate bodies of literature, each under the aegis of a different group of scholars (e.g., psychologists vs. sociologists) employing widely varying methodologies. In addition, studies that have been conducted on helping in later life focus primarily on formal helping, hence omitting from consideration the informal help provided by the elderly (or considering such help under a different rubric, such as "caregiving"; Midlarsky, 1994). Separately, as older adults may more frequently participate in informal modes of helping (see Chapter 5), studies limited to formal helping, or volunteering, may underreport the total number of older helpers and erroneously conclude that older adults are more likely to be "takers" than "givers." Such studies may also conclude that in lieu of volunteering, older adults are inactive or self-indulgent, ignoring the other forms of helping undertaken by older adults and the barriers that may exist to formal helping by this population (Chambré, 1987; Fischer & Schaffer, 1993).

Even when informal helping has not been excluded from community surveys (e.g., Independent Sector, 1986, 1988, 1990), questions about the nature and type of helping behavior have not been as detailed as necessary to account fully for the differences between formal and informal helping. In contrast to voluntary organization participation which, by its very nature, is clear regarding type and amount of help provided, informal helping is more subject to personal interpretation. For example, men surveyed in our research reported that they were "helpers" when they listened to their wives' troubles and ran household errands. Women, on the other hand, made no such attribution based upon help given to their spouses. Most reserved the term *helping* for intensive involvement in caregiving or for extrafamilial volunteering.

In our research, the preponderance of older adults interviewed in a survey of the Detroit metropolitan area portrayed helping others as a characteristic activity and one that was highly valued. Unlike studies that depict a curvilinear relationship between age and helping (Herzog et al., 1989; Independent Sector, 1988), our work found that when all types of helping and giving were considered, most people said that their help giving stayed the same as they aged or decreased slightly. In addition, 18% of the sample reported significant increases in the amount of help given in later years. Furthermore, the majority of subjects reporting decreases were among the "old-old" (85+) respondents and/or those citing multiple obstacles to helping—often relating to finances, serious illness, and the lack of adequate transportation.

The importance of factors such as finances, transportation, and illness as barriers to helping behavior is underscored by findings of the two experiments reported in Chapter 4. Thus, in the study on donation behavior, the removal of financial barriers changed the curvilinear relationship between age and generosity to a linear relationship. In a separate study on helping in emergencies, when financial and transportation barriers were removed, older adults were more likely to enroll in first aid classes than individuals in any of the other age groups.

Of additional significance is the nature of some older adults' responses to open-ended survey questions, in which many reported increases in helping in late life or were providing help for the first time (see Chapter 5). These resilient people stated that traumatic losses or the onset of frailty in their own lives spurred new or renewed helping. For example, a 75-year-old woman who was newly widowed reported that during a period of depression, with a concomitant sense of meaninglessness and alienation, she joined a bereavement group in order to "get on with" her life. Finding bereaved others who seemed even more upset and helpless than she, she spontaneously began to "help the (group) helper" by working with other group members. According to an 82-year-old widower, who had previously led "an entirely self-centered existence," his first response to losing both of his legs as a result of diabetes was to utterly give up hope. Tiring of self-pity at last, he "distracted" himself from his troubles by taking up painting and then social activism (through numerous letters to the editor). Despite of considerable success in both pursuits, he found that helping by "checking up" by telephone on frail older neighbors who lived alone "made more sense" than continuing to focus on his own achievements.

Still another obstacle to helping in later life is the perceived lack of opportunity to help others. Some unusual older persons, like those described in the above paragraph, may create their own opportunities. However, what about those who are less assertive or resourceful but who wish to help others nonetheless? Unlike younger people and employed people of any age, retired people are cut off from the information about volunteer opportunities that is frequently available in the workplace. Among those who telephone voluntary agencies on their own in order to offer help, many report that the initial assumption by agency staff is that they are calling to request help for themselves rather than to offer help.

Our research, as well as the research of others, suggests that one of the best predictors of helping is perceived competence which, in turn, is based on success (Midlarsky, 1971, 1984; Midlarsky & Kahana, 1985a, 1985b; Midlarsky & Midlarsky, 1973; Morrow-Howell & Mui, 1989). If initial attempts to help are misinterpreted or spurned, then the most probable result is that no further spontaneous helping attempts will be made.

When one considers the obstacles to helping encountered by older people, including the spurning and misinterpretation of help offers and the paucity of information available about volunteer opportunities, then it is not surprising that personal, word-of-mouth solicitation is a very effective way to recruit volunteers from this population. In the experiment reported in Chapter 6, for example, people exposed to a personal appeal to volunteer responded not only by helping but with increases in self-esteem. Older adults to whom an appeal for help was directed reported that they felt as if their help was needed and that it was expected to be effective (see Chapter 6).

Studies by other investigators indicate that voluntary agencies often use personal contacts to recruit volunteers (Morrow-Howell & Mui, 1989) and that personal contact is more effective than other recruitment strategies (Chambré, 1987). In a recent review of the literature, Piliavin and Charng (1990) found that personal requests are among the most powerful predictors of volunteering and, in fact, older nonvolunteers often respond to questions about their lack of participation by saying that no one asked for their help (Marriott Seniors Volunteerism Study, 1991; Midlarsky & Kahana, 1981).

Above all, results of our research program on helping in later life suggest that the giving of help is viewed as important and meaningful by older helpers. Helping is a mode of responding that results in positive self-conceptions and from which meaning is derived—particularly when it springs from intrinsic motivation, most notably the desire to be of service to others. Even when barriers to helping exist, the identification and removal of such barriers may lead to increases in helping and donating. When help is given by older adults, it may well be effective, both in aiding needy recipients and in helping to create meaning for its benefactors.

IMPLICATIONS OF LATE-LIFE HELPING
FOR POLICY, RESEARCH, AND PRACTICE

Recent years have witnessed welcome shifts away from stereotypes portraying the elderly as sick, dependent, and useless to
society, both in the professional literature and in the media. Ironi-
cally, however, the negative but often compassionate stereotypes
that portray older adults as constantly in need of assistance (Carver
& del la Garza, 1984) have been replaced by somewhat more
negative stereotypes of the aged as affluent, independent, and
often greedy. These more recent stereotypes have emerged from
political concerns about intergenerational equity and, in particular, about the fu
    nding of entitlements for the old at the expense of the young.

In the social redefinition from passive to active, the *elderly have*
been increasingly depicted in the media not as *having* a problem
but as *being* the problem. Notions about today's "well and resourceful" elderly have not translated into altruistic and helpful
images. Rather, the elderly have often been viewed as selfish and
uninterested in giving to others while, at the same time, draining
society's limited resources. In addition, older people are viewed
as constituting a self-interest group that often demands fulfillment
at the expense of other groups in society. Social policy initiatives
have moved first from demanding resources for the elderly to,
more recently, placing constraints upon entitlements for the elderly. In fact, funding of the Clinton health care reform package is
predicated on cuts in Medicare spending. In the intergenerational
equity debate, it has been demanded that the old must "give
back" to society by relinquishing entitlements such as Medicare
and Social Security, so that these funds can be redistributed to the
young.

A vivid counterpoint to images of selfish aging can be found by
examining the contributions older persons make to their families
and communities (Sainer & Zander, 1971). The fact that older
adults receive entitlements need not be seen as detracting from
other helping behaviors. These two separate aspects of life in the
later years can be reconciled when we consider that some entitlements may function to enhance the health, independence, and

financial well-being of the elderly, thus facilitating their ability to make contributions to the community. Even as older adults continue to gain political power and protect their right to remain in the workforce, an anticipated misuse of power has not materialized among this population. In fact, further demonstrating their humanitarian values, older adults involved in political action groups have taken an interest in the welfare of all generations (Butler, Lewis, & Sunderland, 1990).

Social and political meanings of successful aging which involve helping and contributory roles for older adults have important implications for our aging society. Hudson (1987) argues that exposure to older adults as potential providers, rather than recipients of aid, will lead to new social expectations of this group, translating into new images of older consumers as purchasers of goods for other family members and potential donors to charities. Recognition of older adults as "givers" rather than "takers" in social exchanges also has notable implications for public policy. Replacing more negative, traditional stereotypes with compassionate stereotypes of aging (Binstock, Chow, & Schulz, 1982) could result in a greater understanding of diversity in late life. Thus some segments of the older population would be clearly recognized as being in need of support and assistance programs, whereas others would be seen as able to participate actively in caring for others.

Demographic trends within American society may also shape the characteristics of older cohorts in ways that could engender helping behaviors. Increased health and longevity of older cohorts provides a constituency of potential helpers with time, personal resources, and stamina to support helping roles (Chambré, 1987; Morrison, 1986). Social policies and societal expectations may act in synchrony with the growing proportion of older adults to establish a fertile environment for the emergence of the older helper as a norm.

Research Implications

The lagging societal appreciation of contributions by the elderly is not only reflected in public perception and attitudes but also permeates the research community. Consistent with the societal emphasis placed on funding that addresses the problems and vulnerabilities of older adults, there has been a notable absence of research on productive, generative, and altruistic behaviors in late life. This absence is illustrated by the paucity of research relating to several important areas involving contributions by the elderly. By encouraging researchers to turn their attention to these contributions, new and fertile areas for inquiry in the social sciences can be explored.

Heightening research interest in late-life helping will result in increasingly sophisticated conceptualizations and operationalizations of research on late-life helping. The studies reported in this book represent an initial, systematic effort toward investigating the nature and antecedents of late-life helping. Having presented some empirically-based insights about helping and altruism among the elderly, we recognize that many questions remain. Indeed, because of the newness of this domain of inquiry, there are as yet far more questions than empirically-based responses.

Assistance provided by older adults to their children and grandchildren exemplifies a neglected area of research among gerontologists. Although there is extensive documentation of social supports received by the elderly (Antonucci, 1990; Sauer & Coward, 1985), there is little documentation of the extensive aid flowing from older parents to younger family members (Butler et al., 1990). Another understudied area is the provision of informational support by older to younger adults. In a society wherein advice given by parents and grandparents is frowned upon, the elderly often note that they feel disenfranchised by their families since "no one asks my opinion about anything anymore." There is great potential for the study of imparting wisdom and values from older to younger people. Research on intergenerational communication may hold an important key to understanding factors which impede the utilization of the elderly's helping potential as well as the intergenerational transmission of values (Bengtson & Black, 1973).

For researchers concerned with altruism and helping behavior, the finding that help-giving is a characteristic activity in old age may provide a foundation for the much-needed shift from laboratory to field-based research. Findings about apparent increases in altruistic motivation in late life may provide an initial empirical basis for research on life-span moral development in the cognitive, affective, and behavioral domains. Research suggesting high rates of helping even under conditions of stress may spur efforts to untie what currently appears to be a Gordian knot of relationships between stress and helping in late life. The most fundamental questions, including who, among the elderly, provides help, in what contexts, and why, still remain to be empirically addressed. Questions about the nature and magnitude of the costs versus the benefits received, by both the older helpers and help recipients, are also fruitful areas for future research.

Practice and Policy Implications

A better understanding of altruism and helping in late life will not only inform the research community but may also provide some useful guidelines for practice and policy. The mobilization of helping skills and motivations among older adults presupposes an acknowledgment by the health, social service, and mental health establishments that the desire to help others remains an enduring value throughout life. It presupposes altering societal views to embrace a broader understanding of well-being, wherein helpers receive a benefit intrinsic to meaningful, value-congruent involvement in the welfare of others. In addition, it requires that practitioners make a fundamental shift from their perception of older adults as passive clients whose "cases must be managed" to active, resourceful human beings who can teach the service establishment about creative avenues for helping others.

We will first address considerations for practice that relate to older individuals and then turn to policy issues relevant to older cohorts in society. Recognition of the contributory roles of elders through research focusing on giving as well as receiving leads to a major reconsideration of one of the most widely studied transactions in gerontology: that of caregiving. We will illustrate some of the reconceptualizations of this field that are likely to affect programs and treatment efforts for chronically ill elders and their caregivers. We will then turn to a critical area of programming for

older adults—that of volunteering—in our discussion of practice
implications of contributions by the elderly.

Caregiving/Carereceiving

One area of research in which helping behaviors among the elderly
have been extensively examined is within the realm of caregiving.
A normative helping role for older adults is that of caregiver to a
chronically (or acutely) ill spouse or family member. The pressure
to assume the caregiving role within the family structure is a
powerful one, often resulting in a high cost to the helper.

Research by gerontologists has typically focused on the burdens
and adverse physical and psychological effects of caregiving
(Chiriboga, Weiler, & Nielson, 1990). For this reason, older adults
caring for spouses with chronic illness have been depicted as
paying a high price for rendering aid; social life and physical and
mental health have been found to suffer (Kahana, Young, Kercher,
& Kaczinsky, 1993). Therefore, it is not surprising that recommen-
dations for assisting older caregivers have focused on respite
programs designed to temporarily relieve the caregivers of their
"burden" and support groups wherein caregivers could share
their problems with others in similar situations (Biegel, 1994).

On an individual level, psychotherapeutic efforts have also
centered on the management of caregiver burden. Limited social
and personal resources among older caregivers can become over-
taxed by the caregiving role and may, in some cases, serve as a
deterrent to engaging in helping behaviors within the community
context. The competing aspects of family and community-oriented
helping are demonstrated in data suggesting more limited involvement in volunteering and community-bound helping among
the married versus the widowed elderly (Biegel, 1994). There are
also positive consequences of helping for older caregivers and,
increasingly, attention is being focused on the uplifts received and
satisfaction derived from caregiving (Kinney & Stephens, 1989).
Caregiving activities may reinforce the feeling of being needed
and provide a sense of meaningfulness for older persons who
espouse and act on altruistic values.

Whereas the caregiver is often depicted as a burdened victim of obligatory helping, the carereceiver is also narrowly defined in gerontological literature. According to research on Alzheimer's disease sufferers and their caregivers, the carereceiver is generally depicted as a passive recipient of aid. There is very little acknowledgement of active involvement or the potential for the carereceiver to contribute to the household and/or provide assistance to the caregiver. The common reference to the carereceiver as the "patient" further serves to reduce the evaluation of a dyadic relationship to a unidirectional active-passive exchange of help. However, the benefits of helping received by the caregiver and the therapeutic aspects of helping potential for the carereceivers are also worth noting (Midlarsky, 1994).

Even frail elderly receiving care have a great deal to offer within the framework of family relationships. They are likely to make both instrumental contributions to the household and provide critical affirmational or affective support to their caregivers. It is not uncommon for a physically frail spouse to answer the phones, pay the bills, and conduct the family correspondence. In addition, affective support expressed by the carereceiver can play an important role in the maintenance of the caregiver's psychological well-being. This support, given by the carereceiver, can serve as a critical buffer against the stresses of caregiving, and it may affect psychological outcomes for the caregiver as well as the carereceiver (Biegel, 1994).

It is useful to recognize that "catastrophic" caregiving relationships, wherein a spouse has a severe and incapacitating illness, such as a stroke or Alzheimer's disease, are less common than dyadic situations, wherein both members of the couple alternatively provide and receive care. A more likely scenario is one in which a wife, who has previously suffered a heart attack, is driven to the doctor by her husband while, the next day, she provides assistance to him for his chronic arthritis.

To the extent that the carereceiver's opportunities for contributing to the household and the relationship are reinforced, a sense of control and reestablishment of normalcy in the lives of both the caregiver and carereceiver become possible. Building up perceived competence and self-efficacy by acknowledging the benefits of giving for the caregiver may be a highly effective alternative for practice with older caregivers. Practitioners can further encourage and foster helping by the carereceiver in their efforts to enhance the well-being of both members of the caregiving/carereceiving dyad.

Volunteering

A second area of practice and policy in which helping roles and behaviors of the elderly have major implications is in the realm of volunteering in a community context. In addition to benefits to the older volunteer, there are clear benefits to society. With an increase in highly skilled and educated individuals in the older cohorts, the volunteer potential among this group represents an ever expanding resource. In addition, the maintenance of relatively good health well into old age results in a vigorous and fit group of older volunteers.

Intergenerational programs represent a particularly promising area for such volunteer efforts. Whereas the past emphasis in such programs has been on visitation by children of frail elders in nursing homes, more recently the potential for older volunteers to provide child care, to make educational contributions, and to act as role models for youth has also been documented. Volunteer opportunities in which mutual helping is coordinated constitute a promising area for development. Innovative volunteer programs may match college students with bilingual (ethnic) older adults willing to provide language instruction and opportunities for the students to converse in their native tongue. One successful and sophisticated volunteer program (Ehrlich, 1979a, 1979b) promoted an organized, community-based mutual helping network for older adults. In the framework of this program, participants bartered needed services, ranging from home health care to transportation and home repair services. Because assistance was provided to neighbors, participants not only had an investment in helping familiar persons but could also readily assess both the need for help and the benefits for those being provided with assistance. Presumably as a result of these factors, it was found that participants provided far more aid than required by their official involvement in the program.

The value of creating meaningful and effective volunteer opportunities for older adults has been widely recognized and should not be underestimated. Nevertheless, such programs have not been systematically implemented as public policy initiatives. Instead, there have been only scattered grassroots volunteer programs for older adults sponsored by church groups, charitable organizations, and specific communities. An important goal for organizers of volunteer programs relates to older adults recognizing, and even seeing first hand, how their volunteer activities may benefit others. To the extent that a volunteer program fulfills the desire of older volunteers to help in ways that truly benefit others, success is likely to be enhanced. On the other hand, where older volunteers are treated in a patronizing manner, or where it is clear that they are clients of a service that provides them with perfunctory or "make work" activities, emotional benefits are far less likely to be evident. The older adult stuffing envelopes for a social event is less likely to feel fulfilled than one doing home repairs for a neighbor who will visibly benefit from these efforts.

Findings of our research reported in this book underscore the value of informing volunteers about the need for help and the opportunities for helping, and, matching the helping activities to both the resources and values of program participants. A further implication of research data relates to removing unnecessary situational constraints and costs related to volunteer activities by improving access to volunteer opportunities and reducing some of the physical demands that may be too difficult for elders to meet.

The need for contributions of elderly volunteers, as well as the utilization of the volunteer potential of older people, is likely to be affected by public policies. Specifically, the need for volunteer involvement and provisions of informal aid may rise as there is a decline in government expenditures on social welfare. The Social Security Administration reports that during the 1980s, there was a decrease in social welfare spending from 54.3% to 47.7% of total government spending. The Reagan years witnessed simultaneous declines in welfare spending and calls for greater volunteerism,

particularly among the elderly, as government-sponsored programs established in the 1960s and 1970s, including the Retired
Citizens Volunteer Program, and the Foster Grandparent and
Senior Companionship Programs, fell by the wayside. In 1985 the
publication of *Prime Time*, an official newspaper focusing on volunteer programs for older adults, came to a halt due to funding
cuts. At the same time organizations representing older adults,
such as the American Association of Retired Persons (AARP) and
the Grey Panthers, called for volunteer initiatives on the grassroots
level, arguing that self-initiated and citizen-sponsored volunteer
activities will enhance the quality of life for older Americans. As
such, to the extent that the expectations and opportunities regarding helping roles for the elderly are limited, society allows a
valuable resource to remain dormant (Turner, 1992).

Many older adults desiring to provide aid to others have resources,
skills, and, additionally, the time to give. Systematic efforts to
foster volunteering may yield benefits to the older volunteers, the
beneficiaries of the programs, and society at large.

CONCLUDING REMARKS

We began our volume with a quote from Psalm 92 about the
human potential to be vital and productive well into old age. We
return to the view embedded in this quote in our concluding
remarks. A consideration of altruistic activities in late life opens
up a window through which one can access the "fountain of age"
(Friedan, 1993). Those who want to give, have something to give,
and are empowered by the compassion, sense of competence, and
personal meaning that comes along with giving can, within this
model, remain "full of sap and freshness" to the end of their days.

References

Abeles, R. P., & Ory, M. G. (1991). *ICPSR Bulletin*, 1-5.

Adamchak, D. J., & Friedmann, E. A. (1983). Societal aging and generational dependency relationships: Problems of measurement and conceptualization. *Research on Aging, 5*, 319-338.

Adams, B. N. (1968). *Kinship in an urban setting.* Chicago: Markham.

Adler, A. (1964). *Social interest: A challenge to mankind.* New York: Capricorn.

Akiyama, H., & Antonucci, T. C. (1986, November). *Sex differences in social support among older adults.* Paper presented at the meeting of The Gerontological Society of America, Chicago.

Aldwin, C. (1986). What is successful aging? *Adult Development and Aging News, 13,* 4-5.

Allen, N., & Rushton, J. P. (1983). The personality of community volunteers. *Journal of Voluntary Action Research, 12,* 36-49.

Allport, G. W. (1954). The historical background of modern social psychology. In G. Lindzey (Ed.), *Handbook of social psychology* (Vol. 1, pp. 3-56). Cambridge, MA: Addison-Wesley.

Allport, G. W. (1961). *Pattern and growth in personality.* New York: Holt, Rinehart & Winston.

Antonucci, T. (1990). Social supports and social relationships. In R. H. Binstock & L. K. George (Eds.), *Handbook of aging and the social sciences.* New York: Academic Press.

Antonucci, T., & Akiyama, H. (1987). Social networks in adult life and a preliminary examination of the Convoy model. *Journal of Gerontology, 42,* 519-527.

Ardrey, R. (1962). *African genesis.* New York: Atheneum.

Aristotle. (1962). *The politics* (E. Barker, Ed. & Trans.). New York: Oxford University.

Aronfreed, J. (1968). *Conduct and conscience.* New York: Academic Press.

Aronfreed, J. (1969). The concept of internalization. In D. A. Goslin (Ed.), *Handbook of socialization theory and research* (pp. 263-323). Chicago: Rand McNally.

Arrow, K. (1979). Values and collective decision making. In F. Hahn & M. Hollis (Eds.), *Philosophy and economic theory* (pp. 110-126). New York: Oxford University Press.

Atkinson, R. (1985). *Meaning in old age: Parts of a life linked together.* Paper presented at the meeting of the International Congress of Gerontology, New York.

239

Aubrey, J. (1898). *Brief lives* (A. Clark, Ed.). Oxford: Clarendon.

Austin, W. G., & Worchel, S. (Eds.). (1979). *The social psychology of intergroup relations.* Monterey, CA: Brooks/Cole.

Avorn, J., & Langer, E. (1982). Induced disability in nursing home patients: A controlled study trial. *Journal of the American Geriatrics Society, 30,* 397-400.

Babic, A. L. (1972). The older volunteer: Expectations and satisfactions. *The Gerontologist, 24,* 292-298.

Back, S. H. (1982). Adjustment to and satisfaction with retirement. *Journal of Gerontology, 37*(5), 616-624.

Baldwin, J. O., & Baldwin, J. I. (1981). *Beyond sociobiology.* New York: Elsevier.

Baltes, M. (1988). The etiology and maintenance of dependency in the elderly. *Behavior Therapy, 19,* 301-319.

Baltes, M., Hann, S., Barton, E., Orzech, M., & Lago, D. (1983). On the social ecology of dependency and independence in elderly nursing home residents. *Journal of Gerontology, 38,* 556-564.

Baltes, P. B., & Labouvie, G. V. (1973). Adult development of intellectual performance. In C. Eisdorfer & M. P. Lawton (Eds.), *The psychology of adult development and aging* (pp. 157-219). Washington, DC: American Psychological Association.

Baltes, P. B., & Willis, S. L. (1977). Toward psychological theories of aging & development. In J. E. Birren & K. W. Schaie (Eds.), *Handbook of the psychology of aging* (pp. 128-154). New York: Van Nostrand Reinhold.

Barnett, M., King, L., & Howard, J. (1979). Inducing affect about self or other. *Developmental Psychology, 15,* 164-167.

Bar-Tal, D. (1976). *Prosocial behavior: Theory and research.* Washington, DC: Hemisphere.

Bar-Tal, D., & Raviv, A. (1982). A cognitive-learning model of helping behavior development. In N. Eisenberg (Ed.), *The development of prosocial behavior* (pp. 199-217). New York: Academic Press.

Bar-Tal, D., Raviv, A., & Leiser, T. (1980). The development of altruistic behavior. *Developmental Psychology, 16,* 516-524.

Barton, E., Baltes, M., & Orzech, M. (1980). Etiology of dependence in older nursing home residents during morning care. *Journal of Personality and Social Psychology, 38,* 423-431.

Batson, C. D., Duncan, B., Ackerman, P., Buckley, T., & Birch, K. (1981). Is empathetic emotion a source of altruistic motivation? *Journal of Personality and Social Psychology, 50,* 212-220.

Batson, C. D., Duncan, B., Ackerman, P., Buckley, T., & Birch, K. (1981). Is empathetic emotion a source of altruistic personality? *Journal of Personality and Social Psychology, 50,* 212-220.

Baumann, D. J., Cialdini, R. B., & Kenrick, D. T. (1983). Mood and sex differences in the development of altruism as hedonism. *Academic Psychology Bulletin, 5,* 299-307.

Becker, E. (1975). *Escape from evil.* New York: Free Press.

Bengston, V. L., & Black, K. D. (1973). Intergenerational relations and continuities in socialization. In P. Baltes & K. W. Schaie (Eds.). *Life-span developmental psychology: Personality and socialization.* New York: Van Nostrand Reinhold.

Benton, A. L., Eslinger, P. J., & Damasio, A. R. (1981). Normative observations on neuropsychological test performances in old age. *Journal of Clinical Neuropsychology, 3,* 33-42.

Berkowitz, L., & Daniels, L. (1967). Responsibility and dependency. *Journal of Abnormal and Social Psychology, 5*, 217-225.

Berkowitz, L., & Lutterman, K. (1968). The traditionally socially responsible personality. *Public Opinion Quarterly, 37*, 169-185.

Biegel, D. (1984). *Building support networks for the elderly: Theory and applications.* Beverly Hills, CA: Sage.

Biegel, D. (1994). Effectiveness of interventions for caregivers. In E. Kahana, D. Biegel, & M. Wykle (Eds.), *Caregiving across the life span.* Newbury Park, CA: Sage.

Binstock, R. H., Chow, W. S., & Schulz, J. H. (Eds.). (1982). *Internal perspectives on aging: Populations and policy challenges.* New York: United Nations Fund for Population Activities.

Blalock, H. M., Jr. (1971). *Causal models in the social sciences.* Chicago: Aldine Atherton.

Blau, P. M. (1964). *Exchange and power in social life.* New York: John Wiley.

Blau, Z. (1973). *Old age in a changing society.* New York: New Viewpoints.

Boulding, K. (1981). *A preface to grants economics.* New York: Praeger.

Brabeck, M. (1989). *Who cares?* New York: Praeger.

Bradburn, N. M. (1969). *The structure of psychological well-being.* Chicago: Aldine Atherton.

Bray, D. W., & Howard, A. (1983). The AT&T longitudinal studies of managers. In K. W. Schaie (Ed.), *Longitudinal studies of adult psychological development* (pp. 266-312). New York: Guilford.

Brehm, J. (1966). *A theory of psychological reactance.* New York: Academic Press.

Brickman, P., Rabinowitz, V. C., Karuza, J., Jr., Coates, D., Cohn, E., & Kidder, L. (1982). Models of helping and coping. *American Psychologist, 37*, 368-384.

Brody, E. (1977). Environmental factors in dependency. In A. Exton-Smith &. J. Evans (Eds.), *Care of the elderly: Meeting the challenge of dependency* (pp. 81-95). New York: Academic Press.

Brody, E. (1985). Parent care as a normative family stress. *The Gerontologist, 25*, 19-29.

Bromberg, E. M. (1983). Mother-daughter relationships in later life: The effect of quality of relationships upon mutual aid. *Journal of Gerontological Social Work, 6*, 75-92.

Brown, B. (1939). *The wisdom of the Chinese.* New York: Garden City.

Brown, H. L. (1974). The very special joys of elderly ladies. In M. H. Huyck (Ed.), *Growing older* (pp. 157-158). Englewood Cliffs, NJ: Prentice Hall.

Bryan, J. H., & London, P. (1970). Altruistic behavior in children. *Psychological Bulletin, 73*, 200-211.

Bryan, J. H., & Test, M. A. (1967). Models and helping. *Journal of Personality and Social Psychology, 6*, 400-407.

Budd, L. J. (1956). Altruism arrives in America. *American Quarterly, 8*, 40-52.

Buhler, C. (1961). Old age and fulfillment of life with considerations of the use of time in old age. *Acta Psychologica, 19*, 126-148.

Buhler, C. (1962). Genetic aspects of the self. *Annals of the New York Academy of Sciences, 96*, 730-764.

Buie, D. H. (1981). Empathy: Its nature and limitations. *Journal of the American Psychoanalytic Association, 29*, 281-307.

Busse, E. W., & Blazer, D. (1980). The theories and processes of aging. In E. W. Busse &. D. Blazer (Eds.), *Handbook of geriatric psychiatry* (pp. 3-27). New York: Van Nostrand Reinhold.

Butler, R. (1975). *Why survive?* New York: Harper & Row.

Butler, R., & Lewis, M. (1982). *Aging and mental health: Positive psychological approaches* (3rd ed.). St. Louis, MO: C. V. Mosby.

Butler, R., Lewis, M., & Sunderland, T. (1990). *Aging and mental health.* New York: Macmillan.

Campbell, D. T. (1965). Ethnocentric and other altruistic motives. In D. Levine (Ed.), *Nebraska symposium of motivation* (pp. 283-311). Lincoln: University of Nebraska Press.

Campbell, D. T. (1975). On the conflict between biological and social evolution and between psychology and moral tradition. *American Psychologist, 30,* 1103-1126.

Campbell, D. T. (1983). The two distinct routes beyond kin selection to ultrasociality. Implications for the humanities and the social sciences. In D. L. Bridgeman (Ed.), *The nature of prosocial development* (pp. 11-41). New York: Academic Press.

Campbell, D. T., & Stanley, J. C. (1963). *Experimental and quasi-experimental designs for research.* Chicago: Rand McNally.

Cantor, M. (November, 1973). *Life space and the social support system of the inner city elderly of New York.* Paper presented at the annual meeting of the Gerontological Society of America, Miami Beach.

Cantor, M., & Myer, A. J. (1978). Factors in differential utilization and services by urban elderly. *Journal of Gerontological Social Work, 1,* 47-61.

Carnegie Hero Fund Commission. (1987). *Annual report.* Pittsburgh, PA: Author.

Carr, E. H. (1961). *The romantic exiles.* Boston: Beacon.

Carver, C. S., & del la Garza, N. H. (1984). Schemata-guided information search in stereotyping of the elderly. *Journal of Applied Social Psychology, 14,* 69-81.

Cerella, J., Poon, L. W., & Williams, D. M. (1980). Age and the complexity hypotheses. In L. W. Poon (Ed.), *Aging in the 1980s* (pp. 332-340). Washington, DC: American Psychological Association.

Chambré, S. (1984). Is volunteering a substitute for role loss in old age? *The Gerontologist, 24,* 292-298.

Chambré, S. (1987). *Good deeds in old age: Volunteering by the new leisure class.* Lexington, MA: Lexington Books.

Chambré, S. (1993). Volunteerism by elders: Past trends and future prospects. *The Gerontologist, 33,* 221-228.

Chappell, N. L. (1990). Aging and social care. In R. Binstock & L. George (Eds.), *Handbook of aging and the social sciences* (3rd ed., pp. 438-454). New York: Academic Press.

Chappell, N. L., & Havens, B. (1983). Who helps the elderly person? A discussion of informal and formal care. In W. A. Peterson & J. Quadragno (Eds.), *Social bonds in later life* (pp. 211-227). Newbury Park, CA: Sage.

Chellam, G. (1977-1978). Awareness of death and self-engagement in later life. *International Journal of Aging and Human Development, 8,* 11-27.

Cherry, D. L., Benest, R. F., Gates, F., & White, J. (1985). Intergenerational service programs: Meeting shared needs of young and old. *The Gerontologist, 25,* 126-129.

Chiriboga, D. A., Weiler, P. G., & Nielsen, K. (1990). The stress of caregivers. In D. E. Biegel & A. Blum (Eds.), *Aging and caregiving: Theory research and policy* (pp. 121-138). Newbury Park, CA: Sage.

Christenson, J. A. (1977). Generational differences. *The Gerontologist, 16,* 353-362.

Cicirelli, V. G. (1983). Adult children's attachment and helping behavior to elderly parents: A path model. *Journal of Marriage and the Family, 45,* 815-825.

Clark, M., & Anderson, B. (1967). *Culture and aging.* Springfield, IL: Charles C Thomas.

Clary, E. G., & Snyder, M. (1991). A functional analysis of altruism and prosocial behavior: The care of volunteerism. In M. S. Clark (Ed.), *Review of personality and social psychology: Vol. 12. Prosocial behavior* (pp. 119-148). Newbury Park, CA: Sage.

Clements, W. M. (1990). Spiritual development in the fourth quarter of life. In J. Seeber (Ed.), *Spiritual maturity in the later years* (pp. 55-69). Belmont, CA: Wadsworth.

Coase, R. H. (1976). Adam Smith's view of man. *Journal of Law and Economics, 38,* 529-546.

Cohler, B. (1983). Autonomy and interdependence in the family of adulthood: A psychological perspective. *The Gerontologist, 23,* 33-39.

Cohler, B., Borden, W., Groves, L., & Lazarus, L. (1989). Caring for family members with Alzheimer's disease. In B. Lebowitz & E. Light (Eds.), *Alzheimer's disease, treatment, and family stress: Directions for research* (pp. 50-105). Washington, DC: U.S. Government Printing Office.

Cohler, B., & Galatzer-Levy, R. M. (1990). Self, meaning, and morale across the second half of life. In R. A. Nemiroff & C. A. Colarusso (Eds.), *New dimensions in adult development* (pp. 207-256). New York: Basic Books.

Coke, J. S., Batson, C. D., & McDavis, K. (1978). Empathic mediation of helping: A two-stage model. *Journal of Personality and Social Psychology, 36,* 752-766.

Comte, A. (1875-1877). *System of positive polity.* London: Longmass.

Cornaro, L. (1913). *The art of living long* (W. F. Butler, Trans.). Milwaukee: W. F. Butler.

Costa, P. T., Jr., & McCrae, R. R. (1985). Hypochondriasis, neuroticism and aging: When are somatic complaints unfounded? *American Psychologist, 40,* 19-28.

Covey, H. C. (1991). Old age and historical examples of the miser. *The Gerontologist, 31,* 673-678.

Coward, R. T. (1987). Factors associated with the configuration of the helping networks of noninstitutionalized elders. *Journal of Gerontological Social Work, 10,* 113-132.

Cowgill, D. O. (1986). *Aging around the world.* Belmont, CA: Wadsworth.

Craik, F. (1977). Age differences in human memory. In J. E. Birren & K. W. Schaie (Eds.), *Handbook of the psychology of aging* (pp. 384-420). New York: Van Nostrand Reinhold.

Crandall, J. E. (1981). *Theory and measurement of social interest.* New York: Columbia University Press.

Crowne, D. P., & Marlowe, D. (1960). A new scale of social desirability independent of psychopathology. *Journal of Consulting Psychology, 24,* 349-354.

Crum, J. (1988, December 11). Service is spice of life for retirees. *The Gainesville Sun.*

Cumming, E., & Henry, W. E. (1961). *Growing old: The process of disengagement.* New York: Basic Books.

Dawkins, R. (1976). *The selfish gene.* New York: Oxford University Press.

Dewey, J. (1964). *Experience and education.* New York: Collier.

Dovidio, J. F. (1984). Helping behavior and altruism: An empirical and conceptual overview. In *Advances in experimental social psychology* (Vol. 17, pp. 361-427). New York: Academic Press.

Dowd, J. J. (1980). Exchange rates and old people. *Journal of Gerontology, 35,* 596-602.

Dowd, J. J. (1984). Beneficence and the aged. *Journal of Gerontology, 39*, 102-108.

Downs, A. (1957). *An economic theory of democracy.* New York: Harper & Row.

Dressel, S., & Midlarsky, E. (1978). The effect of models' exhortations, demands and practices on children's donation behavior. *Journal of Genetic Psychology, 132*, 211-233.

Durkheim, E. (1951). *Suicide.* New York: Free Press.

Dye, D., Goodman, M., Roth, W., Bley, N., & Jensen, K. (1973). The older adult volunteer compared to the non-volunteer. *The Gerontologist, 13*, 215-218.

Ehrlich, P. (1979a). *Mutual help for community elderly: Mutual help model* (Final report, Vol. 1). Carbondale: Southern Illinois University.

Ehrlich, P. (1979b). *Mutual help for community elderly: Mutual help model* (Final report, Vol. 2). Carbondale: Southern Illinois University.

Eibl-Eibesfeldt, I. (1971). *Love and hate: The natural history of behavior patterns.* New York: Holt, Rinehart & Winston.

Eisenberg, N. (1979). Development of children's prosocial moral reasoning. *Developmental Psychology, 15*, 128-137.

Eisenberg, N. (1982). *The development of prosocial behavior.* New York: Academic Press.

Eisenberg, N. (1983). The relation between empathy and altruism: Conceptual and methodological issues. *Academic Psychology Bulletin, 5*, 195-207.

Eisenberg-Berg, N., & Hand, M. (1979). The relationship of preschoolers' reasoning about prosocial moral conflicts to prosocial behavior. *Child Development, 50*, 356-363.

Ekstein, R. (1972). The facilitation of positive human qualities. *Journal of Social Issues, 28*, 71-85.

Encyclopedia of the Social Sciences, Vol. 8. New York: Macmillan.

Erikson, E. H. (1963). *Childhood and society.* New York: Norton.

Erikson, E. H. (1968). *Identity: Youth and crisis.* New York: Norton.

Erikson, E. H. (1977). *Adulthood and world views.* Paper presented at the American Academy Conference on Love and Work in Adulthood, Palo Alto, CA.

Erikson, E. H., Erikson, J. M., & Kivnick, H. Q. (1986). *Vital involvement in old age: The experience of old age in our time.* New York: Norton.

Eron, L. (1987). The development of aggressive behavior from the perspective of a developing behaviorism. *American Psychologist, 42*, 435-442.

Exton-Smith, A. N., & Evans, J. G. (Eds.). (1977). *Care of the elderly: Meeting the challenge of dependency.* New York: Academic Press.

Fairchild, T., Pruchno, R., & Kahana, E. (1978, November). *Implications of social exchange theory for understanding the effect of reciprocity among the aged.* Paper presented at the annual Gerontological Society of America meeting, Dallas.

Feldman, S. S., Biringen, Z. C., & Nash, S. C. (1981). Fluctuations in self-related self-attributions as a function of stage of family life-cycle. *Developmental Psychology, 17*, 24-35.

Fengler, A. P., & Goodrich, N. (1980). Money isn't everything: Opportunities for elderly handicapped men in a sheltered workshop. *The Gerontologist, 20*, 636-641.

Fenichel, O. (1945). *The psychoanalytic theory of neuroses.* New York: Norton.

Fischer, D. (1977). *Growing old in America.* New York: Oxford.

Fischer, L. R., & Schaffer, K. B. (1993). *Older volunteers.* Newbury Park, CA: Sage.

Fischer, W. F. (1963). Sharing in preschool children as a function of the amount and type of reinforcement. *Genetic Psychology Monographs, 68*, 215-245.

Fishbein, G. (1975). Congregate housing—with a difference. *Geriatrics, 30*, 124-128.

Fisher, J. D., Nadler, A., & Whitcher-Alagna, S. (1983). Four theoretical approaches for conceptualizing reactions to aid. In J. D. Fisher, A. Nadler, & B. DePaulo (Eds.), *New directions in helping* (Vol. 1, pp. 51-84). New York: Academic Press.

Foa, U., & Foa, E. (1975). *Resource theory of social exchange.* Morristown, NJ: General Learning Press.

Foss, R. D. (1983). Community norms and blood donation. *Journal of Applied Social Psychology, 13,* 281-290.

Foster, G. (1965). Peasant society and the image of limited good. *American Anthropologist, 67,* 293-315.

Fowler, J. W. (1981). *Stages of growth.* San Francisco: Harper & Row.

Frankl, V. E. (1963). *Man's search for meaning.* New York: Washington Square Press.

Freud, A. (1937). *The ego and mechanisms of defense.* London: Hogarth.

Freud, S. (1930). *Civilization and its discontents.* London: Hogarth.

Freud, S. (1933). *New introductory lectures on psychoanalysis.* London: Hogarth.

Freud, S. (1959). Analysis terminable and interminable. In S. Freud, *Collected papers* (Vol. 5, pp. 316-357). New York: Basic Books.

Friedan, B. (1993). *The fountain of age.* New York: Simon & Schuster.

Fries, J. F., & Crapo, T. M. (1981). *Vitality and aging.* San Francisco: W. H. Freeman.

Fromm, E. (1973). *The anatomy of human destructiveness.* New York: Holt, Rinehart & Winston.

Gadow, S. (1983). Frailty and strength: The dialectic in aging. *The Gerontologist, 23,* 144-147.

Garland, R. (1987). Greek geriatrics. *History Today, 137,* 12-18.

Gelfand, D. M., & Hartmann, D. P. (1982). Response consequences and attributions: Two contributions to prosocial behavior. In N. Eisenberg (Ed.), *The development of prosocial behavior* (pp. 167-196). New York: Academic Press.

Gelfand, D. M., Hartmann, D. P., Cromer, C. C., Smith, C. L., & Page, B. C. (1975). The effects of instructional prompts and praise on children's donation rates. *Child Development, 46,* 980-983.

George, L. K. (1981). Subjective well-being. In C. Eisdorfer (Ed.), *Annual review of gerontology and geriatrics* (Vol. 2, pp. 345-382). New York: Springer.

Gergen, K. J., & Gergen, M. M. (1981). *Social psychology.* New York: Harcourt Brace Jovanovich.

Gergen, K. J., Greenberg, M. S., & Willis, R. H. (Eds.). (1980). *Social exchange. Advances in theory and research.* New York: Plenum.

Giele, J. Z. (1980). Adulthood as transcendence of age and sex. In N. Smelser & E. H. Erikson (Eds.), *Themes of work and love in adulthood* (pp. 151-173). Cambridge, MA: Harvard University Press.

Gilligan, C. (1982). *In a different voice: Psychological theory and women's development.* Cambridge, MA: Harvard University Press.

Goldfarb, A. I. (1969). Institutional care of the aged. In E. W. Busse & E. Pfeiffer (Eds.), *Behavior and adaptation in late life* (pp. 289-313). Boston: Little, Brown.

Goodman, C. C. (1984). Natural helping among older adults. *The Gerontologist, 24,* 138-143.

Gould, R. (1972). The phases of adult life: A study in developmental psychology. *American Journal of Psychiatry, 129,* 521-531.

Gould, R. (1980). Transformational tasks in adulthood. In S. I. Greenspan & G. H. Pollock (Eds.), *The course of life: Vol. 3. Adulthood and aging process* (pp. 55-90). Bethesda, MD: National Institute of Mental Health.

Greenberg, J. S., & Becker, M. (1988). Aging parents and family resources. *The Gerontologist, 28,* 786-791.

Gurr, T. (1970). *Why men rebel.* Princeton, NJ: Princeton University Press.

Gutmann, D. (1977). The cross-cultural perspective: Notes toward a comparative psychology of aging. In J. E. Birren & K. W. Schaie (Eds.), *Handbook of psychology and aging* (pp. 302-326). New York: Van Nostrand Reinhold.

Gutmann, D. (1987). *Reclaimed powers: Toward a new psychology of men and women in later life.* New York: Basic Books.

Harel, Z., & Lindberg, R. E. (1981). Community service opportunities and older Americans. *Journal of Sociology and Social Welfare, 8,* 111-121.

Harris, L., & Associates, Inc. (1975). *The myth and reality of aging in America.* Washington, DC: The National Council on Aging.

Hartley, J., Harker, J. D., & Walsh, D. A. (1980). Contemporary issues and new directions in adult development of learning and memory. In L. Poon (Ed.), *Aging in the 1980s: Psychological issues* (pp. 239-252). Washington, DC: American Psychological Association.

Hartmann, H., Kris, E., & Loewenstein, R. M. (1947). Comments on the formation of psychic structure. In A. Freud, H. Hartmann, & E. Kris, (Eds.), *The psychoanalytic study of the child* (Vol. 2, pp. 11-38). New York: International Universities Press.

Harvey, W. (1635). *Works.* London: New Sydenham Society.

Hatfield, E., Walster, G. D., & Piliavin, J. A. (1978). Equity theory and helping relationships. In L. Wispé (Ed.), *Altruism, sympathy, and helping* (pp. 115-139). New York: Academic Press.

Havighurst, R. J. (1975). Lifestyle transitions related to personality after age fifty. Paper presented at the International Society for the Study of Behavioral Development symposium, *The problem of transitions in the human life cycle,* Kiryat Kiravim, Israel.

Haynes, M. S. (1963). The supposedly golden age for the aged in ancient Greece. *The Gerontologist, 3,* 26-35.

Hazan, H. (1982). Beyond disengagement: A case study of segregation of the aged. *Human Organization, 41,* 355-359.

Heidbreder, E. (1933). *Seven psychologies.* New York: Appleton.

Hendricks, J., & Hendricks, C. D. (1986). *Aging in mass society: Myths and realities.* Boston: Little, Brown.

Herzog, A. R., & House, J. S. (1991). Productive activities and aging well. *Generations, 15,* 49-54.

Herzog, A. R., Kahn, R. L., Morgan, J. N., Jackson, J. S., & Antonucci, T. C. (1989). Age differences in productive activities. *Journal of Gerontology: Social Sciences, 44,* S129-S138.

Hess, B. (1972). Friendship. In M. Riley & S. Johnson (Eds.), *Aging and society* (Vol. 3, pp. 357-393). New York: Russell Sage.

Hesse, S. B., & Williamson, J. (1984). Resource theory and power in families: Life cycle considerations. *Family Process, 23,* 261-278.

High, D. M. (1991). A new myth about families of older people? *The Gerontologist, 31,* 611-618.

Hildebrand, H. P. (1990). The other side of the wall: A psychoanalytic study of creativity in late life. In R. A. Nemiroff & C. A. Colarusso (Eds.), *New dimensions in adult development* (pp. 455-474). New York: Basic Books.

Hill, R. (1970). *Family development in three generations*. Cambridge, MA: Schenkman.

Hobbes, T. (1958). *Leviathan*. New York: Bobbs-Merrill.

Hoffman, M. L. (1978). Empathy: Its developmental and prosocial implications. In C. B. Keasey (Ed.), *Nebraska symposium on motivation* (Vol. 25, pp. 169-218). Lincoln: University of Nebraska Press.

Hoffman, M. L. (1982). Development of prosocial motivation: Empathy and guilt. In N. Eisenberg (Ed.), *The development of prosocial behavior* (pp. 281-313). New York: Academic Press.

Hollingshead, A. B., & Redlich, F. (1958). *Social class and mental illness*. New York: John Wiley.

Holmes, S. J. (1945). The reproductive beginnings of altruism. *Psychological Review, 52*, 109-112.

Holmes, T., & Rahe, R. (1967). The social readjustment scale. *Journal of Psychosomatic Research, 11*, 213-218.

Homans, G. (1961). *Social behavior: Its elementary forms*. New York: Harcourt Brace.

Horner, A. J. (1980). *Object relations and the developing ego in therapy*. New York: Jason Aronson.

Hornstein, H. A. (1976). *Cruelty and kindness: A new look at aggression and altruism*. Englewood Cliffs, NJ: Prentice Hall.

Hornstein, H. A. (1978). Promotive tension and prosocial behavior: A Lewinian analysis. In L. Wispé (Ed.), *Altruism, sympathy, and helping: Psychological and sociological principles* (pp. 177-207). New York: Academic Press.

Hospers, J. (1961). *Human conduct: An introduction to the problems of ethics*. New York: Harcourt Brace & World.

Hudson, R. B. (1987). Policy analysis and aging. In G. Maddox (Ed.), *Encyclopedia of aging* (pp. 526-528). New York: Springer.

Hultsch, D. F. (1974). Learning to love in adulthood. *Journal of Gerontology, 29*, 302-308.

Hume, D. (1973). Morality, self-love, and benevolence. In R. D. Milo (Ed.), *Egoism and altruism* (pp. 37-51). Belmont, CA: Wadsworth.

Independent Sector. (1986). *Americans volunteer—1985*. Washington, DC: Author.

Independent Sector. (1988). *Giving and volunteering in the United States*. Washington, DC: Author.

Independent Sector. (1990). *Giving and volunteering in the United States*. Washington, DC: Author.

Isen, A., & Noonberg, A. (1979). The effect of photographs of the handicapped on donation to charity: When a thousand words may be too much. *Journal of Applied Social Psychology, 9*, 426-431.

Jahoda, M. (1958). *Current concepts of positive mental health*. New York: Basic Books.

Jensen, G., & Oakley, F. (1982-1983). Ageism across cultures and in perspective of sociologic and psychodynamic theories. *International Journal of Aging and Human Development, 18*, 17-26.

Johnson, C. L. (1980, November). *Obligation and reciprocity in caregiving during illness: A comparison of spouses and offspring as family supports*. Paper presented at the annual meeting of the Gerontological Society of America, San Diego, CA.

Jones, E. J. (1953-1957). *The life and work of Sigmund Freud, Volume 3*. New York: Basic Books.

Jung, C. G. (1933). *Modern man in search of a soul*. New York: Harcourt, Brace, and World.

Jung, C. G. (1960). *Collected works* (H. R. Read et al., Eds.). Princeton, NJ: Princeton University Press.

Kahana, B. (1982). Social behavior and aging. In B. Wolman (Ed.), *Handbook of developmental psychology* (pp. 871-886). New York: Prentice Hall.

Kahana, B., and Kahana, E. (1971). Theoretical and research perspectives on grandparenthood: A theoretical statement. *Aging and Human Development, 2,* 261-268.

Kahana, B., & Kahana, E. (1980). *Grandparents' attitudes toward grandchildren as a function of marital-divorce status of their children.* Paper presented at the annual meeting of the American Orthopsychiatric Association, Toronto, Canada.

Kahana, B., Kahana, E., Harel, Z., & Segal, M. (1986). Victim as helper. *Humboldt Journal of Social Relations, 13,* 357-373.

Kahana, E. (1972). *The aged and their significant others.* Paper presented at the annual meeting of the American Psychological Association, Honolulu, Hawaii.

Kahana, E. (1974). *The role of homes for the aged in meeting community needs* (Final Report, NIMH Grant R01M721465-01). Washington, DC: U.S. Government Printing Office.

Kahana, E. (1982). A congruence model of person-environment interaction. In M. P. Lawton, P. Windley, & T. Byerts (Eds.), *Aging and the environment* (pp. 97-121). New York: Springer.

Kahana, E., & Coe, R. M. (1969). Staff and self-conceptions of institutionalized aged. *The Gerontologist, 9*(4), 264-277.

Kahana, E., & Felton, B. (1977). Social context and personal needs—A study of Polish and Jewish aged. *Journal of Social Issues, 33,* 56-74.

Kahana, E., & Kahana, B. (1983). Environmental continuity, discontinuity, futurity, and adaptation of the aged. In G. Rowles & R. Ohta (Eds.), *Aging and milieu* (pp. 205-228). New York: Academic Press.

Kahana, E., & Kahana, B. (1993, July). *Proactivity in later life adaptation.* Paper presented at the International Gerontological Society meetings, Budapest, Hungary.

Kahana, E., & Midlarsky, E. (1982, November). *Is there help beyond exchange? Contributory options in late life adaptation.* Paper presented at the annual meeting of the Gerontological Society of America, Boston, MA.

Kahana, E., & Midlarsky, E. (1983, November). *Altruism in late life: Nature and salience.* Paper presented at the annual meeting of the Gerontological Society of America, San Francisco, CA.

Kahana, E., Midlarsky, E., & Kahana, B. (1987). Beyond dependency, autonomy, and exchange: Prosocial behavior in late-life adaptation. *Social Justice Research, 1,* 439-459.

Kahana, E., Young, R. F., Kercher, K., & Kaczynski, L. (1993). Testing a symmetrical model of caregiving outcomes during recovery from heart attacks. *Research on Aging, 15,* 371-399.

Kakar, S. (1978). *The inner world: A psychoanalytic study of idea and its healing tradition.* New York: Knopf.

Kalish, R. A. (1969). *Dependencies of old people.* Ann Arbor: University of Michigan Press.

Kalish, R. A. (1979). The new ageism and the failure of models: A polemic. *The Gerontologist, 19,* 398-402.

Kant, I. (1949). *Critique of practical reasoning* (L.W. Beck, Trans.). Chicago: University of Chicago Press.

Karuza, J., Jr., Rabinowitz, V., & Zevon, M. (1986). Implications of control and responsibility on helping the aged. In M. Baltes & P. Baltes (Eds.), *Aging and the psychology of control*. Hillsdale, NJ: Lawrence Erlbaum.

Kaufmann, S. (1986). *The ageless self: Sources of meaning in late life*. New York: New American Library.

Kausler, D. H. (1982). *Experimental psychology and human aging*. New York: John Wiley.

Keith, J. (1982). *Old people as people: Social and cultural influences on aging and old age*. Boston: Little, Brown.

Kelly, G. A. (1955). *The psychology of personal constructs*. New York: Norton.

Kermis, M. D. (1984). *The psychology of human aging*. Boston: Allyn & Bacon.

Kernberg, O. F. (1979). *Object relations theory and clinical psychoanalysis*. New York: Jason Aronson.

Kieffer, J. A. (1986). The older volunteer resource. In Committee on an Aging Society (Ed.), *Productive roles in older society* (pp. 51-72). Washington, DC: National Academy Press.

Kimmel, D. (1988). Ageism, psychology, and public policy. *American Psychologist, 43*, 175-178.

Kinney, J. M., & Stephens, M. A. P. (1989). Hassles and uplifts of giving care to a family member with dementia. *Psychology and Aging, 4*, 402-408.

Kohlberg, L. (1969). Stage and sequence. In D. Goslin (Ed.), *Handbook of socialization theory and research* (pp. 347-480). Chicago: Rand McNally.

Kohlberg, L. (1973). Continuities in childhood and adult moral development revisited. In P. B. Baltes & K. W. Schaie (Eds.), *Life-span developmental psychology: Personality and socialization* (pp. 179-204). New York: Academic Press.

Kohlberg, L. (1984). *The psychology of moral development: Essays on moral development*. San Francisco: Harper & Row.

Kohlberg, L., & Wasserman, E. (1980). The cognitive developmental approach and the practicing counselor. *Personnel and Guidance Journal, 58*, 559-567.

Krause, C. A. (1978). *Grandmothers, mothers, and daughters*. New York: American Jewish Committee.

Krebs, D., & Miller, D. (1985). Altruism and aggression. In G. Lindzey & E. Aronson (Eds.), *The handbook of social psychology* (Vol. 11, pp. 1-71). Reading, MA: Addison-Wesley.

Kropotkin, P. (1902). *Mutual aid: A factor of evolution*. New York: McClure Phillips.

Kubler-Ross, E. (1975). *Death. The final stage of growth*. Englewood Cliffs, NJ: Prentice Hall.

Kurtines, W., & Gewirtz, J. (1984). *Morality, moral behavior, and moral development*. New York: John Wiley.

Kuypers, J. A., & Bengtson, V. L. (1973). Social breakdown and competence: A model of normal aging. *Human Development, 16*, 181-201.

Labouvie-Vief, G. (1981). Proactive and reactive aspects of constructionism. In R. M. Lerner & N. A. Busch-Rossnagel (Eds.), *Individuals as producers of their own development: A life span perspective* (pp. 197-230). New York: Academic Press.

Labouvie-Vief, G. (1982). Dynamic development and mature autonomy: A theoretical prologue. *Human Development, 25*, 161-191.

Labouvie-Vief, G., Hakim-Larson, J., & Hobart, C. (1987). Age, ego level, and the life-span development of coping and defense processes. *Psychology and Aging, 2*, 286-293.

Lachman, M. (1986). Locus of control in aging research. *Psychology and Aging, 1*, 34-40.

Lachman, M. E., & McArthur, L. Z. (1986). Adulthood age differences in causal attributions for cognitive, physical and social performance. *Psychology and Aging, 1*, 127-132.

Langer, E. J. (1980). *Old age: An artifact?* Washington, DC: National Research Council.

Langer, E. J. (1983). *The psychology of control.* Beverly Hill, CA: Sage.

L'Armand, K., & Pepitone, A. (1975). Helping to reward another person: A cross-cultural analysis. *Journal of Personality and Social Psychology, 31*, 189-198.

LaRue, A., Bank, L., Jarvik, L., & Hetland, M. (1979). Health in old age: How do physicians' ratings and self-ratings compare? *Journal of Gerontology, 34*, 678-691.

Latané, B. (1981). Psychology of social impact. *American Psychologist, 36*, 343-346.

Latané, B., & Darley, J. M. (1969). Bystander "apathy." *American Scientist, 57*, 244-268.

Lawton, M. P. (1975a). The Philadelphia Geriatric Morale Scale. *Journal of Gerontology, 30*, 85-89.

Lawton, M. P. (1975b). The impact of the environment on aging and behavior. In J. Birren & K. W. Schaie (Eds.), *Handbook on the psychology of aging* (pp. 276-301). New York: Van Nostrand Reinhold.

Lawton, M. P. (1989). Environmental proactivity in older people. In V. L. Bengtson & K. W. Schaie (Eds.), *The course of later life: Research and reflections* (pp. 15-23). New York: Springer.

Lawton, M. P., & Nahemow, L. (1973). Ecology and the aging process. In C. Eisdorfer & M. P. Lawton (Eds.), *Psychology of adult development and aging* (pp. 619-674). Washington, DC: American Psychological Association.

Lawton, M. P., Windley, P. G., & Byerts, T. O. (1982). *Aging and the environment.* New York: Springer.

LeMare, L., & Krebs, D. (1983). Perspective-taking and styles of prosocial behavior. *Academic Psychology Bulletin, 5*, 289-298.

Leon, G. R., Gillum, B., Gillum, R., & Gouze, M. (1979). Personality stability and change over a 30-year period—middle age to old age. *Journal of Consulting and Clinical Psychology, 47*, 517-524.

Leventhal, G. (1976). The distribution of rewards and resources in groups and organizations. In L. Berkowitz & E. Walster (Eds.), *Advances in experimental social psychology* (Vol. 9, pp. 91-131). New York: Academic Press.

Levy, O. (Ed.). (1910). *The complete works of Friedrich Nietzsche.* Edinburgh: T. N. Foules.

Liang, J., Dvorkin, L., Kahana, E., & Mazian, F. (1980). Social integration and morale: A reexamination. *Journal of Gerontology, 35*, 746-757.

Lieberman, M. (1975). Adaptive processes in later life. In N. Datan & L. Ginsburg (Eds.), *Life-span developmental psychology* (pp. 135-160). New York: Academic Press.

Lifton, R. J. (1988). *Understanding the traumatized self.* New York: Plenum.

Light, L. (1991). Memory and aging: Four hypotheses in search of data. *Annual Review of Psychology, 42*, 333-376.

Linn, B., & Linn, M. (1980). Objective and self-assessed health in the old and very old. *Social Science and Medicine, 14A*, 311-315.

Loevinger, J. (1976). *Ego development.* San Francisco: Jossey-Bass.

Lorenz, K. (1963). *On aggression.* New York: Harcourt, Brace & World.

Losco, J. (1981, August). *Understanding altruism*. Paper presented at the annual meeting of the Annual American Political Science Association, New York City.

Lowenthal, M., & Robinson, B. (1976). Social networks and isolation. In R. Binstock & E. Shanas (Eds.), *Handbook of aging and the social sciences* (pp. 432-456). New York: Van Nostrand Reinhold.

Lowenthal, M., Thurnher, M., & Chiriboga, D. (1975). *Four stages of life*. San Francisco: Jossey-Bass.

Lozier, J. (1975). Accommodating old people to society: Examples from Appalachia and New Orleans. In N. Datan & L. Ginsburg (Eds.), *Life-span developmental psychology* (pp. 287-298). New York: Academic Press.

Lynch, J. G., & Cohen, J. L. (1978). The use of subjective expected utility theory as an aid to understanding variables that influence helping behavior. *Journal of Personality and Social Psychology, 36*, 1138-1151.

Maas, H. S., & Kuypers, J. A. (1974). *From thirty to seventy*. San Francisco: Jossey-Bass.

Macaulay, J. R., & Berkowitz, L. (1970). *Altruism and helping behavior*. New York: Academic Press.

MacPherson, C. B. (1962). *The political theory of possessive individualism: Hobbes to Locke*. New York: Oxford University Press.

Maddi, S. R. (1970). The search for meaning. In A. Williams & M. Pages (Eds.), *The Nebraska symposium on motivation* (pp. 134-183). Lincoln: University of Nebraska Press.

Maddox, G. L. (1970). Themes and issues in sociological theories of human aging. *Human Development, 13*, 17-27.

Mancini, J. A. (1980). Friend interaction, competence, and morale in old age. *Research on Aging, 2*, 416-431.

Markides, K. S., & Krause, N. (1986). Older Mexican Americans. *Generations, 10*, 31-34.

Marriott Seniors Volunteerism Study. (1991). Commissioned by Marriott Senior Living Services and U.S. Administration on Aging. Washington, DC: Marriott Senior Living Services.

Maslow, A. H. (1954). *Motivation and personality*. New York: Harper & Row.

Maslow, A. H. (1968). *Toward a psychology of being* (rev. ed.). Princeton, NJ: Van Nostrand.

Masters, R D. (1978, August). *Classical political philosophy and contemporary biology*. Paper presented at the conference for the Study of Political Thought, Chicago.

Matter, J. A. (1974). *Love, altruism and world crisis: The challenge of Pitirim Sorokin*. Chicago: Nelson-Hall.

Mauss, M. (1954). *The gift: Forms and functions of exchange in archaic societies*. Glencoe, IL: Free Press.

McClelland, D. C. (1986). Some reflections on the two psychologies of love. *Journal of Personality, 54*, 334-357.

McDonald, G. W. (1981). Structural exchange and marital interaction. *Journal of Marriage and the Family, 43*, 825-839.

McDougall, W. (1908). *An introduction to social psychology*. London: Methuen.

Meachem, J. A. (1989). Autonomy, despair, and generativity in Erikson's theory. In P. S. Fry (Ed.), *Psychological perspectives of helplessness and control with the elderly* (pp. 63-98). North-Holland: Elsevier.

Medawar, P. B. (1955). The definition and measurement of senescence. In *Ciba Foundation colloquia on aging* (Vol. 1, pp. 75-121). Boston: Little, Brown.

Mehrabian, A., & Epstein, N. (1972). A measure of emotional empathy. *Journal of Personality, 40*, 525-543.

Mergler, N. L., & Goldstein, M. D. (1983). Why are there old people? *Human Development, 26*, 72-90.

Metchnikoff, E. (1912). *The prolongation of life.* London: Putnam.

Midgley, M. (1978). *Beast and man: The roots of human nature.* Ithaca, NY: Cornell University Press.

Midlarsky, E. (1968). Aiding responses: An analysis and review. *Merrill Palmer Quarterly, 14*, 229-260.

Midlarsky, E. (1971). Aiding under stress: The effects of competence, dependency, visibility, and fatalism. *Journal of Personality, 39*, 132-149.

Midlarsky, E. (1984). Competence and helping: Notes toward a model. In E. Staub, D. Bar-Tal, J. Karylowski, & J. Reykowski (Eds.), *Development and maintenance of prosocial behavior* (pp. 291-308). New York: Plenum.

Midlarsky, E. (1991). Helping as coping. In M. S. Clark (Ed.), *Review of personality and social psychology: Vol. 12. Prosocial behavior* (pp. 238-264). Newbury Park, CA: Sage.

Midlarsky, E. (1992). Helping in late life. In P. Oliner, S. Oliner, L. Baron, L. Blum, D. Krebs, & E. Smolenska (Eds.), *Embracing the other* (pp. 253-276). New York: New York University Press.

Midlarsky, E. (1994). Helping through the life course. In E. Kahana, D. Biegel, & M. Wykle (Eds.), *Family caregiving through the life course* (pp. 69-95). Newbury Park, CA: Sage.

Midlarsky, E., & Bryan, J. H. (1967). Training charity in children. *Journal of Personality and Social Psychology, 5*, 408-415.

Midlarsky, E., Bryan, J. H., & Brickman, P. (1973). Aversive approval: Interactive effects of modeling and reinforcement on altruistic behavior. *Child Development, 44*, 321-328.

Midlarsky, E., & Hannah, M. (1985). Competence, reticence, and helping by children and adolescents. *Developmental Psychology, 21*, 534-541.

Midlarsky, E., & Hannah, M. E. (1989). The generous elderly: Naturalistic studies of donations across the life span. *Psychology and Aging, 4*, 346-351.

Midlarsky, E., Hannah, M. E., & Kahana, E. (1983, November). *Who cares? Naturalistic studies of altruism across the life span.* Paper presented at the Gerontological Society of America meeting, San Francisco, CA.

Midlarsky, E., Hannah, M. E., & Kahana, E. (1985, August). *The generous elderly: Perspectives from naturalistic research.* Paper presented at the American Psychological Association meeting, Los Angeles, CA.

Midlarsky, E., & Kahana, E. (1981, November). *Altruism in the aged.* Paper presented at the annual meeting of the Gerontological Society of America, Toronto, Canada.

Midlarsky, E., & Kahana, E. (1983a). *Altruism in late life: Nature and salience.* Paper presented at the annual meeting of the Gerontological Society of America, San Francisco, CA.

Midlarsky, E., & Kahana, E. (1983b). Helping by the elderly: Conceptual and empirical considerations. *Interdisciplinary Topics in Gerontology, 17*, 10-24.

Midlarsky, E., & Kahana, E. (1984). *From helplessness to helpfulness—Prosocial behavior among the elderly.* Paper presented at the annual meeting of the American Psychological Association, Toronto, Canada.

Midlarsky, E., & Kahana, E. (1985a). *Altruism and helping among the elderly* (Final Report to the National Institute on Aging, for Grant No. RO1 AGO3068-01). Detroit: Center for the Study of Development and Aging, University of Detroit.

Midlarsky, E., & Kahana, E. (1985b). *Helping by the elderly: A proactive option in late life adaptation.* Paper presented at the annual meeting of the International Gerontological Association, New York.

Midlarsky, E., & Kahana, E. (1986). Altruism, meaningfulness, and the sense of mastery in late life. *Adult Development and Aging News, 13,* 5-6.

Midlarsky, E., Kahana, E., & Corley, R. (1987, August). *Altruist or hedonist? Correlates of moral reasoning among the elderly.* Paper presented at the Gerontological Society of America meeting, Chicago.

Midlarsky, E., & Midlarsky, M. (1973). Some determinants of aiding under experimentally-induced stress. *Journal of Personality, 41,* 305-327.

Midlarsky, E., & Suda, W. (1978). Some antecedents of altruism in children: Theoretical and empirical perspectives. *Psychological Reports, 43,* 187-208.

Moberg, D. O. (1983). The ecological fallacy: Concerns for program planners. *Generations, 8,* 12-14.

Monk, A., & Cryns, A. G. (1974). Predictors of voluntaristic intent among the aged. *The Gerontologist, 14,* 425-429.

Montague, M. F. A. (1950). The origin and nature of social life and the biological basis of cooperation. In P. Sorokin (Ed.), *Explorations in altruistic love and behavior: A symposium* (pp. 74-92). Boston: Beacon.

Montgomery, J. (1972). The housing patterns of older people. *Family Coordinator, 21,* 37-46.

Morgan, L. A. (1983). Intergenerational economic assistance to children: The case of widows and widowers. *Journal of Gerontology, 38,* 525-531.

Morrison, M. H. (1986). Work and retirement in an older society. In A. Pifer & L. Bronte (Eds.), *Our aging society: Paradox and promise* (pp. 341-365). New York: Norton.

Morrow-Howell, N., & Mui, A. (1989). Elderly volunteers: Reasons for initiating and terminating service. *Journal of Gerontological Social Work, 13,* 21-33.

Moss, M. K., & Page, R. A. (1972). Reinforcement and helping behavior. *Journal of Applied Social Psychology, 2,* 360-371.

Myerhoff, B. (1978). *Life's career: Aging.* Beverly Hills: Sage.

Nagel, T. (1970). *The possibility of altruism.* Oxford: Clarendon.

Nahemow, L., & Lawton, M. P. (1975). Similarity and propinquity in friendship formation. *Journal of Personality and Social Psychology, 32,* 205-213.

National Advisory Council on Aging. (1990). *The NACA position on community services in health care for seniors.* Ottawa, Canada: Author.

National Council on the Aging. (1975). *The myth and reality of aging in America.* Washington, DC: Author.

Neugarten, B. L. (1964). *Personality in middle and late life: Empirical studies.* New York: Atherton.

Neugarten, B. L. (1977). Personality and aging. In J. E. Birren & K. W. Schaie (Eds.), *Handbook of the pyschology of aging* (pp. 626-649). New York: Van Nostrand Reinhold.

Neugarten, B. L. (1979). Time, age, and the life-cycle. *American Journal of Psychiatry, 136,* 887-894.

Nieburg, H. L. (1969). *Political violence: The behavioral process.* New York: St. Martins Press.

Okun, M. A., & Eisenberg, N. (1991). *Motivation for community service volunteering among elders: A review and preliminary study.* Unpublished manuscript, Arizona State University.

Olweus, D., Block, J., & Radke-Yarrow, M. (1986). *Development of antisocial and prosocial behavior.* New York: Academic Press.

Otten, J., & Shelley, F. D. (1977). *When your parents grow old.* New York: Signet.

Palmore, E. (1981). *Social patterns in normal aging: Findings from the Duke Longitudinal Study.* Durham, NC: Duke University Press.

Parmelee, P. A. (1983). Spouse versus other family caregivers: Psychological impact on impaired aged. *American Journal of Community Psychology, 1,* 337-349.

Payne, B. P. (1977). The older volunteer: Social role continuity and development. *The Gerontologist, 17,* 355-361.

Payne, B., & Bull, C. N. (1985). The older volunteer: The case for interdependence. In W. A. Peterson & J. Quadagno (Eds.), *Social bonds in late life* (pp. 251-272). Beverly Hills, CA: Sage.

Peck, R. (Ed.). (1968). Psychological developments in the second half of life. In B. L. Neugarten (Ed.), *Middle age and aging* (pp. 88-92). Chicago: University of Chicago Press.

Perkinson, M. A. (1980). Alternate roles for the elderly: An example from a Midwestern retirement community. *Human Organization, 39,* 219-226.

Petersen, M. (1981). *The assessment of service provider attitudes toward older clients in an urban social service system.* Unpublished doctoral dissertation, Portland State University.

Pfeiffer, E., & Busse, E. (Eds.). (1973). *Mental illness in later life.* Washington, DC: American Psychiatric Association Press.

Piaget, J. (1952). *The origins of intelligence in children.* New York: International Universities Press.

Piliavin, J., & Charng, H. W. (1990). Altruism: A review of recent theory and research. *Annual Review of Sociology, 16,* 27-65.

Piliavin, J., Dovidio, J., Gaertner, S., & Clark, R. (1981). *Emergency intervention.* New York: Academic Press.

Plato. (1954). *The Republic* (Francis Cornford, Trans.). New York: Penguin.

Poon, L. W. (1985). Differences in human memory with aging. In J. E. Birren & K. W. Schaie (Eds.), *Handbook of the psychology of aging* (pp. 427-462). New York: Van Nostrand Reinhold.

Press, I., & McKool, M. (1972). Social structure and status of aging: Toward some valid cross-cultural generalizations. *International Journal of Aging and Human Development, 3,* 297-306.

Prohaska, T. R., & McAuley, W. N. (1984). Turning the tables on assistance: The elderly as care providers. *Academic Psychology Bulletin, 6,* 191-202.

Pruchno, R. (1979). *Social networks of the elderly: An exchange analysis.* Unpublished master's thesis, Oakland University.

Rachman, S. V. (1978). *Fear and courage.* San Francisco: Freeman.

Raj, D. (1968). *Sampling theory.* New York: McGraw Hill.

Reece, D., Walz, T., & Hagebaek, H. (1983). Intergenerational care providers of non-institutionalized frail elderly: Characteristics and consequences. *Journal of Gerontological Social Work, 5,* 21-34.

Reichard, S., Livson, F., & Peterson, P. G. (1962). *Aging and personality: A study of 87 older men.* New York: John Wiley.

Reisberg, B. (1981). *A guide to Alzheimer's disease.* New York: Free Press.

Riessman, M. (1976). How does self-help work? *Social Policy, 7,* 41-45.

Riger, S., & Gordon, M. T. (1981). The fear of rape: A study in social control. *Journal of Social Issues, 37,* 71-92.

Riley, M., & Foner, A. (1968). *Aging and society.* New York: Russell Sage.

Riley, M., & Foner, A. (1978). *Aging and society: Vol. 1. An inventory of research findings.* New York: Russell Sage.

Robertson, J. F. (1977). Grandmotherhood: A study of role conceptions. *Journal of Marriage and the Family, 38,* 165-174.

Rockstein, M., Chesky, J., & Sussman, M. (1977). Comparative biology and evolution of aging. In G. E. Finch & L. Hayflick (Eds.), *Handbook of the biology of aging* (pp. 202-207). New York: Van Nostrand Reinhold.

Rodin, J. (1986). Aging and health: Effects of the sense of control. *Science, 233,* 1271-1276.

Rosenberg, M. (1965). *Society and the adolescent self-image.* New York: John Wiley.

Rosenfeld, J. P. (1979). Bequests from resident to resident. Inheritance in a retirement community. *The Gerontologist, 19,* 594-600.

Rosenhan, D. (1969, August). *Determinants of altruism: Observations for a theory of altruistic development.* Paper presented at the annual meeting of the American Psychological Association, Washington, DC.

Rosenhan, D. L. (1978). Toward resolving the altruistic paradox: Affect, self-reinforcement and cognition. In L. Wispé (Ed.), *Altruism, sympathy, and helping: Psychological and sociological principles* (pp. 101-113). New York: Academic Press.

Rosenthal, A. M. (1964). *Thirty-eight witnesses.* New York: McGraw-Hill.

Rosow, J. (1967). *Social integration of the aged.* Glencoe, IL: Free Press.

Rouseau, J. J. (1950). *The social contract and discourses.* New York: Dutton.

Rotter, J. B. (1966). Generalized expectancies for internal versus external control of reinforcement. *Psychological Monographs, 80,* 1-28.

Rowe, J. W., & Kahn, R. L. (1987). Human aging: Usual and successful. *Science, 237,* 143-149.

Rushton, J. P. (1982). Altruism and society: A social learning perspective. *Ethics, 92,* 425-446.

Rushton, J. P., Chrisjohn, R. D., & Fekken, G. D. (1981). The altruistic personality and the Self-Report Altruism Scale. *Personality and Individual Differences, 2,* 293-302.

Rushton, J., Fuller, D., Neale, M., Nias, D., & Eysenck, J. (1986). Altruism and aggression: The heritability of individual differences. *Journal of Personality and Social Psychology, 50,* 1192-1198.

Rushton, J. P., & Sorrentino, R. M. (1981). *Altruism and helping behavior.* Hillsdale, NJ: Lawrence Erlbaum.

Rushton, J. P., & Teachman, G. (1978). The effect of positive reinforcement, attributions, and punishment on model-induced altruism in children. *Personality and Social Psychology Bulletin, 4,* 322-325.

Ryan, T. (1960). Significance tests for multiple comparison of proportions, variances and other statistics. *Psychology Bulletin, 57,* 318-328.

Rycroft, C. (1985). *Psychoanalysis and beyond.* London: Hogarth.

Ryff, C. (1984). Personality development from the inside: The subjective experience of change in adulthood and aging. In P. B. Baltes & O. G. Brim, Jr. (Eds.), *Life-span development and behavior* (Vol. 6, pp. 243-279). Ontario, FL: Academic Press.

Ryff, C., & Heincke, S. G. (1983). The subjective organization of personality in adulthood and aging. *Journal of Personality and Social Psychology, 44,* 807-816.

Sagi, A., & Hoffman, M. L. (1976). Empathic distress in the newborn. *Developmental Psychology, 12,* 175-176.

Sainer, J., & Zander, M. (1971). Guidelines for older person volunteers. *The Gerontologist, 11,* 201-204.

Salthouse, T. A., & Somberg, B. L. (1982). Time-accuracy relationships in young and old adults. *Journal of Gerontology, 37,* 349-353.

Saltz, R. (1971). Aging persons as child care workers in a foster grandparent program: Psychosocial effects and work performance. *Aging and Human Development, 3,* 314-340.

Sampson, E. E. (1988). The debate on individualism: Indigenous psychologies of the individual and their role in personal and societal functioning. *American Psychologist, 43,* 15-22.

Sanders, N. (1988). The dynamics of helping behavior in congregate housing. *Activities, Adaptation, and Aging, 12,* 13-26.

Sandler, A. M. (1982). Psychoanalysis and psychoanalytic psychotherapy of the older patient: A developmental crisis in an aging patient. Comments on development and adaptation. *Journal of Geriatric Psychiatry, 15,* 11-53.

Sandler, J., & Freud, A. (1985). *The analysis of defense: The ego and the mechanisms of defense revisited.* New York: International Universities Press.

Sankar, A. (1984). It's just old age. In D. Kertzer & J. Keith (Eds.), *Age and anthropological theory* (pp. 250-280). Ithaca, NY: Cornell University Press.

Sauer, W. J., & Coward, R. T. (Eds.). (1985). *Social support networks and the care of the elderly.* New York: Springer.

Savage, R. D., Gaber, L. B., Britton, P. G., Bolton, J., & Cooper, A. (1977). *Personality and adjustment in the aged.* London: Academic Press.

Schaie, K. W. (1974). Translations in gerontology—from late to life: Intellectual functioning. *American Psychologist, 29,* 802-807.

Schaie, K. W., & Parham, I. (1976). Stability of adult personality traits: Fact or fable? *Journal of Personality and Social Psychology, 34,* 146-158.

Scheier, C. J., & Geller, S. (1979). Analysis of random effects in modeling studies. *Child Development, 50,* 752-757.

Schulz, R. (1986). Successful aging: Balancing primary and secondary control. *Adult Development and Aging News, 13,* 2-4.

Sechrest, L., & Cohen, R. (1983). Evaluating outcomes in health care. In G. Stone, F. Cohen, & N. Adler (Eds.), *Health psychology* (pp. 369-394). San Francisco: Jossey-Bass.

Seidler, V. J. (1986). *Kant, respect and injustice: The limits of liberal moral theory.* London: Routledge & Kegan Paul.

Seidler, V. J. (1993). Rescue righteousness and morality. In P. M. Oliner, S. Oliner, L. Baron, L. Blum, D. Krebs, & Z. Smolenska (Eds.), *Embracing the other* (pp. 48-65). New York: New York University Press.

Selig, S., Tomlinson, T., & Hickey, T. (1991). Ethical dimensions of intergenerational reciprocity: Implications for practice. *The Gerontologist, 31,* 624-638.

Seligman, M. E. P. (1975). *Helplessness: On depression, development, and death.* San Francisco: W. H. Freeman.

Shanas, E. (1962). *The health of older people: A social survey.* Cambridge, MA: Harvard University.

Shanas, E. (1967). Family help patterns and social class in three countries. *Journal of Marriage and Family, 29,* 257-266.

Shane, M., & Shane, E. (1990). The struggle for otherhood. In R. A. Nemiroff & C. A. Colarusso (Eds.), *New dimensions in adult development* (pp. 475-486). New York: Basic Books.

Shapiro, E. G. (1978). Help-seeking. *Journal of Applied Social Psychology, 8,* 163-173.

Sharabany, R. (1984). The development of capacity for altruism as a function of object relations development and vicissitudes. In E. Staub, D. Bar-Tal, J. Karylowski, & J. Reykowski (Eds.), *Development and maintenance of prosocial behavior* (pp. 201-222). New York: Plenum.

Sharma, I. C. (1965). *Ethical philosophies of India.* London: Allen & Unwin.

Shaw, G. B. (1903). *Man and superman.* London: Constable.

Simon, H. (1979). From substantive to procedural rationality. In F. Hahn & M. Hollis (Eds.), *Philosophy and economic theory* (pp. 65-86). New York: Oxford University Press.

Singer, I. (1992). *Meaning in life.* New York: Free Press.

Singer, P. (1979). *Practical ethics.* Cambridge, UK: Cambridge University Press.

Sivley, J. P., & Fiegener, J. J. (1984). Family caregivers of the elderly. *Journal of Gerontological Social Work, 8,* 23-34.

Skinner, B. F. (1953). *Science and human behavior.* New York: Macmillan.

Skinner, B. F. (1971). *Beyond freedom and dignity.* New York: Knopf.

Slaby, R. G., & Crowley, C. G. (1977). Modification of cooperation and aggression through teacher attention to children's speech. *Journal of Experimental Child Psychology, 23,* 442-458.

Smith, A. (1976). *The theory of moral sentiments* (D. Raphael & A. Macfie, Eds., reprint ed.). Oxford: Clarendon. (Original work published 1759)

Smith, M. B. (1978). Perspectives on selfhood. *American Psychologist, 33,* 1053-1063.

Smith, P., & Midlarsky, E. (1985). Empirically-derived conceptions of femaleness and maleness. *Sex Roles, 12,* 313-328.

Smith, W. C. (1979). *Faith and belief.* Princeton, NJ: Princeton University.

Sorokin, P. A. (1950). *Altruistic love.* Boston: Beacon.

Sorokin, P. A. (1954). *Forms and techniques of altruistic and spiritual growth.* Boston: Beacon.

Spencer, H. (1897). *The principles of psychology.* New York: Appleton.

Spratling, C. (1982, October 11). Helping gilds golden years. *Detroit Free Press.*

Staub, E. (1974). Helping a distressed person: Social, personality, and stimulus determinants. In L. Berkowitz (Ed.), *Advances in experimental social psychology* (Vol. 7). New York: Academic Press.

Staub, E., Bar-Tal, D., Karylowski, J., & Reykowski, J. (Eds.). (1984). *Development and maintenance of prosocial behavior.* New York: Plenum.

Stewart, B. J., & Smith, C. L. (Ed.). (1983). Prosocial behavior for and by older persons. In D. L. Bridgeman (Ed.), *The nature of prosocial behavior* (pp. 309-340). New York: Academic Press.

Stirner, M. (1907). *The ego and his own.* New York: B. R. Tucker.

Stoller, E. P. (1983). Parental caregiving by adult children. *Journal of Marriage and the Family, 45,* 851-858.

Stoller, E. P. (1984). Self-assessments of health by the elderly: The impact of informal assistance. *Journal of Health and Social Behavior, 25,* 260-270.

Stoller, E. P. (1989). Formal services and informal helping: The myth of service substitution. *Journal of Applied Gerontology, 8,* 37-52.

Streib, G. F., Folts, W. F., & Greca, A. (1983). *Process and problems related to entry in the study of retirement communities.* Paper presented at the annual meeting of the Gerontological Society of America, San Francisco.

Stueve, A. (1982). The elderly as network members. *Marriage and Family Review, 5,* 59-87.

Sullivan, H. S. (1953). *The interpersonal theory of psychiatry.* New York: Norton.

Sussman, M. (1965). Relationships of adult children with their parents in the United States. In E. Shanas & G. Streib (Eds.), *Social structure and family: Generational relations* (pp. 62-92). Englewood Cliffs, NJ: Prentice Hall.

Sussman, M. B., & Romeis, J. C. (1982). Willingness to assist one's elderly parents: Responses from United States and Japanese families. *Human Organization, 41,* 256-259.

Thomae, H. (1980). Personality and adjustment to aging. In J. Birren & R. B. Sloane (Eds.), *Handbook of mental health and aging* (pp. 285-309). Englewood Cliffs, NJ: Prentice Hall.

Thomasma, D. C. (1984). Freedom, dependency, and the care of the very old. *Journal of the American Geriatrics Society, 32,* 906-914.

Tillich, P. (1952). *The courage to be.* New Haven, CT: Yale University Press.

Tolstoy, L. (1983). *Confession* (D. Patterson, Trans.). New York: W. W. Norton.

Trimakas, K. A., & Nicolay, R. D. (1974). Self-concept and altruism in old age. *Journal of Gerontology, 29,* 434-439.

Trivers, R. (1983). The evolution of cooperation. In D. L. Bridgeman (Ed.), *The nature of prosocial development* (pp. 43-60). New York: Academic Press.

Troll, L. E. (Ed.). (1984). The psychosocial problems of older women. In G. Lesnoff-Caravaglia (Ed.), *The world of the older woman: Conflicts and resolutions* (pp. 21-35). New York: Human Services Press.

Troll, L. E., Miller, S., & Atchley, R. (1979). *Families of later life.* New York: Human Sciences Press.

Tullock, G. (1978). Altruism, malice, and public goods. *Journal of Social and Biological Structures, 1,* 3-9.

Turner, H. B. (1992). Older volunteers: An assessment of two theories. *Educational Gerontology, 18,* 41-55.

Uhlenberg, D. (1979). Older women: The growing challenge to design constructive roles. *The Gerontologist, 19,* 236-241.

Underwood, B., & Moore, B. (1982). Perspective-taking and altruism. *Psychological Bulletin, 91,* 141-173.

Vaillant, G. (1977). *Adaptation to life.* Boston: Little, Brown.

Veroff, J., Reuman, D., & Feld, S. (1984). Motives in American men and women across the adult life span. *Developmental Psychology, 20,* 1142-1158.

Vogler, R. E., Masters, W. M., & Morrill, G. S. (1970). Shaping cooperative behavior in young children. *Journal of Psychology, 74,* 181-186.

Volunteer Action Center. (1986). *Volunteer opportunities guide for community service in Macomb, Oakland, Wayne.* Detroit: United Community Services.

Wack, J., & Rodin, J. (1978). Nursing homes for the aged: The human consequences of legislation-shaped environments. *Journal of Social Issues, 34,* 6-21.

Walker, A. (1982). Dependency and old age. *Social Policy Administration, 16,* 115-135.

Wallach, M. A., & Wallach, L. (1983). *Psychology's sanction for selfishness: The error of egoism in theory and therapy.* San Francisco: W. H. Freeman.

Waller, W. W., & Hill, R. (1951). *The family: A dynamic interpretation.* New York: Dryden.

Walster, E., Walster, G. W., & Berscheid, E. (1978). *Equity: Theory and research.* Boston: Allyn & Bacon.

Wan, T. (1982). *Stressful life events, social support networks, and gerontological health.* Lexington, MA: Lexington Books.

Ward, R. A. (1977). Services for old people. *Journal of Health and Social Behavior, 18,* 61-70.

Ward, R. A. (1979a). The impact of subjective age and stigma on older persons. *Journal of Gerontology, 32,* 227-232.

Ward, R. A. (1979b). The meaning of volunteer association participation to older people. *Journal of Gerontology, 34,* 438-445.

Ward, R. A. (1981-1982). Aging, the use of time, and social change. *Aging and Human Development, 14,* 177-187.

Waterman, A. S. (1981). Individualism and interdependence. *American Psychologist, 36,* 762-773.

Weiner, B., & Graham, S. (1989). Understanding the motivational role of affect: Life span research from an attributional perspective. *Cognition and Emotion, 3,* 401-419.

Weiss, R. F., Boyer, J. L., Lombardo, J. P., & Stich, M. H. (1973). Altruistic drive and altruistic reinforcement. *Journal of Personality and Social Psychology, 25,* 390-400.

Weisskopf-Joelson, E. (1968). Meaning as an integrating factor. In C. Buhler & F. Massarik (Eds.), *The course of human life* (pp. 359-383). New York: Springer.

Wentowski, G. J. (1981). Reciprocity and the coping strategies of older people: Cultural dimensions of network building. *The Gerontologist, 21,* 600-609.

White, R. W. (1959). Motivation reconsidered. *Psychological Review, 66,* 297-333.

Whitehouse, M. (1989). *Ageism: A new look at an old problem.* Unpublished manuscript, University of Detroit.

Wilson, D. S. (1980). *The natural selection of populations and communities.* Menlo Park, CA: Benjamin Cummings.

Wilson, E. O. (1975). *Sociobiology: The new synthesis.* Cambridge, MA: Belknap Press.

Wilson, E. O. (1978). *On human nature.* Cambridge, MA: Harvard University Press.

Winiecke, L. (1973). The appeal of age-segregated housing for the elderly poor. *Aging and Human Development, 4,* 396-406.

Wispé, L. G. (Ed.). (1978). *Altruism, sympathy, and helping.* New York: Academic Press.

Wittgenstein, L. (1979). *Notebooks 1914-1916* (2nd ed., G. Anscomae, Trans.). Chicago: University of Chicago Press.

Wong, P. T. P. (1989). Successful aging and personal meaning. *Canadian Psychology, 30,* 516-525.

Wong, P. T. P., & Sproule, C. F. (1984). Attributional analysis of locus of control and the Trent Attributional Profile (TAP). In H. M. Lefcourt (Ed.), *Research with the locus of control construct: Limitations and extensions* (Vol. 3, pp. 310-357). New York: Academic Press.

Wright, D. (1971). *The psychology of moral behavior.* Middlesex, England: Penguin.

Yarrow, M. R., & Waxler, C. (1976). Dimensions and correlates of prosocial behavior in young children. *Child Development, 47,* 118-125.

Yates, F. (1965). *Sampling methods in censuses and surveys.* London: Griffin.

Yordy, D. K. (1986). Current and future developments in health care. *Bulletin of the New York Academy of Medicine, 62,* 27-38.

Zola, I. (1983). The medicalizing of society. In I. K. Zola (Ed.), *Socio-medical inquiries* (pp. 241-296). Philadelphia: Temple University Press.

Zuckerman, M., & Reis, H. T. (1978). Comparison of three models for predicting altruistic behavior. *Journal of Personality and Social Psychology, 36,* 498-510.

Index

About the Authors

Elizabeth Midlarsky, Ph.D., is Professor in the Department of Clinical Psychology and Director of the Center for Lifespan and Aging Studies at Teachers College, Colombia University. She received her doctorate in clinical psychology from Northwestern University, Evanston. She is past editor of the *Academic Psychology Bulletin,* and is a Fellow of the American Psychological Association, and the American Orthopsychiatric Association, and the American Psychological Society. Her ongoing research projects include predictors and consequences of altruism and helping from childhood through late life, in siblings of people with disabilities, and among non-Jewish rescuers of Jews during the Holocaust, as well as psychotherapy with diverse populations, and gender roles. Her research has appeared in journals such as *Psychology and Aging, Journal of Personality and Social Psychology, Developmental Psychology,* and *Sex Roles,* and in edited books. She is currently Principal Investigator of a study on predicators and barriers to mental health-care utilization and help-seeking by older adults.

Eva Kahana, Ph. D., is Pierce T. and Elizabeth D. Robson Professor of Humanities, Chair of the Department of Sociology, and Director of the Elderly Care Research Center at Case Western Reserve University. She received her doctorate in human development from the University of Chicago and did a postdoctoral fellowship with the Midwest Council on Social Research in Aging. She has received the Gerontological Society of America Distinguished

Mentorship Award. She is currently a Mary E. Switzer Distinguished Fellow of the National Institute of Disability and Rehabilitation. In the past year she has received the Heller Award from the Menorah Park Center for the Aged and was named the Distinguished Gerontological Researcher in the State of Ohio. She has published extensively in the areas of stress, coping and health of aged, late-life migration, and environmental influences on older persons.